M000309811

WHATEVER IT TAKES

THE INSIDE STORY OF THE FIFA WAY

WHATEVER IT TAKES

THE INSIDE STORY
OF THE FIFA WAY

BONITA MERSIADES

POWDERHOUSE
PRESS

CHEYENNE, WYOMING, USA

Copyright © 2018 by Bonita Mersiades

Powderhouse Press

1910 Thomes Avenue

Cheyenne, WY, USA 82001

www.powderhousepress.com

ISBN: 978-0-999643-1-0-5

Cover design and typeset by Leslie Priestley

All rights reserved. No part of this publication may be reproduced, distributed, stored or transmitted in any form or by any means (electronic, mechanical photocopying, recording or otherwise), without the prior written permission of the publisher. Any person who does any unauthorized act in relation to this publication may be left liable to criminal prosecution and civil claims for damages.

The right of Bonita Mersiades to be identified as the author of this work has been asserted by her.

This book is sold subject to the condition that it shall not, by the way of trade or otherwise, be lent, resold, hired out, or otherwise circulated without the author's prior consent in any form of binding or cover other than that in which it was published and without a similar condition including this condition being imposed on the subsequent purchaser.

Publisher's Note: This is a work of non-fiction. The work represents the author's story (memoir) based on her experience, point of view, recollection, contemporaneous notes, investigations, interviews, research and the public record. Except where otherwise noted, all currency is in Australian dollars.

For real football people everywhere, those who love the game and who believe in fair play in everything

POWDERHOUSE
PRESS

100% of the author's proceeds
from the sale of this book will go to
the Australian Sports Foundation's fundraising campaign for the
'Pararoos' to participate in the 2019 IFCPF World Cup

Contents

Foreword

I DIDN'T WANT to do this. I said to Bonita, you've got a great, great story, just get on with telling it. Mouth turned down. A day later I thought better. So here is what you need to know.

Firstly, never mind the recent day trippers who peered over the FIFA wall and proclaimed themselves experts. I've yet to meet them on the road. This is the only book written by somebody who was - and still is - deeply involved in both campaigns of 2018 and 2022.

A real football official who worked on her national bid, Bonita Mersiades travelled the world for two years and she tells the story from the inside. It's not a good story and she is the only one with the courage to tell the truth. And she knows more about football than most. The players on the national squad thought so when they admired her as their operations manager.

She went further. She tracked down the anonymous source who supplied the material used by *Sunday Times* reporters who, oh so selectively, then claimed they knew who won the World Cup for Qatar. But they didn't - it was nonsense.

She sipped tea in the kitchen of the source, warmed her hands on his Aga and listened to his amazement at the binning of 90 per cent of the material. Unhelpful to their cause. She didn't need any help identifying the billionaires who benefited so much. It's a stunning read.

Her bid leaders were no better. They spent millions on crooked 'consultants' and were comprehensively screwed. Blatter knew - and everybody on the inside knew. But not the poor saps putting up long lists of reasons why they deserved the tournament.

Unlike all the other officials from initially dozens of bidding countries, she alone kept her head - and her principles. That cost her the job, months before the corrupt votes, demanded by the 'consultants.'

Slowly, the tide has turned. Now officials have briefed her on what really happened. She has been welcomed by authorities around the world and told a pile of truths. This is bad news for the callous scavengers who operated the multiple, criminal scams.

It's great news for football. Less so for others. I hope you enjoy - I did, hugely.

Andrew Jennings

Cumbria, England

January 2018

Introduction

THIS BOOK HAS been a long time coming.

I was sacked from Australia's World Cup bid towards the end of January 2010, ten months before the votes for Russia 2018 and Qatar 2022 that caused shock waves across the world.

It took a little while to gather my thoughts and think coolly, calmly and objectively about what I had witnessed, observed and heard; and what it is that I had railed against and asked questions about.

I began writing about that experience later in 2010 - in some cases, almost word-for-word conversations based on my personal contemporaneous notes and my recollection. I finished the first draft in 2011. Since publishing extracts of the first draft in 2012, there have been many people who urged me to publish the entire account. I didn't for a number of reasons, one of which was that I always thought the story wasn't finished.

I was right.

I already knew that people entered the World Cup bidding contest knowing how decisions were made at FIFA, content to play the FIFA way as long as they won. I knew that so many pointed the finger at the winners but were unwilling to examine, or admit to, their own conduct or behaviour.

What I have learned subsequently was how powerful and influential people joined forces in an attempt to overturn the decision, especially in relation to Qatar.

Even before FIFA President Sepp Blatter opened the envelope and showed the world 'Qatar' as the winners of the 2022 World Cup tournament - his own disdain clearly etched on his face - there were people around the world working to make sure that a tournament in Qatar wouldn't happen. When Qatar was announced as the host, amidst instantaneous shock, horror, disbelief and cynicism, the work didn't stop. It just regrouped, stepped-up a notch, and used every means at their disposal, drawing on significant resources.

I found myself part of the story also, not merely an insider as a reluctant senior executive of a bid team, but for years afterwards.

It is time to share the story of what I know about the FIFA way, through exposure to the World Cup bidding process of 2018 and 2022, and about how some will do whatever it takes to win, to get their way, to be proven right, or to stay in power.

To the extent that this is about Australia's bid, it is illustrative of what drove the system that developed around FIFA. The bidding process and the subsequent decision were a manifestation of the secret deals, counter deals and double deals that drove the way FIFA conducted its business for decades.

Bidding nations opted to be part of that, to one extent or another, and for better or worse, knowing full well that the decision was never going to be made on the basis of merit. Anyone who suggests otherwise is either lying or was born yesterday.

While Russia and Qatar emerged as the winners, all of us - other bidders, football officials, broadcasters, sponsors, players, fans - before and after, were diminished.

What follows is based on a combination of personal notes, recollection, research, documents, investigation, information already in the public domain, meetings and discussions with a large number of people - some of whom are off-the-record - as well as formal interviews.

I grew up in football. As someone for whom football has been a leitmotif of my life, it is the corrupt core of world football and its implicit injustice that drove me to complain, question and speak out - and, finally, to publish this book. I did so knowing I had everything to lose and nothing to gain - except for one thing. I am on the right side of history.

Bonita Mersiades

Sydney, Australia

January 2018

CHAPTER 1
A backstory emerges

London: February 2015

AN AWARD FOR investigative journalism in the United Kingdom wouldn't normally be something I'd take a lot of notice of.

I did in 2015.

That was when Jonathan Calvert and Heidi Blake of *The Sunday Times* were co-winners with Richard Brooks and Andrew Bousfeld of *Private Eye* for the UK's pre-eminent award for investigative journalism, the annual Paul Foot Award.

A Paul Foot Award winner could expect accolades, attention, more work and a handy cash reward. It's a career game-changer and more coveted than many journalists care to admit.

On the evening of the award for 2014 being announced, the convenor of the award, *Private Eye* editor Ian Hislop, took to the stage to announce the winners. A short, jolly-looking man with a mind like a steel-trap, Hislop told the audience it was a tough choice. All the finalists were worthy but the two co-winners couldn't be split.

Hislop said that Brooks and Bousfield won for their work in unravelling details of 'decades of bribery' in arms deals involving the UK and Saudi Arabia. There was warm applause as the two men - Brooks a previous winner, Bousfield a younger man - made their way to the small stage.

Calvert and Blake won for their reports known as *The FIFA Files* which were published in *The Sunday Times* as the World Cup got underway in Brazil the year before.

The reports caused a sensation.

Hislop said *The Sunday Times* team won because 'they spilled the secrets of a bombshell cache of hundreds of millions of secret documents.' The citation read:

In forensic detail, they reported on an extraordinary campaign waged by Mohamed Bin Hammam, Qatar's top football official, and how he exploited his position to help secure the votes Qatar needed to win the bid to host the 2022 World Cup.

Whoa. Wait a sec. Really?

The citation continued.

The team spent two months in a secret data centre outside London painstakingly piecing together a timeline of Bin Hammam's activities, going through emails, faxes, phone records, letters, flight logs, accounts and bank transfer slips, examining tens of thousands of gigabytes of data using forensic search technology and a network of offshore supercomputers.

What?

Calvert and Blake showed in impressive detail how Mohamed Bin Hammam paid millions to a large number of people in the football world. Lots and lots.

But hang on: most of the people that Calvert and Blake listed did not have a vote on 2 December 2010 to decide the hosts of the 2018 and 2022 World Cup tournaments. That decision was the exclusive domain of the FIFA Executive Committee. Only two of the many people catalogued by Calvert and Blake were Executive Committee members; Jack Warner of Trinidad and Tobago and Reynald Temarii of Tahiti.

For anyone who knew the football world, it was perplexing to suggest that the gratitude of the likes of a football association president from Gambia, Guinea, Bangladesh or Mongolia would have any influence on the 24 members of FIFA's elite.

What *The FIFA Files* revealed was not a blueprint for how Bin Hammam won the hosting rights for the 2022 World Cup, but Bin Hammam's plan to win the FIFA presidency in 2011.

Because every football association president voted in the FIFA presidential election, every act of generosity counted. And like many in world football, Bin Hammam thought that, by 2011 when the next presidential election was due, 13 years was more than enough time for Sepp Blatter to be in charge. As early as 2008, Bin Hammam was campaigning for the FIFA Presidency.

Astonishingly, Calvert and Blake didn't appear to see any of this. Instead, they chose a narrative that since 2006, Bin Hammam waged a secret campaign to win the World Cup.

Using the power and reach of their broadsheet newspaper - part of the vast media empire owned by American-Australian Rupert Murdoch - Calvert and Blake gave the world a rationale. It was widely accepted by most because it was *The Sunday Times*. It sounded plausible. It was convenient. And so many people around the world wanted a way to explain Qatar's win and, more importantly, find a way to take the 2022 World Cup off them.

The problem was, while there were aspects to the story that did have an impact on voting, such as a gas deal between Qatar and Thailand, it didn't ring entirely true.

One incident they wrote about was an issue I knew well. It involved a visit to the Emir of Qatar in October 2009 by Franz Beckenbauer of Germany, former playing great and then a FIFA Executive Committee member, together with Fedor Radmann, his long time trusted aide. Radmann, in secret, was a highly-paid consultant to the Australian bid, for which I worked. The understanding was that Beckenbauer's vote belonged to Australia.

According to Calvert and Blake, the visit was initiated by Bin Hammam so the Emir could lean upon Beckenbauer to support Qatar in return for Bin Hammam having supported Germany for their 2006 World Cup bid.

Not so. The fact is both Beckenbauer and Radmann were in Doha on the business of the Australian bid. They were on a mission to convince the Emir to withdraw the Qatar bid altogether.

Calvert and Blake wouldn't know this from their search of the treasure trove of documents from a window-less room in the high street of Beeston, a town outside Nottingham, from which they compiled *The FIFA Files*. This aspect of their story was deduced solely from an email detailing a trip to Doha by Beckenbauer and Radmann as guests of Bin Hammam.

I called Calvert to let him know the true purpose of the trip. His reaction was not what I expected.

He wasn't interested. He didn't ask for details. He didn't want to verify it. He simply didn't want to know.

Then it dawned on me.

'Your source is Frank Lowy.' Frank Lowy was the billionaire head of the Australian football association who was humiliated when Australia received just one vote after spending around $50 million of taxpayers' money to bid for the World Cup.

'That is very funny. Who is putting that around?'

I replied 'You know it makes sense.'

It made sense because there was no other reason why a journalist of Calvert's reputation and standing - he was nominated for the Paul Foot Award on four previous occasions - was not interested.

When an insider - namely me - just informed him that Radmann was a consultant to the Australian bid, and the true purpose of the trip, wouldn't you contact Australia's FA to ask them for their view? After all, if Calvert and Blake were right, Australia should feel outraged, or hurt, or disappointed, that their consultant and one of their high profile supporters visited Qatar without their knowledge. Wouldn't the reaction have added to the story?

It was too late to correct the published newspaper report, but I reasoned he could correct it for the book he and Blake were writing that was to be published later in 2015. Not so.

With Calvert's stony disinterest came the realisation that there was a backstory unfolding before me almost as intriguing as how Russia and Qatar managed to win the 2018 and 2022 World Cup tournaments. I wanted to find out more.

As I reflected on my conversation with Calvert, I couldn't help but remember another conversation long ago. Five years beforehand, in June 2009, Frank Lowy said to me that when it came to the World Cup bid, he would do 'whatever it takes' to win.

CHAPTER 2
We've only just begun

Germany: June 2006

LIKE EVERY AUSTRALIAN who ventured to Germany for the 2006 FIFA World Cup, Frank Lowy loved being there.

The diminutive billionaire property developer especially loved it when fellow Aussies would stop him in the streets of Berlin or Munich or Stuttgart and tell him what a 'champion' he was for making qualification happen. Lowy was elected to the position of Australian federation president with the support of the government of the day three years before, armed with a mandate, a government loan, and a lot of goodwill to help football live up to its potential.

Dizzy with the combined effects of the June sunshine, German organisational efficiency, the hundreds of thousands of supporters of many shapes, sizes, ages and cultures happily milling around the Brandenburg Gate, Lowy said he wanted to bring the World Cup to Australia.

He told reporters he would 'dare to dream and do whatever it takes' to make sure it happened as quickly as possible. Then 76 years of age, Lowy described time as being in 'short commodity'.

It wasn't the first time Australians dreamed big about hosting the World Cup. Four years earlier, when football in Australia was in the midst of government-led governance reforms prior to Lowy becoming Australia's federation president, several of Australia's state premiers announced they would support a bid. It went nowhere.

But by 2006, Lowy knew how FIFA worked and what made world football's elite sit up and take notice. He knew that money talked.

He had endeared himself to FIFA elites two years earlier.

At the 2004 Athens Olympics, he moored the larger of his two luxury yachts, Ilona IV, in Piraeus Harbour and set about wining and dining football and Olympics power brokers at his own expense. He was helped by the powerful Australian vice-president of the International Olympic Committee, John Coates. Ever since, the invitations to Lowy from football's elite rolled-in, a fact he acknowledged many years later when he claimed that he was 'very popular' with world football's elite after the hospitality he showed in Athens.

Even before Australia formally joined the Asian Football Confederation in January 2006, Lowy was top of the invitation list of Bin Hammam, the Asian confederation's president. Lowy was always an honoured guest at Bin Hammam's table at events from Kuala Lumpur to Abu Dhabi and cities in-between.

Other guests would include Bin Hammam's fellow FIFA Executive Committee members, past and present: men such as Jacques Anouma of Cote d'Ivoire, Ismail Bhamjee of Botswana, Worawi Makudi of Thailand, Junji Ogura of Japan, Dr Moon-Jung Chung of South Korea, Hany Abo Rida of Egypt, Reynald Temarii of Tahiti, Jack Warner of Trinidad and Tobago, Michel Platini of France, the silent man Geoff Thompson of England and the main man himself, FIFA President Sepp Blatter.

The FIFA power brokers would be joined by one or more close associates.

Swiss Hungarian consultant Peter Hargitay was a regular guest at Bin Hammam's events. He later took credit for Australia's move from the little Oceania confederation into the Asian confederation. It was a claim that astonished FFA executives of the time.

Franz Beckenbauer's most trusted associate Fedor Radmann, and Rio-based Lebanese racehorse owner Elias Zaccour, were also regulars. And there were the lads from two of the biggest TV rights wheelers-and-dealers, World Sports Group and Dentsu. Lowy was on friendly terms with all of them.

From time-to-time the next generation of FIFA leaders would also be warmly welcomed at Bin Hammam's events: Gianni Infantino, the General Secretary of UEFA, Tarek Bouchamaoui of Tunisia, Hargitay's good friend, Peter Kenyon of Chelsea Football Club, Nirwan Bakrie of Indonesia and Danny Jordaan of South Africa.

LOWY STARTED TO lay the groundwork for what he saw as his ultimate legacy to the game, a FIFA World Cup in Australia.

He confided in Bin Hammam who was happy to support his new friend. In fact, Bin Hammam saw this as a win-win situation. He could support Australia's aspirations to host the World Cup and bring it to Asia. And he could also shore-up his own ambition to become the next FIFA President when the election rolled around in 2011.

Lowy also let Sepp Blatter know that Australia would bid. The two, who were similar in stature and not too far apart in age, enjoyed a friendly relationship. Blatter said that when he first met Lowy in 2004 that the two of them were 'like people who have known one another a long time.'

For a start, Blatter admired anyone who made lots of money on their own, as Lowy had. Plus Blatter had a genuine soft spot for Australia; his only daughter Corinne worked with the Australian federation pre-Lowy days and he enjoyed many visits to the land down under.

Blatter told Lowy that the people he needed to talk with were the Germans. Bin Hammam agreed. The Germans had the key to winning - not just on the park, but also off it.

President of the German Football Federation (DFB) Theo Zwanziger, and General Secretary Horst Schmidt, welcomed Lowy with open arms.

By September 2007, the FFA and the German FA had signed a cooperation agreement. Finalising its negotiation was one of the first tasks of the FFA's new chief executive.

Ben Buckley started in the job at the end of 2006. Lowy found him far more amenable than his predecessor, John O'Neill, who was inclined to lend a cautionary voice to Lowy's plans.

The German FA were generous considering the relative pecking order of the two countries in football terms. Not that every part of the agreement was written down.

Soon after the agreement was finalised, Australia withdrew its bid to host the 2011 Women's World Cup. The official reason given was that it was uneconomic for Australia to host it, despite the more modest infrastructure requirements of the 16-team women's tournament compared with the 32-team men's tournament. It was a nonsense argument, especially when less than 18 months later, Australia also bid for the 2015 Asian Cup - also a 16-team tournament.

Australia's withdrawal from the 2011 Women's World Cup bid meant that Germany was confirmed as favourites to host the tournament, which it eventually did.

They promised international friendlies between the men's and women's teams.

They also promised help in putting together a bid for the World Cup and exclusive access to the German representative on the FIFA Executive Committee, Franz Beckenbauer. With Beckenbauer came his support team which included two men who worked in the shadows. They were Fedor Radmann and his close friend, Andreas Abold.

This trio of Beckenbauer, Radmann and Abold had proven success in shaking down bidding countries. The 2006 World Cup, the 2010 World Cup, the 2009 and 2010 Club World Cup.

Lowy was ecstatic. Everybody was on board. With Blatter's and Bin Hammam's encouragement, the German FA's help, Beckenbauer's support, and exclusive use of Radmann and Abold, he was confident he would win!

All he needed now was the money to pay for the bid.

Unfortunately, the Australian football association was broke. In the previous financial year, they made an $11 million loss.

While Lowy could easily pay for a bid himself, he thought it better to use taxpayers' money.

Fortunately, in Australia it was election time.

The 13-year government of the incumbent Prime Minister was struggling in the polls, and it looked like there would be a change of government. What would have everyone cheering for a government, whether it be a new one or the return of an old one?

Lowy told everybody who would listen that a World Cup in Australia would be an enduring legacy - not just for him, and for football, but for the country. He said that every time Australia hosted a major world event, the country pushed ahead on the global stage: 1956 Melbourne Olympics, 1988 World Expo, 2000 Sydney Olympics. The World Cup in 2018 would be the same.

Over the years of building the world's biggest retail property company, Lowy learned to play all sides of politics around the world. A donation here, a donation there, a board room lunch, a phone call at the right time. For extra clout, he had also been on the Board of the Australian Reserve Bank for a decade.

Lowy knew that his quest was helped by Australia hosting the AFC Awards in Sydney in November 2007 - a favour from Bin Hammam. The following year would be even bigger with the whole circus coming to Australia for the FIFA Congress. The ever-helpful Blatter helped make sure that happened.

Never mind the battle to lead the country. Both the Prime Minister and the Opposition Leader found time in their hectic election schedules in the last weeks of the campaign in November 2007 to meet with Lowy. The government promised $16 million towards FFA operational costs and money for the World Cup bid. The opposition upped the ante with a $32 million promise as well as money for the World Cup bid.

Lowy was delighted the stars were aligning so well. So much support from the powerful people in world football, and now both sides of politics at home.

KEVIN RUDD WON.

Lowy was sorry that his friend, Prime Minister John Howard, lost the election at the end of November 2007. Fortunately, the new Prime Minister of Australia, Kevin Rudd, was happy to be a friend also.

Rudd was younger, ambitious, energetic, and wanted to get things done. A former diplomat, Rudd also wanted to make his mark on the international stage.

This suited Lowy's football plans, as well as another long-held private interest. Lowy is a high profile Jewish person in Australia, who fought with the Haganah in Israel before joining the remaining members of his family in Australia in January 1952. He has close and continuing links to Israel's power elite, and funds and chairs the Institute for National Security Studies in Israel. In 2003, he established the Lowy Institute for international policy in Australia which quickly established a reputation as an international policy think-tank of significance.

So it was no great surprise when the Prime Minister's office called me on a Saturday afternoon in February 2008 to say the Prime Minister would be at the A-League Grand Final the next day to announce funding for Australia's World Cup bid.

With less than three months in charge, Rudd had already made an apology to Aboriginal Australians known as the 'Stolen Generation' for being forcibly removed from their families as babies and children. He had signed the Kyoto Protocol.

And he told the assembled media ahead of the grand final that the World Cup bid was another 'nation-building gesture' that would help the overall international reputation of the country.

After the announcement, I watched Rudd as he stood by himself towards the back of the VIP suite overlooking the Sydney Football Stadium, holding a cup of tea and a biscuit.

The officials who'd circled him at the pre-match reception made their way to their seats under a cloudless bright blue Sydney sky as the anthem was belted-out. Rudd stayed to talk to the VIPs again at half-time and then quietly left before the end of the game.

IT WASN'T LONG before we were brought back to earth.

My role at FFA was not about the World Cup bid. I was head of communications and corporate affairs covering all of our operations after a career as a senior executive in the public and non-government sectors. I didn't want to work on the bid at all.

Many years later, one of the international authorities who interviewed me in relation to the bidding process, asked me why.

'I knew what FIFA was like,' I told them. 'I knew that the decision wouldn't be taken on merit. If we won, it would have been because we paid someone something. If someone else won, it was because they did. I didn't want to be distracted from the day-to-day business of football - which I love - for that.'

But it wasn't to be. I spent more and more time on bid matters and less and less time on other matters - despite my many protestations to Lowy and my boss, the chief executive Ben Buckley.

Not long after the Prime Minister's announcement, Ben, a colleague Stuart Taggart and I were in Australia's capital, Canberra, to meet with government officials. Stuart was handling technical issues for the bid which involved matters such as host cities, stadiums and venue selection and relationships with state governments and the three other football codes.

We were accompanied. Lowy sent Mark Ryan, his fixer from Westfield, Lowy's global retail property empire, to be with us.

There were two things to achieve: enlisting government help in convincing China not to bid, and getting hold of the money the Prime Minister promised.

A possible bid from China - which was hosting the Olympic Games later that year - hung over us. We thought if they did throw their hat into the ring, it would be all over.

'If we're going to convince China not to bid, what do we tell them that we'll do in return?' asked a policy advisor from the Prime Minister's office.

'We can assist them with a future bid. They can be part of our organising committee and learn from us,' suggested Stuart.

Everyone knew that wouldn't cut the mustard. We all sat silently for a few moments. Some of us looked out the window at a glorious autumn day; others down at the large, polished mahogany table. The Prime Minister's advisor raised his eyebrows.

'We'll do what we can,' said the Prime Minister's man.

WE WERE SENT to the money men.

Although the Prime Minister was an enthusiastic supporter of the World Cup bid, not everyone in government was. The Treasurer and the Health Minister - from whose budget the money would come - were against it. The Prime Minister's own departmental head, the most senior civil servant in the country, advised him that government money shouldn't go towards the bid because it would end up in brown paper bags. The view from many within the bureaucracy was that Lowy could have funded the bid himself.

The executive now chairing the meeting in the Prime Minister's department told us he would be responsible for shepherding us through the bureaucracy so we got the promised money. His attention turned immediately to Mark Ryan.

'What role does Westfield have in this?' the executive asked.

'What do you mean?' replied Ryan.

'Are we giving this money to FFA or to Westfield?'

'FFA of course,' Ryan replied sharply.

'So my question remains,' the executive insisted.

'Frank Lowy wanted me here,' said Ryan.

The executive rocked back on his heels a little and looked down his nose. 'Doesn't he trust this lot?' he gestured towards Ben, Stuart and me.

'Of course he does,' Ryan said, his tone becoming more terse. 'This is a very important issue for him and he wants to be kept informed every step of the way.'

'Isn't that what a CEO is for?' again gesturing to Ben.

Ryan didn't have an answer for that.

Undeterred, the executive continued. 'Let's just cut to the chase. If we've got to do this – and it seems we have to as Rudd wants it – I'll tell you exactly what's going to happen.'

The temperature rose as he continued.

'The money doesn't just turn up in a brown paper bag you know.' He smiled at his little joke and continued. 'We want a submission to Cabinet in September and that means the money will start flowing from next year.'

'But it's only March. We were hoping for some money before the end of June,' said Ben.

The executive sat back in his chair and put his hands together, his fingers touching one another in a triangle, looking straight ahead.

'Is that because you're broke?' he said.

There was silence. FFA was - and he knew it. But Lowy wasn't, and he knew that too.

'It's because we have already commissioned some work and we need to pay for it,' Ben replied.

Ben explained that consulting firm PricewaterhouseCoopers was working on four projects: an infrastructure audit, an economic impact analysis, a bid budget and how Australia's three other football codes - of Australian Rules, rugby league and rugby union - could hold their traditional domestic competitions at the same time as the World Cup.

The executive grunted. 'You do realise that the other codes are a huge issue.'

It was a statement. He didn't wait for a response.

'Huge. Do you seriously think that the management of Aussie Rules and Rugby League will just move aside for a World Cup?'

He didn't expect an answer. He waved airily at us again, still looking ahead.

'You can tell us later. In the meantime, we'll do what we can to help, won't we?'

He turned to his three colleagues. He gave partly a smile, partly a grimace. It was accompanied by a roll of his eyes, and a look that wondered how it came to be his lot in life that he - a serious economist - was left to deal with an impoverished sporting organisation run by a billionaire who wanted the taxpayer to fund a bid for a World Cup in a sport he didn't even like.

Sydney: April 2008

IT DIDN'T TAKE long for the first FIFA Executive Committee member to pay a visit once the Prime Minister made our bid official.

The President of the Oceania Football Confederation, Reynald Temarii, and the chief executive, Tai Nicholas, visited Lowy and Ben a few weeks later in April.

Later the same day, Ben handed me a single, typewritten piece of paper as we sat across from each other at the round table in his office. It looked as if it had been folded and re-folded a few times.

'This is what Reynald wants,' he said as he handed me the paper. 'Don't write it down. Don't tell anyone. You never saw it. Just memorise it.'

It was quite a list. They wanted the television rights to Australia's A-League in the Oceania Confederation; vehicles for the ten technical directors in each Oceania nation, other than New Zealand; an extension of funding of the salary of the Oceania Director of Coaching – an expense Australia had been meeting since our move from Oceania to the Asian Football Confederation in 2006; an Oceania team in the A-League; funding for a conference on children and sport. And they wanted a new headquarters building in Auckland.

'What else did he say?' I asked.

'That we've got his vote.'

With 24 FIFA Executive Committee members, 13 votes were needed to win. I did a quick calculation.

'That's some shopping list for one vote. If this is how much one vote costs, it's going to cost us $52 million to get 13.'

Ben ignored me. 'You need to raise $4 or $5 million by the end of next month for the headquarters building,' Ben said.

I told him that we wouldn't get money from government for a headquarters building.

'We have to get it,' he said. 'We need Temarii's vote locked-in before we can take the next step. And we have to get it by the end of May.'

'It's impossible to get money from government in that timeframe even if they actually agreed to it - which they won't. Frank would be better paying for it personally,' I said.

Ben looked at me as if to say that wasn't going to happen.

'Frank wants to meet with each of the Executive Committee members knowing that Reynald's support is locked-in. Plus Frank and I are going to New Caledonia for the Oceania Congress and Frank wants to announce it there.' He was referring to the Oceania Football Confederation Congress being held immediately after the FIFA Congress.

He watched me as I made notes.

'Oh. And by the way, we need the same amount for both Asia and Africa.'

Canberra: May 2008

THE THREE SENIOR executives from the Australian Government's overseas aid agency sitting across the sofa from us listened politely. We let them know that Oceania wanted money for a headquarters building, and we casually explained we would need even more money for Asia and Africa.

The looks on their faces suggested they thought we were at best, naïve or at worst, crazy.

They told us their existing Sport for Development program was fully committed. More to the point, New Zealand - where Temarii wanted the building - wasn't a priority for Australian aid. And also - no surprise - they couldn't possibly fund a capital item such as a building.

But because the World Cup bid was a high priority for the new government, the agency knew they had to assist us.

Soon afterwards, one of the officials we met with came to Sydney. He wanted to know what the urgency was.

'Oceania says they'll vote for us if we deliver what they want,' I told him. 'Lowy and

Buckley are heading to New Caledonia next week to tell them it's a done deal.'

He was about to say something but I put up my hand to stop him. 'I know this is not how you fund things. I know you can't give approval today to $4 million. And I know you can't fund a building.'

He drew breath, and then let it out with a puff. He was the quintessential Canberra public servant. Proper. Precise. Cautious.

'We're under no illusion that we have to give you this money somehow even though it's outside normal guidelines and funding,' he said.

'So here's what you need to do. Come up with something that's a partnership between governments in the Pacific, Oceania confederation, us representing the Australian government and you. Something that directly relates to the health and wellbeing of children, and especially girls. And then we can go from there.'

CHAPTER 3

You better watch out, you better take care

Sydney: May 2008

THE FIFA CONGRESS was coming to town.

The 75-strong FIFA staff who travelled from Zurich to manage the Congress set-up residence in the Sheraton on the Park hotel in the centre of Sydney. The lobby was abuzz with activity for a Saturday morning.

The concierge welcomed Lowy deferentially as he opened the rear door of one of Lowy's chauffeured black Mercedes-Benz vehicles.

Lowy was a trim, fit man for his almost 78 years. A full head of thick white hair, pale blue eyes, dressed in a dark navy blazer, light blue shirt and tie, with the lapel pin of the highest Australian civilian honour. His shoes were always highly polished.

Lowy greeted me warmly, gripping my forearms in his hands as he gave me a kiss. He was nervous.

'Now these people aren't going to say anything stupid, are they?' he asked me as we moved upstairs. He was referring to a group of local journalists, waiting upstairs to meet with the FIFA President, Sepp Blatter.

Lowy didn't have much time for journalists who asked difficult questions.

'They understand it's rare for them to have an opportunity to meet with the FIFA President,' I replied.

A few weeks before Ben and I briefed local journalists on the state of play with the A-League, the FIFA Congress and the bid. We asked them to 'dial-down any cynicism' they might have had while the Congress was in Sydney. It was an unnecessary request in many ways as most of the the journalists who made their living from only reporting on football were fully supportive of Australia's bid from the outset.

High profile journalists and commentators who were familiar with how FIFA operated had no reservations about what it would take to win the right to host the World Cup.

'We all know what FIFA's like. Frank knows too. He knows what he's getting into. If anyone can pull off a World Cup, it will be Frank. He knows whose tree to shake and whose palms to grease,' more than one veteran journalist said to me in the period since Rudd's announcement.

From our vantage point at the top of the grand stairway, Lowy and I saw Blatter before he saw us.

'Mr President,' Lowy said, his arms spread wide.

Blatter looked up, saw Frank and smiled warmly, his brown eyes crinkling. 'Mr President,' Blatter returned. As he got to the top of the stairs, the two men shook hands and then embraced in one fluid action.

Blatter is a little more than five years younger than Lowy. The two men shared the same short stature, but Blatter was thicker set and rounder - the physique of an old-fashioned opera tenor. He wore a grey suit, almost the same colour blue shirt as Lowy and a striped blue, silver and white tie. I noticed he also had highly polished shoes. He looked every inch the well-heeled, older European gentleman.

'How are you my friend?' Blatter asked, the two of them still clutching each other's arms.

'I am very well. And you?' Lowy asked the question with an upward inflection on 'you'.

'Oh a little tired. I got in last night. It is a long way. But I am very happy to be here and to meet your media.'

His eyes darted around wondering where they were.

'It is very good of you Mr President. We are very honoured,' was Lowy's reply.

Lowy introduced us. We had met previously on two occasions. Once when I was operations manager of the men's national team, the Socceroos. It was an Oceania confederation event where the ubiquitous official banquet included country karaoke. We sang *You are my sunshine.* The other time was after I returned to the public sector, and was privately advocating for change in the administration of the game that eventually led to Lowy being in charge.

'Hello,' Blatter said clasping both his hands over mine. 'It is good to see a lovely lady working in an important job in football.'

Lowy beamed. 'We are very lucky to have her.'

Moments later, we were seated in a nondescript internal meeting room. Blatter and Lowy were at the front of the room with Blatter's communications head and me either side. The journalists, all men, sat facing them in a semi-circle.

'Welcome gentlemen. And lady,' he turned to me and smiled.

'It is wonderful to be in Australia again. I have a great interest in football in Australia. I have been a regular visitor here since 1977. The first World Youth Cup was held here in 1981 and then again in 1993. It didn't take much effort for you to organise the wonderful football tournament in 2000 for the Olympics. My daughter worked here for a while – some of you may know her? And she had a wonderful time. But I do want to say this.'

He finally drew breath. He leaned forward a little, his hands clasped in front of him on the table. The 20 or so journalists, picked up their pencils and checked their sound recorders before he continued. Like the showman he was, he waited until they were ready.

'Other footballs here are not football,' he said emphatically. He was referring to Australia's three other football codes of Australian Rules, Rugby League and Rugby Union.

'There is only one football. These others? They are pretenders.'

Blatter turned down the corners of his mouth.

'My only sadness when I come here is little Oceania. It was a big loss for them when you left and went to Asia. It is an open file in FIFA since Australia left Oceania. It is little, but there is so much to do. So much development. So much that needs to be done.'

He let that sink in a little.

'And Australia should be helping. I have told Reynald that,' he said it slowly.

I gave Reynald Temarii a mental tick. Only weeks after his shopping list visit, Blatter was telling us in no uncertain terms that we needed to do something for Oceania.

'And the other thing is, I am very happy that you are going to have a second division. This is important.'

In unison, the journalists looked up from their notebooks in disbelief.

The A-League had just finished its third season. A second division was not on the agenda.

Lowy realised the discussion was in dangerous territory and cut in to prevent any questions. What he said privately to Blatter about a second division in a previous meeting was not something he wanted discussed with journalists.

'A big hearty welcome to you, Mr President, and the whole of the Executive Committee,' Frank said in a booming and cheery voice. He was usually quietly spoken. When he spoke loudly, it meant he was anxious.

'We have very big plans for the national league and for Australia. That is why it is a very big deal for us to have the FIFA Congress here. And that is why we are bidding for 2018,' Lowy said.

It worked for now. The journalists didn't ask a potentially embarrassing question about a second division. Instead, they wanted to know from Blatter whether he would allow only one bid from each Confederation.

'I spoke with Michel Platini and Mohamed Bin Hammam about this.' Platini was the head of UEFA, the powerful European football confederation, Bin Hammam the head of Asian football. 'They both want to make sure there is only one bid for each confederation.'

He continued. 'But of course everyone has the right to bid for the World Cup. There is a lot of interest around the world. I've met with a high level delegation from England. I've been to Russia. I believe Spain and Portugal are interested, and the Netherlands and Belgium. In Asia, I know that Qatar, China, Japan and,' he paused for dramatic effect, 'the independent island of Australia are all interested. Plus there's North America.'

He had a sip of water.

'I want to calm the market a bit,' he continued. 'I do not want this to get out of hand. There is already a lot of lobbying going on. In the universality of football, it should go to all continents.

I think we will have a package of two World Cups at once, 2018 and 2022.' He said it as 'two twenty two'. It is more attractive to sponsors and commercial partners to offer two World Cups at once.'

There were rumours of this happening for months. By 2018 Europe would not have hosted the World Cup for twelve years. It was assumed the powerful European confederation would be determined to have it there.

From Australia's point-of-view, the money men in government saw combining the two tournaments as a double chance. If we didn't get 2018, we might get 2022. We also knew that while the Prime Minister was committed to funding the bid, not everyone in government agreed.

There was another advantage to a dual bidding process. It meant we could swap votes with another bidder. But so could others.

Blatter was asked what Australia's biggest challenge was for 2018.

'Some countries who are powerhouses in world football think they have the right to host it. I don't think so. You don't have to be a powerhouse. Some say Australia is too far away, but I don't see this as a handicap for the World Cup when people spend weeks here. I think it is for a shorter tournament.'

It was another pointed comment from Blatter. We had submitted a bid to host the 2009 and 2010 Club World Cup tournaments and were up against Abu Dhabi and Japan. It was clear from his comments that we were not in the running for the week-long Club World Cup tournament.

'Who said we're too far away?' Lowy interrupted. 'Too far away from whom? Europe? Europe isn't the world. If it goes to Europe, what is it going to do for Europe? We will fight this view,' he said.

Blatter said nothing. He was asked who he would vote for.

The showman emerged again. He pulled a face that let the journalist feel as if he was being cheeky by trying to get an exclusive. 'Let's put it this way. If you get 12 votes, you will have 13.'

That seemed as good a place as any to stop. Despite his communications chief hovering anxiously, Blatter answered one-on-one questions for 90 minutes afterwards. He moved on for photographs, as well as radio and television interviews. He was patient, polite and friendly. He never stopped smiling.

THE DECISION to 'bundle' the bids for the 2018 and 2022 World Cups into one bidding process, to which Blatter alluded, was confirmed by the FIFA Executive Committee a few days later.

We immediately declared we would bid for both. Within the bid team, we knew that our better chance was 2022 and that was where our strategy was focussed, but our public position remained focussed on 2018 for another two years.

At that stage – long before it was mandated by the FIFA Executive Committee that 2018 would go to Europe – we thought the secret to winning 2018 was to get as many second preference votes as possible and be the last man standing. We called it the 'Steven Bradbury Strategy' after the unlikely Australian who won a Winter Olympics Gold medal in speed skating when all his opponents fell away due to mishap or injury.

We knew we had Reynald Temarii's vote - as long as we found $4 million. We were confident of Franz Beckenbauer's vote because of the arrangement with Germany. The public reasoning was that this put us in good position to win 2018 on the basis of second preference votes as other bidders fell away. Or, if that didn't work, find a partner from amongst the European bidders with whom we could swap votes for 2022.

The seemingly illogical focus on 2018 was seen by many as a stubborn wish of Lowy's because of his age. It wasn't.

If anyone asked publicly, the response was that 2018 was preferred because it would give the quickest financial return to FFA and football. The $32 million grant that the new federal government gave as an election promise would run out in 2012. The game still had significant financial challenges. Winning the right to host the tournament at the end of 2010 when the vote took place would be a turbo-boost to the game just when it was needed.

The reality was that bidding for both was similar to making the opening move in a game of chess.

CHAPTER 4
Islands in the sun

Sydney: May 2008

LOWY KNEW FROM the wining and dining on his yacht in Piraeus Harbour at the Athens Olympics almost four years before, and the countless events as a guest of Asian Football Confederation chief Mohamed Bin Hammam since, just what was needed to impress the FIFA Executive Committee.

Conspicuous wealth.

There were very few places in Australia that could compete with the sumptuous surrounds of Lowy's harbourside mansion.

Early in the week of the FIFA Congress, he hosted an intimate, private dinner for the Executive Committee members who attended along with their partners. During the week, Lowy also provided hospitality for each Executive Committee member individually.

Accompanying FIFA Executive Committee member Franz Beckenbauer to Lowy's mansion for the formal dinner, Fedor Radmann admired his surroundings and the man who owned them. Lowy was a self-made man who built an empire with a combination of diligence, risk-taking, and business acumen. He also had a willingness to do whatever it takes to get ahead.

The decor was elegant and understated. Radmann's practiced eye could see it was all class. The Persian rugs, the artwork, the Lladro figurines, the photographs of Lowy with world figures, the grand piano - not to mention the sunset view of Sydney Harbour.

Executive Committee members were delighted when they were ushered into the dining area to discover bespoke dinner plates with their names embossed in gold plate.

Another nice touch were the gifts. $100,000 worth of exclusive Paspaley pearls. Cufflinks for the men and pendants for the partners. They went down a treat.

Jewellery connoisseur, Jack Warner, was dismayed when there was no pearl pendant for his wife. It was one of the rare occasions Maureen Warner did not travel with him so no gift was made available for her. As he circled the enormous terrace and adjacent reception room, champagne glass in hand, he made a note to himself to make sure he got one for her.

FIFA SPENT $20 million on the 2008 Congress in Sydney.

Football images lit up the Sydney Harbour Bridge. FIFA street banners adorned main roads.

'Welcome to the new FIFA Opera House in Sydney,' Blatter joked in his opening remarks, reflecting the strong presence FIFA had in the city.

The Concert Hall of the Opera House was set up with its extended stage, the backdrop backlit in FIFA blue with a huge FIFA logo. The Opening Ceremony was slick and professional. There were Aboriginal dancers, a didgeridoo player and a jazz trumpeter. I wondered whether FIFA's overwhelmingly male officials might have preferred Kylie Minogue.

Prime Minister Rudd was warmly received. The applause after he gave a clear message of the government's financial support for the bid was even warmer.

The ceremony over, I was posted on the lookout for Asian football officials.

As discreetly as possible, our mission was to usher Mohamed Bin Hammam and other Asian Executive Committee members, Worawi Makudi from Thailand, Manilal Fernando from Sri Lanka and Yousuf Al-Serkal of the UAE into the restaurant adjacent to the Opera House for a private meeting with the Prime Minister and Lowy. There were others from the FFA Board too.

Blatter had announced at the Congress opening ceremony that Qatar was expected to bid also, as he told the journalists in the briefing a few days before.

The first thing Bin Hammam said to the small group meeting with Rudd was that he did not believe that Qatar would bid. He pointed out that the 2011 Asian Cup, which was being held in Qatar, was moved to January because it was too hot in Doha in summer. He said that if it was too hot for the Asian Cup, it would be too hot for the World Cup, and the World Cup couldn't be moved.

He also repeated what Blatter said a few days before; that his preference was for only one bidder from the Asian confederation, but like Blatter, he also knew he couldn't enforce it.

Bin Hammam assured the Prime Minister that he and Lowy were 'working closely and diligently to realise the dream of Asia and Australia of hosting the World Cup in Australia.'

He also told the Prime Minister he knew just the way to help Australia's bid. Vision Asia. It was a development program that handed out money to needy football associations throughout the Asian confederation. Bin Hammam chaired Vision Asia, as well as the equivalent committee within FIFA that was responsible for allocating close to $1 billion every four years.

Bin Hammam told the Prime Minister that Vision Asia would greatly enhance our prospects.

He was so keen to help us that a week later he wrote to Rudd and Lowy. He mentioned the countries that needed assistance within the Asian confederation.

And he made another suggestion. If we also gave money for Africa, Bin Hammam wrote to Rudd, it 'would be very helpful to promote Australia in other continents.'

He invited Lowy to meet him in Kuala Lumpur in June so they could plan how to make it happen, after he met with African officials.

A few weeks after telling the government's aid agency that we needed money for Oceania, Asia and Africa, the need was confirmed by both Blatter and Bin Hammam.

AT THE CLOSING media conference of a rather dull Congress, Sepp Blatter was asked a general question about the dual bidding process agreed by the Executive Committee earlier in the week.

Referring to the 2010 and 2014 World Cup tournaments being held in the southern hemisphere, Blatter told a packed media conference that 'It is perhaps logical that Australia concentrates on the 2022 tournament.'

As he said it, he realised he might have put his foot in it. His eyes darted wildly around the room. He saw Ben and me at the back of the room. He tried to make amends.

He didn't.

'It is better for Australia in 2022 because the 2022 tournament might not be as tough to win as 2018.'

We could see the media pack craning their necks to make sure Ben hadn't left, keen to get a comment from him.

A few moments later, Ben told them what was to be our public position for the next two years – that is, we didn't accept we were out of the race for 2018, that we knew there would be strong competition from Europe, 'but our 100 per cent dedication and focus will be towards 2018.'

Brisbane: June 2008

'MINISTER, IS IT APPROPRIATE to be spending taxpayers' money on the World Cup bid in light of Sepp Blatter's comments on Friday?'

It was the Australian Broadcasting Corporation's (ABC) Sunday political affairs program, Insiders. The Minister being interviewed was the Finance Minister, one of the top people in the government and a strong supporter of football.

'The Government supports the judgement of the Football Federation, Barrie,' the Minister told the host.

But the host didn't want to let go. Half an hour later he was hosting another show, *Offsiders*, a sports program. He asked the same question.

Roy Masters, journalist and former sports official went for the jugular.

'This is a wicked, wilful waste of money. 60 million bucks. Australia is going to make the Salt Lake City Olympics Bid look like a tea party. We're wining and dining football officials all over the world for something that absolutely is not going to happen. Don't forget that soccer already gets 32 million bucks – this is on top of the $60 million – and that money comes out of the Australian Sports Commission.'

Where did Roy's $60 million figure come from?

I telephoned Lowy and Ben in New Caledonia where they had travelled the previous morning with Blatter and FIFA General Secretary, Jerome Valcke, for the Oceania Congress. The four were about to return to Australia for a World Cup qualifier between Australia and Iraq.

Lowy kept his promise to Reynald Temarii. He told the Oceania Congress members that their wishlist would be met - even though we didn't yet have the money from government.

Over the phone I could hear a discussion in the background.

'Bonita, the President wants to clarify his comments from Friday. Could you arrange a media conference at our hotel prior to the match?' Lowy asked.

THERE ARE VIPs and then there are VVIPs – very very important people. It really is a category.

The latter includes Blatter and the entire FIFA Executive Committee. They stay in the best hotels in town, enjoy chauffeured limousines, many have private aircraft like Frank Lowy, and they enjoy 'Head of State' status, such as green light corridors. What that means is that there's no waiting at traffic lights and a trouble-free run wherever you want to go.

I called the hotel where both Blatter and Lowy were staying asking for a media conference room. They gave me short shrift. 'Oh, madam, we are so sorry, but we don't have anyone who can look after a function inquiry on duty on Sunday.'

It was time to name-drop.

'Oh that's a shame,' I said. 'I'll have to let Mr Lowy know that you were not able to help.'

There was a small intake of breath. A pause. A hand was placed over the mouthpiece while he conferred with someone else. He came back to me quickly.

'Mr Lowy wants a small meeting room with full audio-visual facilities for a media conference today? And afternoon tea? For how long? 30 minutes you said? We'll have it set up in the next two hours so you can check it out before they arrive.'

By the time I arrived at the hotel about an hour before the media conference, a small army had descended on the lobby.

There was hotel security, FIFA security, FFA security, Blatter's personal staff, Lowy's personal assistant, the hotel executive management team, my colleague Stuart Taggart with a clipboard tucked under his arm, and me with copies of a media release and large print speaking points for Blatter and Lowy.

The hotel manager looked aghast when the journalists started arriving. In their casual gear, with TV cameras, sound recorders and laptops slung over their shoulders, they looked out of place in the understated and pristine elegance of the hotel lobby.

The manager summoned me. 'You have to get those men out of my lobby,' he said.

The questions and comments from the media came thick and fast as I ushered them upstairs. In Australia's small football media community, the same journalist who rushes to meet a deadline after a World Cup qualifier is also expected to cover issues of football politics.

'What's all this about then?'

'You do realise it's a bloody nuisance to have to come here when there's a game on? Now we've just got to get back again.'

'This better not take too long.'

'They better be on time.'

'You've got to be kidding,' another said. 'Sepp be fast! Not possible, my friend.'

BLATTER AND LOWY sprang out of the back of their chauffeured limousine. The hotel manager greeted them effusively, deferentially bowing his head and handing them their room keys. Valcke and Ben, who were following in the second limousine, quickly caught up with their bosses.

Lowy pulled me aside. 'I am tired. I have talked to him for four hours. The entire trip home. He knows what he needs to say.'

Why didn't this fill me with confidence?

'Oh, lovely lady again. How are you?' asked Blatter strolling across to join us. He gave me three kisses, Swiss-style.

'I'm fine thanks Mr Blatter. How was New Caledonia?'

'It was very lovely. Very nice. But a very quick trip. I am tired. But don't worry, I will fix this for my Aussie friends.' He pronounced Aussie as 'Ossie'.

I looked at the two septugenarians in front of me. They both said they were tired. Behind their smiling facades they looked it, and it would be another seven hours before their duties were complete for the evening.

Blatter felt at home in front of microphones and cameras. He strode to the front of the room and beckoned Lowy to sit next to him. Ben and I stood just inside the closed door.

'The first thing I want to say is that I did not say that Australia should forget about bidding for the 2018 tournament because you do not have a chance.'

I looked at the floor and tried not to laugh. It was exactly what he had said. The journalists were staring at him, nonplussed. He continued.

'It does not matter if you are not successful. You can still go for the next one. But you should go for 2018.'

It might have been alright if he had stopped there. He felt compelled to continue.

'Although I must say that the Europeans would be favourites. You have to remember that the next World Cup in 2010 is in South Africa and the one after that is in South America.'

Lowy interrupted: 'What the President means is that if we are not successful in 2018, it does not rule out 2022.'

The two men looked at each other and smiled.

'How are relations with Oceania, Mr Lowy?' asked one journalist.

Lowy beamed. 'We have reacquainted ourselves with one another. And we are interested in helping the Oceania confederation to get established in football,' he replied.

'What does that mean exactly?' the journalist asked.

'Well, for a start, Oceania confederation will have television rights to broadcast the A-League. And I have also invited Oceania to create a team of islands to join the A-League as one of the expansion teams.'

The journalists looked up from their notepads. Lowy often talked of A-League expansion, but never before had an Oceania team been mentioned.

Lowy continued. 'And I am very pleased to say we have enlisted the valuable support of Oceania for our bid.'

By now, some of the journalists were starting to pack-up. They were anxious to get back to the stadium. If they heard Frank say that Oceania agreed to vote for us it was mostly - but not entirely - unreported.

Sydney: June 2008

TWO DAYS LATER Ben and I were meeting with Lowy in his office at Westfield headquarters.

Lowy was soon leaving for his customary break in the northern hemisphere. He liked to visit his business interests and spent time either in his large yacht moored in the Mediterranean or one of his homes in New York or Tel Aviv every Australian winter.

'I want to talk to Roy,' Lowy said. He meant Roy Masters who so strongly criticised the bid on television a few days before. 'Bonita. Contact him for me and tell him I would like him to come and see him when I get back. Now, can we trust these journalists not to say anything more?'

'Many of them will have a holiday in July, Frank, and the A-League starts in August so that should take their mind off things to do with the bid,' Ben said. 'But there is another one who's starting to ask a few awkward questions. He's asking us why we're really bidding.'

'Tell him because we want to win. I don't know why these people have to ask questions,' Lowy said.

'It's their job,' I said.

'They are picking on us. Picking on me,' Lowy said crossly.

'I disagree. The Olympics had plenty of questions asked about them. It's a legitimate inquiry for them, especially when we're using public money.'

I felt Ben kick me under the table. He was warning me to stop.

The discussion turned to how much money we'd ask for from the government. I was to prepare the strategy submission over the coming weeks.

Ben said that he thought $90 million was about right.

I was incredulous. 'What could we could possibly need $90 million for?' I asked.

Lowy was distracted by a business phone call. Ben and I stood to move outside to the ante room while he took the call, but Lowy signalled for us to stay in the room. Ben and I continued talking quietly.

'Legacy,' replied Ben.

'Legacy? You mean brown paper bags?'

'You shouldn't say that.'

'In the absence of any other information about what we could possibly need $90 million for, all I can assume when it comes to FIFA is that 'legacy' is a euphemism for brown paper bags.'

There was a period of silence while we waited for Lowy to complete his call.

'We should ask for less than $60 million,' I said.

'Why?' asked Lowy.

'Because that's how much Roy Masters said we were getting and it will show he was wrong.'

There was another option of course.

Some people, especially a prominent local football journalist who regularly called for it, believed Lowy should put his own money into the game. The view was that, by virtue of a $100 million or so 'gift', he could give the game the capital and the impetus it needed to fulfil its potential. Lowy's view was that he gave enough to the sport by virtue of his involvement. He gave it instant credibility, he backed it with his reputation and his standing within government and commercial circles.

I agreed with Lowy in respect of the day-to-day business of the sport. It needed to be developed and managed in a way that made it financially self-sustaining. But I thought the World Cup bid was different.

'Are you sure you don't want to pay for it yourself?' I asked. 'The reason I ask is that we – you - have to be prepared to be fully accountable for taxpayers' money.'

'If the government can't support this, we may as well not do it,' was the reply.

I let it drop, not least because Ben had gone visibly pale under his suntan.

It was agreed that we would ask for funding in two parts. The first part would be under $60 million. The second would flag the need for up to another $30 million for legacy programs.

CHAPTER 5
An idea that was bound to backfire

Sydney: June 2008

WHO WAS THIS man in front of me and why I was meeting him? He had just arrived from Germany. He told me it was a speculative visit to see me and one of my colleagues.

I looked curiously at his business card.

His name was Andreas Abold. It told me that he owned a marketing and events company in Munich.

Tall, slender, with light brown wavy hair, he was immaculately and expensively dressed with an equally expensive looking leather briefcase and the very latest MacBook. He made our shabby office look even more shabby.

He explained that he came to see us because he wanted to work on the Australian World Cup bid. I asked him why. His English was excellent.

'Because I think you are in a winning position,' he said. 'You just hosted the FIFA Congress. The World Cup hasn't been here. Everyone knows how good the Sydney Olympics was. You have a beautiful country. Your bid is very well supported by your government. And Frank Lowy is very successful and knows what needs to happen to win.'

He ran through a presentation that set out his winning strategies for Germany in 2006, South Africa 2010 and the Club World Cup in Abu Dhabi in 2009 and 2010.

It was textbook stuff. Solid, but not rocket science. And no particular sizzle.

He told us more. He is a lifelong Bayern Munich supporter. He met his second and current wife while working on the German bid – she was an employee of the German FA. He said the bid process were some of the happiest days of his life. We would travel the world in five-star luxury. He said he looked forward to showing us what a wonderful time it could be for us too.

'If you pick me, you get a bonus of course,' he said pausing for effect. 'You get Franz also.'

Abold explained his close and long relationship with Executive Committee member, Franz Beckenbauer.

Now I understood. Andreas Abold was part of the deal with the German football association. It was not a speculative visit at all.

Canberra: September 2008

SEVERAL WEEKS LATER I was in Canberra, across the table from six senior public servants who were trying to understand the bid budget before them.

Ben Buckley and Stuart Taggart were in Germany to meet with the German FA and Andreas Abold.

Soon afterwards, Radmann and Abold visited Mohamed Bin Hammam in Qatar to find out more about his ideas for supporting football development activity in Asia and Africa, outlined in Bin Hammam's letters to Prime Minister Rudd and Lowy in June. On Radmann's and Abold's return to Europe, they established a company called Beyond Limits Marketing, registered in Switzerland.

While I developed and wrote the strategy document that gave the narrative to the bid budget, I was not involved in the internal discussions that arrived at the detail of the budget beyond the earlier strategic level discussion with Lowy and Ben about a two-tiered approach.

What we had now was a budget in two parts but it wasn't a whole lot different from the original number of $90 million that Ben had mentioned in Lowy's office. The main operating budget of $54 million which was the subject of the strategy document before us, and a second 'legacy' budget of $28.5 million for which there was no strategy.

I wasn't comfortable. Having previously worked in the federal Finance Department, which monitors all public expenditure and where you're required to be healthily sceptical about all requests for funding, I had a good sense of what the officials might be thinking.

They had a lot of questions: some reasonable, some nit-picking.

How many consultants would we engage? What would the travel money be spent on? What type of office accommodation were we moving to? How many staff would we employ? They asked if we would be participating in government events overseas. They confirmed that if we held an event at an Australian Embassy or High Commission, the cost would come from the bid budget. And then the tough question.

'If we win, how much is it really going to cost us?' asked a Treasury official.

Only the previous week, Lowy and Ben had met with the Tourism Minister and the Sports Minister. The Tourism Minister asked the same question. Ben told me he did some back of the envelope calculations and came up with $1 billion. I repeated the story and the amount.

The Treasury official looked over the top of his glasses at me. 'That seems low,' he said. He looked at his papers. 'You say we'll need a minimum of 12-14 stadiums but we don't have that many. It's going to cost a helluva lot more than $1 billion.'

I thought he was right, but I suggested it would be better if we responded to the questions in writing because it was not my area of responsibility.

'What is this last line in here,' pointing to the strategy document, 'about needing more money for a bid legacy program? Is this on top of the $54 million you want from this submission?'

'Yes,' I said quietly.

'What exactly is a 'bid legacy' program?' he asked.

I did my best to explain.

'That's $84 million you're wanting in total,' he said. I nodded. What could I say? I thought it was ridiculous too.

'You're going to have to give us another submission on that,' he said. 'And we need it by the end of next week.'

I DID NOT want to write the second strategy document for the bid legacy program. But Ben wanted me to. I felt physically ill having to do so.

'What is it for?' I asked Ben. I said again that it sounded to me like we were asking the government for brown paper bag money.

What he did know was that his meetings in Germany made it clear we would need the extra money for bid legacy. 'You're good at putting words together which make sense. Just make it sound like we know what we're doing,' Ben said.

'I have no idea what we're doing.' My voice rose in exasperation.

'Neither do I. But we have to get that money.'

We sent through the strategy - to use the term loosely - for bid legacy the following week.

Sydney: November 2008

I WAS A kid when Australia made it to the World Cup in 1974. It was such a thrilling time for so many to see us make it for the first time. Our group included Chile, East Germany and the eventual winners and hosts, West Germany.

My overriding memory of that tournament was its star. The World Cup winning captain, Franz Beckenbauer.

I was lucky to meet him earlier when he was in Sydney for the FIFA Congress. Now, six months later, Ben told me that Beckenbauer was making a brief visit to Australia. Lowy and he were meeting with him again.

'Why didn't you tell me this before?' I asked. 'We could have arranged a function and some media around his visit.'

'No you couldn't. It's a private meeting. Very hush-hush. You're not to tell anyone.'

I didn't learn it until nine years later when the Garcia Report into the 2018/2022 World Cup bidding process was made public; Beckenbauer was accompanied on that visit by his aide, Fedor Radmann, who was already in regular communication with Lowy and Ben about our bid. In other words, the trio of Franz Beckenbauer, Fedor Radmann and Andreas Abold were on board already - if not formally in a contractual sense, at least unofficially with a wink and a nod.

Sydney: December 2008

IN DECEMBER, CABINET agreed to give us just shy of $46 million, $8 million less than the $54 million we sought for the main grant.

The extra $28.5 million we also wanted for bid legacy was unsurprisingly rejected. We were told instead that we should approach the overseas aid agency to try to divert their modest sports project funding into bid-related activity.

Ben, Stuart Taggart and I were meeting in Ben's office.

'Day one,' said Ben. 'Who do we already have on board?'

Stuart reeled off the consultants we had already engaged.

'PwC for the cost-benefit analysis, the analysis of the winter sports and the environmental impact statement. Andreas is doing the Bid Book, final presentation and technical inspection. ECN is responsible for strategy, lobbying, competitor analysis and international PR,' continued Stuart.

'Who or what is ECN?' I asked.

'Peter Hargitay,' said Ben.

'Who is he?' I asked.

Ben pursed his lips and asked Stuart to leave. He was reluctant to go but he packed up his notebook and shuffled out the door, closing it behind him.

Ben walked to his desk, beckoning me to take one of the seats facing him.

'You really don't know who Peter Hargitay is?'

'No. Should I?'

He went to the tall bookshelf along the wall to his left, ran his finger along the books on the top shelf, and found what he was looking for one-third of the way along.

He handed me 'FOUL!', the book about FIFA corruption by Andrew Jennings that had been published a few years beforehand.

Andrew Jennings was known worldwide for being the bête noire of both the IOC and FIFA.

'Have you read this?'

'I did when it came out.'

'Read it again. Or at least read the bits about Peter Hargitay again,' said Ben. And while you're at it, can you dig around and find out what else you can about him?'

This didn't sound encouraging. I asked how we had come to employ him.

'He's Hungarian. Les Murray recommended him. So did Blatter. So did Bin Hammam. Frank wants him.'

The late Les Murray, who also came from Hungary, enjoyed celebrity status in Australia. He was a TV commentator appointed to the FIFA Ethics Committee on Lowy's recommendation in 2004.

Ben continued, almost as if he needed to convince himself. 'He can open doors for us. To his good mates. Blatter, Bin Hammam, Jack Warner. We've got Beckenbauer. With Reynald too, that's five votes before we even get started.'

Just as I reached the door to leave, Ben said 'You're going to have a fair bit to do with him over the next two years so it's better we both know what we're dealing with.' He moved some papers around on his tidy desk.

'And you're going to have to be nice to him, however difficult that is.'

It was early evening when I returned to Ben's office after a few hours of looking into our new consultant.

'He owes a man in Switzerland quite a lot of money,' I said.

He asked what that was about.

'A Swiss man loaned him some money. He didn't pay it back. His defence seems to be that he shouldn't have to pay it back because it was a long time ago.'

We looked at each other, realising how absurd that was and laughed.

'What's even funnier is, he seems to be winning the argument,' I said. 'But I guess that's Swiss law for you.'

I asked him if he was sure Peter Hargitay was right for our bid.

'It's what Frank wants.'

'Shouldn't we go out to tender?'

'Kate said we didn't have to when they are such specialised services,' he said, referring to the Sports Minister.

I turned to leave. We were heading to Canberra the next morning for another meeting with government.

'By the way, tomorrow, don't mention him if they ask us about consultants.' Ben said. 'And don't mention him to any media either.'

'That's not a good idea. It's bound to backfire,' I said.

'It doesn't matter. It's what Frank and Peter want.'

Sydney: January 2009

'CAN YOU TALK?' It was Matthew Hall. An Australian journalist living in New York. Someone I had known for more than a decade.

'Yes.'

'You don't have to say anything and I'm not going to ask you. I believe Peter Hargitay is working for FFA and the Australian bid. If that is the case, I just want to tell you that the people involved in football now may be 20 rungs or more above the ladder than previous administrations, but they're really not that different.'

I understood what Hall was saying. He and I were part of a group who campaigned for a change in governance and management in Australian football in 2001. I remained silent.

'I also believe Lowy met privately with Jack Warner on his yacht recently. Don't trust Warner. Or Les Murray either.' He hung up.

Moments later, I recounted the conversation with Hall to Ben.

'Shit. How long do you think the fact that Hargitay is working for us will be kept quiet?' Ben asked.

It was only a matter of time. I said again that the best way of managing Hargitay's appointment was to announce it along with other consultancies.

'Frank won't agree,' Ben said. 'In the meantime, this has happened.' He handed me an email. It was from Lowy. It contained a news report emanating from the Caribbean quoting Jack Warner, head of CONCACAF.

Warner criticised Australia for bidding on the basis that we were now part of Asia, and the Asian confederation hosted the World Cup in 2002. Warner added: "If Australia had stayed in Oceania then we could say that Oceania has never had the World Cup and there could be no question that Australia deserves to host in 2018."

Lowy wanted a letter by the end of the day to Sebastian Coe, then the head of the FIFA Ethics Committee, to complain about Warner's comments.

The letter to Coe was with Lowy by the end of the day. But it was never sent. Hargitay told Lowy that he would smooth things over with Warner.

ANDREAS ABOLD WAS visiting us again, accompanied by one of his business partners. He stood before the entire bid team - still only five of us including Ben, Stuart and me - assembled around the board room table. His formula for winning hadn't changed since the previous June.

He started by reminding us of his track record. I noticed it was now updated to include the 2011 Women's World Cup in Germany - without any hint of irony, considering Germany's hosting of the tournament was virtually guaranteed as part of the agreement with the German FA that saw Australia withdraw its bid.

'From now until decision day, we must attend all FIFA events and every event of every confederation. For FIFA, we need to prove our competence, present a strong national image, forge alliances with Executive Committee members and others close to them. Every time we see ExCo members, we give them a present.'

'What type of present?' I interrupted.

'Something that reminds them of your country.'

My mind raced. Stuffed kangaroos? Vegemite? AC-DC recordings?

'What type of thing did you give?' I asked.

'Oh, things like jewellery, cufflinks, watches, handbags for their wives, belts, shoes, ties, pens, that sort of thing. German of course.'

'No BMWs or Audis?' I asked.

Abold looked quizzically at me.

'Bonita's joking,' said Ben.

Abold gave an ever-so-slight smile. 'No, no, never a car, Bonita. But it was always very classy, very elegant, very German. The best. Hugo Boss. Mont Blanc. Wellendorf.'

Who knew Mont Blanc was German?

Ben grabbed my notebook, wrote on it and slid it back to me. I read it. *"You are being very naughty. Stop it."*

Abold continued.

'As well as gifts each time we see them, we must also send Executive Committee members birthday and Christmas gifts.'

So that was it? We send them gifts and we'd win?

'And the Bid Book must leave no question unanswered. The Bid Book for Germany was 1,260 pages,' he said proudly.

I wondered who actually read a Bid Book of that length. I didn't have to wonder for long.

'Of course, none of the ExCo read the Bid Book. But still it must be perfect,' he continued.

'And so must be the FIFA inspection visit and the final presentation. None of these things will win the bid but they must be delivered perfectly. If they are not, they can count against you. They are part of a good impression. FIFA expects they will all be excellent.'

The Bid Book, the FIFA inspection visit and the final presentation. All Abold's responsibility. Yet he just said none of them counted.

I had to ask. 'Why don't they have any influence on the bid outcome?'

Abold looked at me as if I was naïve or stupid or both. He told me there are other things which determine who will win.

'Intangible things,' he said. I swear his eyes twinkled as he said it.

It occurred to me that Andreas Abold had a marvellous business model. He gets paid to produce a Bid Book that no one who actually matters reads. He convinces his clients it's the Bid Book they must have even though they don't really need it. Plus he gets to charge clients highly for his expertise. His contract was for $3.2 million.

On the final afternoon of their week-long visit, Abold gave us a list of 13 do's and don'ts. They were a combination of common sense and basic communications management.

There was one instruction on Abold's list that the Australian bid was unable to meet. It was number six: '*Clear, early definition around timing of venue and city selection*'.

Poor Ben and Stuart. They struggled for almost two years on stadium selection, venue selection, and who would pay for what ended up being the $5 billion worth of work needed to meet FIFA's technical requirements. When it came to the three other football codes, Ben and Stuart endured an even tougher time.

CHAPTER 6
Getting to know you

Sydney: February 2009

THE FIRST THING I noticed about Peter Hargitay was his hands.

I was expecting the gleaming skull, the goatee and the wispy hair from the description by Andrew Jennings in FOUL!

They are big hands. Not large big, but thick big. Thick hands with short, thick fingers; a ring on his little finger and a wedding ring. I thought, 'he doesn't play piano or violin.'

I stretched out my hand to greet Hargitay and took a seat at the small, round meeting table in the corner of Ben's office alongside my colleague Stuart.

It was a hot, early February morning. Australia was in the midst of one of its longest droughts and summer in the south-east was stifling. Conditions had worsened in recent days. Bushfires threatened.

I opened my notebook and pen and prepared to learn from the man who, I was assured, was going to win us the World Cup.

Hargitay gave us a rundown on some of the members of FIFA's Executive Committee and the anticipated changes in the coming months. He imparted this as if we were fortunate to have access to such insights from someone so well connected to the FIFA elite. But my first thoughts, as I listened, were that most of his so-called gems were already public information dressed up by him as exclusive intelligence.

We had compiled extensive research on Executive Committee members with information on their backgrounds, their interests, their marriages (the number not their nature), their children, the languages they spoke, their education and the personal honours they had garnered from our planning for the FIFA Congess in the previous May. It was something we updated constantly so we knew who was who, what they looked like and who was up for election.

We knew that someone from Egypt would be elected to replace Slim Chiboub from Tunisia as the fourth Executive Committee member from the African continent, but we did not know whom – and neither did Hargitay.

'Nothing happens in Egyptian football unless Mubarak's son says so.'

We received the same information from the Australian Embassy in Cairo.

Press reports in recent months had suggested Russian Prime Minister Vladimir Putin wasn't happy with Koloskov, the Russian ExCo member.

'He will want someone close to him,' Hargitay said, referring to Putin.

No kidding.

He told us that Spanish Executive Committee member, Angel Maria Villar Llona, wouldn't vote for us.

'He will vote for the US or Qatar. But he's not worth worrying about.'

Ben explained our Steven Bradbury strategy.

'Of course, Jack is no problem,' said Hargitay, referring to Jack Warner. It was as if he didn't hear Ben explain our strategy. 'He will do whatever I say. And Mohamed's support is critical. In the next two to three weeks, he's going to say something about it.'

'Really?' asked Stuart. 'What can he say? Qatar is bidding.'

Our competitors were confirmed earlier in the week: 13 countries in 11 bids.

For 2018, we were up against joint bids from Belgium and Holland and Spain and Portugal as well as England, Russia, Mexico, the USA and Japan. For 2022, we were up against the same countries plus South Korea, Qatar and Indonesia.

Hargitay sniffed and cleared his throat again, ran a finger around the inside of his collar, and flicked his thumb and forefinger with much the same menace as a tiger flicks its tail. I got the sense Hargitay wasn't used to being questioned.

'Come on man, how can Qatar host the World Cup? It's too hot. It's too small.

No one would go. Mohamed doesn't even support Qatar.'

'But it is in the Middle East,' I said. 'It would be a powerful statement.'

'Yes, but FIFA isn't that stupid,' he said. He looked at me as if I was.

Perhaps because it was his first day with us he also remembered to follow-up with a smile. It was a closed mouth smile that didn't move to his eyes.

Hargitay had written to Bin Hammam the previous December when his company, ECN, was asked by international sports management company, IMG, to assess Qatar's bid chances. He wrote that he and Fedor Radmann agreed that Qatar's chances were 'virtually nil'. Bin Hammam replied that he didn't have a clue about a bid from Qatar.

Part of Hargitay's duties included looking after the international press. Hargitay said that he had excellent relationships with all the media who count. He told us that no other bidder had the level of access he enjoyed either to media or to the movers and shakers in FIFA. He said someone called Charlie Sale would be helpful.

'Who is Charlie Sale?' I asked.

'He's the most important and influential football journalist in England,' he said, looking at me as if I was simple. 'Everyone reads him.'

Hargitay told us he would devise a plan to deal with Lord David Triesman, Chairman of the English FA who was leading their bid. He said that Triesman was an 'idiot'.

He would also make a plan to deal with Michel Platini. Only the previous day, Platini was reported around the world saying that the 2018 World Cup should be in Europe - and in Europe every third time.

Hargitay expressed astonishment at Platini's comments, almost as if it was a personal affront to his consultancy. He added that Platini was a 'dangerous little faggot'. I wrote it down.

'Platini: PJH astounded by comments re 2018. *'dangerous little faggot.'*

Noticing me, Hargitay leaned over the table and said 'don't write that down Bonita.'

Ben laughed and advised Hargitay that I wrote down everything, had a mind like a steel trap, and the memory of an elephant.

'I have a good memory but Bonita's is better than anyone I've known,' he said.

Ben's long, suntanned fingers twisted nervously around the pen he was holding. He hadn't written a word and sounded half-pleased as he said this, perhaps realising that the journey with the 'chief strategist' for our bid would be long and arduous.

Tokyo: February 2009

FIVE DAYS LATER I was sitting in the top floor executive lounge of the Westin Hotel in Tokyo with Frank Lowy. He had asked me to join him for morning coffee.

We were in Tokyo in force. The Socceroos had a World Cup qualifier against Japan in Yokohama in the evening and we had started our bid charm offensive.

Japan was also bidding, but we wanted ExCo member Junji Ogura's second vote even though he would initially support Japan.

We left Sydney on the Monday night after a tragic weekend in Australia. Raging bushfires had killed 173 people. Before leaving, we announced the FFA was donating $100,000 to the bushfire appeal. It was the type of tragedy that binds a nation and its people regardless of where they are, and the Socceroos – nearly all expats – were also donating their match fees to the appeal.

'What did you think of Hargitay?' Lowy asked, knowing we had met the previous Friday.

'He's obviously intelligent.' I said. 'Very quick. Clever. I admire anyone who can speak as many languages as he can.'

'Yes, but what did you think of him?' Lowy insisted.

I weighed up what I knew, together with my first impressions.

What I knew was that Sepp Blatter, Mohamed Bin Hammam and Les Murray recommended him to Lowy. I knew that journalist Matthew Hall was not impressed with him.

Another leading football journalist, the late Michael Cockerill, told me that one of Lowy's most trusted advisors at Westfield described Hargitay to him as 'a walking time bomb' and couldn't believe Lowy engaged him for the World Cup bid.

I had re-read the portrayal of Hargitay in 'FOUL!' as Ben suggested.

Another FFA colleague, who referred to Hargitay as 'Hargy', described him as a 'piece of work.' He said that the FFA's previous CEO, John O'Neill, did not get on with Hargitay when he was hired by Lowy three years previously to help Australia be accepted as a member of the Asian Football Confederation.

'O'Neill used to complain that Hargy did nothing, but claimed all the glory,' the colleague said. 'If things don't go well, he'll find someone else to blame but it's always and only him if it goes right.'

I had some coffee. I knew Lowy respected me because I didn't duck his gaze.

'I only met him briefly in a meeting,' I said. 'He's not my type of person – but that doesn't matter. What's important is whether he can do what he says he can do in a way that we can live with.'

'Do you think he can?'

'I don't know. Do you?'

'I have to. I have to believe.'

Sydney: March 2009

IT WAS THE first day in our new offices. We moved 100 metres up the road in to a high-rise office building.

Ben sat at the head of the meeting table in his spacious white office, looking pleased with his new surroundings.

We were discussing the calendar of events between now and December 2010 when the vote would take place. I asked him to clarify my budget.

'About $7-8 million.'

I put my pen down. 'What?! The budget we put to government was $17 million.'

'They cut us back,' he said.

They cut us back by $8 million in total, and only $2 million in my area of responsibility. 'What happened to the rest of it?'

'We need it for other things.'

The problem was we had already spent half of the new budget amount, paying for creative work that Ben insisted be started last year. The budgets from the agencies we hired were all at premium prices. With this news, I said we would have to cancel the arrangements with two of the agencies because we could no longer afford them.

'You can't give lack of funds as the reason for cancelling the contracts,' Ben said to me.

'Why not?' I said.

'It will look like we don't know what we're doing.'

I looked at him. 'We don't know what we're doing! You've just told me for the first time that you cut my budget in half.'

I asked him where the rest of it was going. He said that I should not have presumed that the budget would be $17 million.

'It's a fair presumption to make. It's what we told government,' I said.

'We've had to take Hargitay's fee out of that.'

'How much is he getting?'

'100,000 or something.'

'What do you mean *'or something'*? 100,000 what? Dollars? Euros? Pounds? Per week?'

'Dollars per month.'

'That accounts for $2.4 million. What about the rest?'

He ignored the question, and instead said that he and Lowy were off to Zurich the following week to meet with Hargitay, Radmann and Abold.

I asked him who was Fedor Radmann.

'Didn't I mention this? He's very close to Beckenbauer.'

'So is Abold.'

'Yes, they're all close. They work together. The three of them. Fedor is a very experienced sports administrator. He ran the German bid. He was involved with the South African bid. He ran the Salzburg bid for the Olympics. Franz Beckenbauer and he are very, very close and he is a trusted confidante. He knows everyone at FIFA,' Ben said.

I was curious. 'When did this happen?' I asked.

He didn't look me in the eye. 'Last year. It's part of the deal with the German FA,' he said.

'What? We get all Germany's secrets plus we get Andreas Abold, Fedor Radmann and Franz Beckenbauer as well?'

'Radmann's part of the deal. I've got absolutely no say in this.' I got up to leave. 'But can you look into him for me and tell me what you find.'

I returned to Ben's office a few hours later. I showed him German newspaper reports by Thomas Kistner and Jens Weinreich which suggested that Radmann had convinced, by way of a payment, the former President of Oceania Football Confederation, and Reynald Temarii's predecessor, Charlie Dempsey to abstain from voting – an act which handed the 2006 World Cup to Germany rather than South Africa. Charlie Dempsey passed away the year before, aged 87.

'There's no proof that happened,' said Ben.

'Just a detailed published account from two reputable German investigative journalists in one of Germany's top broadsheet newspapers,' I said.

'Fedor denies it. Charlie Dempsey never admitted to it. You know you can't believe everything you read in the paper,' Ben replied.

I walked across to the door, closed it and turned around. I asked him if the reason my budget had been reduced was to fund Fedor and his activities.

'What are we doing Ben?' I asked. 'First, Peter Hargitay. Now this Fedor Radmann.'

He sighed. 'There are things going on in this bid that I can't tell you about. It's going to be a very tough two years. The only way we'll get through it is if we stick together.'

I stood in silence for a moment. 'When do we plan on telling the media?'

'We don't. No one is to know that Fedor is working for us. Ever.'

THE BID REGISTRATION document arrived.

Bidders were asked to consider the impact that hosting the event would have on the country, society and the football legacy to the host nation and beyond.

The guidelines also warned not to 'attempt to influence' Executive Committee members. And although FIFA was inviting bids for 2018 and 2022, the guidelines warned against 'unfair collaboration' and vote swapping.

The guidelines were the cause of much hand-wringing between different sets of lawyers associated with FFA. In the end, the relationship with the German FA, Beckenbauer, Oceania and Temarii were deemed irrelevant on a technicality. They were made before the bid registration agreement was signed.

As it turned out, we were not the only bidders to ignore the guidelines.

CHAPTER 7

Did Qatar make an offer FIFA refused?

Sydney: March 2009

FRANK LOWY WANTED to know how we were progressing with Russia.

The Russian bid was backed by President Medvedev and Prime Minister Putin, who later swapped positions as part of their tandem rule. The Russian bid involved their closest allies, most of whom were from St Petersburg.

Putin's first deputy prime minister and money-man, Igor Shuvalov, was chairman of the bid. Vitaly Mutko was Russia's new representative on the FIFA Executive Committee. He was also the Sports Minister, the President of the Russian FA and the spokesperson on their bid committee. It was headed by a former colleague of Putin at the KGB (now FSB), Alexey Sorokin. It had the financial backing of, amongst others, billionaires Alisher Usmanov and Roman Abramovich.

The advice from Australia's consultants was that the Russian bid was not going to lose. Russia wanted 2018. We knew our best chance was 2022, despite our public position on 2018. The consultants said Russia would be a good strategic partner for us.

Our consultants enjoyed solid connections through the network of FIFA insiders, just like them, who were consultants to the Russian bid. Markus Siegler and Andreas Herren, both former FIFA staffers, worked for the Russians.

Between leaving FIFA and joining the Russian bid team, Siegler was in business with Hargitay. They worked briefly together on the English bid until Lord Triesman arrived as FA chairman and found an elegant way to move Hargitay on.

Hargitay offered his services to Australia, Siegler to Russia. The question was whether they really parted ways.

Herren was an 18-year veteran of FIFA's media department and worked as Siegler's deputy for five years. He was known to Hargitay, Radmann and Abold.

'Bonita, I want you talk to Rudd's office about inviting Medvedev here. And find out more about Traktovenko and Zenit,' Lowy said.

He wanted to know whether David Traktovenko had a relationship with Putin, Medvedev or Mutko as part of the St Petersburg clique that formed Russia's power base. Lowy sold much of his remaining stake in Sydney FC to Traktovenko the previous December. A St Petersburg local with a daughter, son-in-law and grandchildren in Sydney, Traktovenko was co-owner of Zenit along with Vladimir Kogan until they sold it to Gazprom in 2006.

Ben's phone vibrated. He looked at who was calling, excused himself, and left the room.

There was silence. I tapped my pen on the notebook. Lowy saw me frown.

'What's the matter, Bonita?'

I looked at him. 'Two things,' I said. 'Can you trust the consultants?'

'Do you?' he asked.

'No. Not if we're looking to win the bid fairly. Andreas, maybe. But the other two definitely not. I think Andreas and his company are just the public face of their operations,' I said.

He ignored it. 'And the second?' he asked.

'All this talk of Russia made me think of something I used to hear someone say when I was young.'

'What was that?' Lowy insisted.

I hesitated, adopting the eastern European accent of the person whom I had heard say it on multiple occasions – more than 40 years ago. Slowly, emphasising each word.

'Never trust a Russian.'

I shifted in my seat and put my pen down. 'It sounds racist, doesn't it? But in context, from the person who said it, it wasn't meant that way.'

Lowy was staring into space but he cut me off. 'I think this person could well have been right. But on this occasion,' he shrugged his shoulders and turned his mouth down, 'I have to. I have no choice. This is how we win. We have to deal with the Russians.'

There was a heavy silence. I thought to myself that we did have a choice.

The side door swung open. Ben walked in.

'I was just explaining to Bonita why we need to get close to the Russians,' Lowy said.

BEN WAS BACK from a lightning visit to Europe with Lowy where they caught-up with Hargitay, Radmann and Abold. Along with Lowy and his two closest Board members, Brian Schwartz and Philip Wolanski, the seven men were the self-styled 'strategy brains trust' of the bid. The group was referred to as the 'A Team'.

The next priority was to fill-out the international match schedule, starting with the Socceroos.

There were no prizes for guessing the priorities. All Executive Committee countries. Nigeria, Cote d'Ivoire, Cameroon, Egypt, Paraguay, Switzerland and Jamaica. I looked up from my notebook when I heard Jamaica.

They didn't have a vote, but the president of the Jamaican FA was 'Captain' Horace Burrell, a friend of Warner and Hargitay. Warner apparently put in a special request.

Reynald Temarii, President of the Oceania confederation had also been in touch again. Temarii told Lowy and Ben that he had been approached by other bidders. If we didn't get the money soon, Oceania would have to reconsider their vote. They issued a deadline. They wanted to sign an agreement at the FIFA Congress in the Bahamas in June. If not with us, then they'd go to one of the other bidders.

'Go back to Canberra. Get the money. Don't come back without it,' Ben told me.

He then closed the door to his office. It was a sign that what he was about to say was extremely confidential.

'We need a letter to the Emir of Qatar from the Prime Minister inviting him to Australia,' he said.

'Why?'

Ben sighed. 'Why do you have to ask *'why'*? Can't you just do it because I told you to?'

'I have to know why so I can give the letter some context. Otherwise it's meaningless. What do I say? *'Dear Emir, please visit Australia as you'll really like it and you could probably buy us out,'* I joked.

'Because we want to talk him out of bidding.' He continued. 'Peter says it's not a genuine bid. He says it's just so they can get noticed on the world stage. The idea is we invite the Emir, Rudd gives him the VVIP treatment, he knows Australia's noticed them, and we talk him out of bidding.'

I guffawed. 'That's ridiculous.'

His voice became sterner, more serious. 'Bonita, you might think it's ridiculous. I might think it's ridiculous. But it's what we're doing. Qatar needs to be convinced to withdraw, and that needs to happen at the highest level. Bin Hammam doesn't even support their bid.'

With Europe destined to get 2018, 2022 would come down to Asia versus USA. We believed we were the natural frontrunner in Asia.

'We need to be the only Asian bidder. Japan and South Korea won't get it and they know it. They're only in it for their own political reasons. Indonesia is not serious. They just want to get what they can out of other bidders, including us. And, by the way, they're coming to see us soon. We just need to convince Qatar to withdraw,' he repeated.

If the other four Asian bidders were out of the way, that would give us four more votes in addition to Temarii and Beckenbauer. In other words, we would be heading into the first round with six votes - even without closing a deal with Russia.

A FEW DAYS later Ben called me back into his office.

He spun around from his desk. He was white. Shellshocked. He told me to close the door and sit down. He asked if I had sent the letter to the Prime Minister's office about the visit by the Emir of Qatar.

'Yes,' I said.

'Get it back.'

'Okay, but why?'

'The Emir has been to see Blatter in Zurich and asked him straight out: *'How much do I need to pay to buy the World Cup.'*

'What!? Do you mean a bribe?'

'No, in terms of underwriting and owning the entire bloody thing.'

'What was the reaction?'

'Blatter said it's not for sale.'

'And who told you this?'

'Hargitay.'

'How does he know?'

'Blatter. Valcke. One or both of them told him. I'm not sure which.'

I sat thinking for a few moments. It didn't sound true to me. Why would the Emir of Qatar, who's a world figure, a head of state, take the risk of going to FIFA to offer 'to buy' the World Cup?

'The Emir isn't stupid. He would know that someone would leak something like that, or eventually it would get out. It doesn't make sense to me,' I said.

'Who's not telling the truth? Hargitay, Valcke, Blatter?'

I shrugged my shoulders. 'Who knows? All of them. Any of them. I guess there's always a possibility that Qatar, or any bidder, could 'buy' the World Cup through an otherwise legitimate backdoor somehow. Such as a bonus on a sponsorship or broadcast contract.'

We sat contemplating the possibilities. Al Jazeera. Qatar Airways. Qatar Gas.

Ben said that, according to Hargitay, it was the best thing that could ever happen. Blatter and Valcke were hopping mad and determined to see Qatar didn't win.

Yet, only days ago, Hargitay and the other consultants said our only serious rival for 2022 was the USA.

I contacted the Prime Minister's office and asked them to return the draft letter.

CHAPTER 8
The art of the deal

London: April 2009

HARGITAY AND HIS son and business partner, Stevie, were kind. They insisted on arranging for their driver to meet me at Heathrow and take me to the hotel before meeting with them mid-morning.

The driver was a large, fit-looking man, from Albania via Macedonia, driving a big Mercedes-Benz that still had the new-car leather smell.

I sat in the front passenger seat with him and we talked about the Balkans, the fact that he had been working for Hargitay ever since arriving in London, and the football VIPs he had driven around. It seems he had met almost everyone but most regularly Blatter, Warner and Bin Hammam.

Ben wanted me to travel to London to brief the Hargitays on the bid brand, our initial promotional film, and the launch of our bid planned for Canberra in June.

After settling-in to the hotel, I was taken on the short drive to what was then the Hargitay office, opposite the back of the exclusive Grosvenor House in Park Street, Mayfair.

It was a lovely Spring day: fine, sunny, an almost perfect temperature. Hargitay's office was a classic brick Mayfair mansion with a semi-basement, a short flight of stairs up to the front entrance and several stories high.

It was home to several businesses. The driver showed me through the front door, and I was greeted by Hargitay who had come down stairs on the other side of the small, marbled lobby. His greeting was warm; he introduced me briefly to the woman at the reception desk.

While Hargitay called Stevie, I was shown into a room at the front of the building tastefully furnished with a sofa, comfortable chairs, coffee table with coffee table books, a decorative desk and some expensive looking artefacts and a fireplace.

Stevie bounded into the room. He was tall, tanned, with a long face, receding hairline and designer stubble. He was lively and friendly. I judged him to be in his mid-to-late 30s. Within minutes, he told me he was a lawyer but now helped his father in all aspects of their business interests. These appeared to be diverse, encompassing strategic consultancy services, security and intelligence advice, making motion pictures and sports public relations, marketing and event management.

I took them through brand imagery, event plans, public relations plans, domestic media issues and briefing them on the issues my colleague Stuart Taggart was grappling with, such as the other sports and stadium selection. We spoke of the international friendlies to be arranged and events with Executive Committee members.

Hargitay said that we needed to employ someone in London to look after international public relations.

'I thought you were doing that,' I said.

'I am responsible for it, yes. But I am the chief strategist for this bid. I can't do the day-to-day media relations work.'

I sat silent for a moment, wondering what to say. This was new. I wondered if he meant another person would cost more money or was within his consultancy fee. Ben told me we were already paying him $100,000 a month. The answer to the budgetary issue soon came.

'For the sake of a little bit extra money, it will make a big difference.'

Hargitay said he would introduce me to the London journalist he had in mind tomorrow.

'But now we're taking you somewhere very special for lunch,' Hargitay said.

We walked down the short flight of stairs to the waiting car. It was a ten minute ride until we pulled up outside Cipriani where we were greeted warmly by the maître d'.

It was popular. Almost every table and seat at the bar was full. It was quite old-fashioned with lots of waiters buzzing around in stiff white jackets, long white tablecloths, heavy dark timber, round-backed timber seats with leather cushions, chandeliers with an ochre hue.

We were shown a large round table at the back of the room with seating for six.

Hargitay's eyes were bright, shining, looking around the room to see who else was there.

'This is where all the beautiful people come,' he said. 'Aren't you impressed?'

Not really. I said nothing.

The menu was in Italian and Hargitay spoke at length with the sommelier in Italian before selecting a wine. I couldn't think of anything worse right at that moment than drinking wine at a swanky restaurant in Mayfair when I was jetlagged and had barely three hours sleep in the past 48 hours. Later that night we were heading to Stamford Bridge to see Chelsea v Everton.

'We are members there, Bonita, and personal friends of Peter Kenyon. We have a wonderful experience for you in the Armani Lounge.'

Peter Kenyon was the CEO of Chelsea Football Club, and previously of Manchester United. He was one of Hargitay's closest associates in football. He was a regular guest of Mohamed Bin Hammam's at Asian Football Confederation events, and would sometimes accompany Bin Hammam and Hargitay on visits within Asia using Bin Hammam's private jet.

A few hours later, and it was exciting to be at Stamford Bridge for my first English Premier League match.

Guus Hiddink was coaching Chelsea and Socceroo, Tim Cahill, was having a great season for Everton.

The Armani Lounge is like many other VIP lounges in stadiums around most of the western world. It was small and, therefore, exclusive.

We were met by two glamorous blonde-haired women – dressed in Armani of course – at the entrance to the lounge. From there, we entered into a small area that had sofas, occasional tables for pre-dinner drinks and canapés which led directly to the outdoor seating with a prime view of the ground. To the left of the lounge area was another room set up with several dining tables.

There was another meal to get through. Peter Kenyon gave a speech to the obviously well-heeled group of people. After dinner, I took my assigned seat next to Kenyon in the front row.

'We got you pride of place, Bonita. Right next to the CEO. How good is that? No-one else could do that for you,' Hargitay said. I thanked him.

It was one of the disadvantages of working in football administration that you became more detached from what drew you to it in the first place. I'd rather be out on the terraces.

The stadium was packed. The match was a fairly dour 0-0 – or maybe it seemed that way because jet lag and tiredness had set-in.

After the match, Kenyon kindly escorted me through the bowels of the stadium, across the pitch and over to the change rooms so I could say hello to Tim Cahill.

I WALKED THE five minutes to the Hargitays' office the next morning before Stevie and I set off for some venue inspections. So focussed were Hargitay and Stevie on the English bid - despite the fact that we didn't consider it a serious rival for 2022 - that a London launch of the Australian bid was also being talked about for later in the year. They said their friend Elle Macpherson could be the star attraction.

Stevie was driving his own vehicle this morning, a luxury SUV.

'We know that Peter will come,' he said. 'You know, Peter Kenyon whom you met last night. And Richard Scudamore.' He lowered his voice a little. 'You know that Richard can't stand Triesman or Anson.'

Richard Scudamore was CEO of the Premier League. Stevie was referring to Lowy's counterpart, Lord David Triesman, and the CEO of the England bid, Andy Anson.

I wasn't shocked because Ben told me the same thing six months before after he met with Scudamore on a visit to London. Ben said Scuadmore told him the EPL would do 'anything' to help the Australian bid beat the English bid - a claim I found astounding.

Stevie continued. 'And all the media. They'll just love the thought of being somewhere like here.' It was a short drive, and we pulled up at a venue called Sketch.

'This is fabulous. It's the place to go,' said Stevie. 'This is the place where everyone will sit up and take notice that we're serious.'

'You don't think our Government's funding of it for $46 million would help people realise we're serious?' I asked quietly.

We breezed in through the front door where Stevie was greeted warmly.

We had a heart-starting coffee in the Parlour, eclectically furnished in a mixture of colour and fabric. Rich red velvet mixed with cottage chintz, brocade wallpaper, timber tables, tray-like tables, tiger print pillows, standard lamps with skulls, spotlights – really, it was anything goes and it worked. The place was packed, even at 9.30 in the morning.

Sketch was very cool – in the 21st century meaning of that term. It was terrific if launching an art or fashion exhibition. But it didn't have much resonance for the Australian World Cup bid. Stevie promised to send me a proposal for us to consider within the next week.

I HADN'T PROGRESSED Hargitay's suggestion from the day before of engaging another person to look after international media. Ben was on a flight to Istanbul where he and I were meeting the next day so I had not been able to talk with him.

Hargitay, his recommended journalist Paul Nicholson, and I were seated in the front downstairs office where I had met with Hargitay and Stevie the previous morning.

Nicholson was not long redundant. He seemed a pleasant enough guy; a genuine sports 'hack'. He told me he knew almost everybody in English football – administrators, players, managers. He knew the English media inside-out.

I asked him about his knowledge of international media, considering that's what Hargitay said the job was needed for.

'Between us – with my considerable contacts – we can cover everywhere,' said Hargitay. 'And in different languages. As you know, Bonita, I speak five.'

'Can I ask how much you're looking for?' I turned to Nicholson.

Hargitay answered for him again. He said we could talk about money later. Hargitay said the job needed to be at least two to three days a week for the rest of the year leading to full time the following year.

I stood and put my hand out to Nicholson. 'It's been nice to meet you. But I'll have to talk with my boss about it. It's not something we've discussed, so we'll talk it over and get back to you via Peter.'

It turned out Hargitay and Nicholson have a history of working closely.

At the same time as Hargitay's ECN was receiving what turned out to be $60,000 a month from us in 2009 and 2010 - not the $100,000 Ben mentioned in vague terms - ECN was also working for Mohamed Bin Hammam. Hargitay was engaged as Bin Hammam's strategy advisor for his campaign to retain his FIFA Executive Committee position within the Asian Football Confederation, as well as for his tilt at the FIFA presidency in 2011.

About one week before we met in London, Hargitay sent Bin Hammam a draft campaign strategy, copying it to his son Stevie and Nicholson, who helped prepare it.

It was entitled The future has begun. Together with other activity associated with the campaign - including 'cooperation with SBS-TV' via Hargitay's friend and then FIFA Ethics Committee member, Les Murray - ECN invoiced Bin Hammam USD$500,000 for the work payable to Hargitay's Swiss bank account.

The invoice was sent by Bin Hammam's offsider, Nirajab Chirakal, to Pierre Kakhia of World Sports Group to make the payment.

On the road to Gallipoli: April 2009

I ARRIVED IN Istanbul from London about midnight. Together with the national goalkeeping coach, Tony Franken, Ben and I were meeting early in the morning for breakfast for the three hour drive to Canakkale, the nearest large town to the Gallipoli Peninsula.

We were visiting Gallipoli for two matches of our under-16 team v Turkey's under-16s as an inaugural Anzac Day series commemorating the Gallipoli campaign in 1915 when many Turkish, Australian, New Zealand and soldiers from other nations perished. The Australian Foreign Minister, Stephen Smith, was in attendance also. Afterwards, in Istanbul, we hosted a small event for the Turkish FA.

After a stop along the road for some thick, strong, sweet Turkish coffee recommended by the friendly local driver we engaged, I talked about my two days in London.

Ben was sitting in the front passenger seat; Tony and I were in the back. Ben was half-twisted in his seat facing me, and I could see his jaw tighten and a pulse tick in his neck as I mentioned the meeting with Hargitay and Paul Nicholson. He wanted to know how much Hargitay said Nicholson should be paid.

'He was a bit vague at first but after Nicholson had gone, he mentioned 70,000 pounds for three days a week and then the full time equivalent next year,' I said.

'For fuck's sake. He's got a nerve. Leave it with me,' Ben said.

Paul Nicholson's name was not mentioned again.

Other than to note that Nicholson was working with Hargitay through an online football news site, I didn't give him a thought for another six years.

Dubai: April 2009

BEN AND I were having a late morning coffee in the lobby of our Dubai hotel. He was debriefing me on the most recent meeting of the 'A' team.

While we had been in flight from Istanbul, FFA had taken ownership of two A-League clubs - majority ownership of Brisbane Roar and full ownership of Adelaide United. We couldn't afford it but there was no choice. We couldn't allow any of the A-League clubs to collapse. It wouldn't look good in the middle of bidding for two teams to fold in an eight-team league.

The other news was that matches against Trinidad and Tobago and Jamaica were confirmed for September.

I was also asked to write to another Executive Committee member, Rafael Salguero of Guatemala, inviting his national team to participate in a mini-tournament.

'We've assigned who's going to look after which ExCo member. Write this down,' he instructed.

'Everyone has Blatter,' he began. 'Frank has Temarii, Beckenbauer and Grondona.'

'Grondona? You know what Grondona said about Jewish people?' I looked up.

Years before, Grondona was recorded in an interview as saying 'Jews don't like hard work' and in another instance *Jews don't like it when it gets rough.'*

'Frank doesn't care about that. They have made a connection,' Ben said.

'What connection? How can Frank make a connection with someone who thinks that?'

'I don't know,' Ben said, shrugging his shoulders. 'Grondona and he seem to like each other a lot.'

'Is that because Frank is rich?' I asked.

He ignored me and continued. 'Fedor has Ogura, Makudi, Chung, Platini, Lefkaritis and Teixeira. And Peter has Mohamed, Geoff Thompson, Erzik, D'Hooghe, Villar Llona, Mutko, Leoz, Salguero, Havelange. And Jack of course.'

'Havelange doesn't vote,' I said.

'Peter says Havelange is the key to Leoz. He'll do whatever Havelange says.'

I moved on to the four African votes, pointing out that they were not on the list.

'They're a special case,' Ben said.

'What do you mean by special case?'

'Nothing.'

'Ben, you can't give me half the information. Why tell me *'they're a special case'* unless you're prepared to say what it means? And what is even meant by 'looked after' anyway? What are we doing with them all?'

He slammed his coffee cup down. Coffee spilt on to the glass-topped table. 'You know what? You are impossible at times. It's never enough for you just to do something. You've always got to ask why. Question-after-question. Argue the point.'

I started to say I wasn't arguing the point. I merely wanted to know what was happening, but he got up and stormed out of the hotel lounge. It was uncharacteristic.

I looked around the lounge at the handful of other people there to see if anyone had noticed. There were some men in Arabic dress conferring over a computer and drinking coffee, two impeccably-coiffed women having a chat, a group of about eight men and women having a late breakfast.

'Would you like another coffee madam?' the waiter asked as they cleared away Ben's cup hurriedly.

'Yes thanks, that would be great.'

I turned on my computer and worked through my emails. Ben appeared about an hour later.

'I'm sorry,' he said.

'No problem. I don't really think you're mad with me.'

He laughed. 'I am you know.'

'No you're not. Not really,' I said. 'You're just mad at the situation. Either you can't answer the questions because you don't know the answer yourself, or you won't answer them because you don't want me to know. So, unless you can give me a plausible explanation to my perfectly reasonable questions, what else can I do but think the worst?'

He didn't respond. 'Where were we?' He thought for a moment. 'I'm in KL next week.'

The Asian Football Confederation Congress was on. Mohamed Bin Hammam was being challenged for the AFC presidency and his FIFA Executive Committee position by Sheikh Salman Bin Ibrahim Al-Khalifa of Bahrain.

We were supporting Bin Hammam because we still saw it was our best - and only - chance of winning the bid.

Canberra: May 2009

I WAS IN Canberra to finally secure the money Reynald Temarii wanted for Oceania.

The two officials had before them a copy of our submission to government from last year seeking $28.5 million for bid legacy. The submission was rejected by government, but we had been advised to ask the government's aid agency for additional money on a case-by-case basis - or, in football terms, a confederation basis. The officials knew we wanted money for Oceania, Asia and Africa.

After talking round-and-round all morning about our first priority, Oceania, we came to an agreement that made everyone more-or-less happy.

'You do realise you're only getting this money because we've been told we have to,' one of the officials said to me. 'But it has been a very useful meeting. We do feel as if we can at least work with the model we've come up with.'

'And it's genuinely very exciting to be trialling the model we've worked up,' his colleague said. 'We've never funded something based on a tripartite agreement before so this is quite innovative. Who knows? If it works, we can apply it elsewhere.'

I called Ben. 'The good news is I'll be back in the office this afternoon,' I said without even saying hello.

'You got the money?' he asked.

'I got the money,' I replied.

'I take back all the mean things I've ever said to you. How much?'

'$4 million over three years.'

'Oh,' I could hear him almost punching the air 'that is the best news I've had all day. All week. All month. You've just earned yourself a big fat bonus! Wait till I tell Frank! He'll be over the moon!' His sentences came out in a series of exclamations. Clearly, this was important.

'A big bonus for delivering a big brown paper bag. How fitting,' I said.

Canberra: June 2009

THE LAUNCH OF the bid was spectacular.

The Great Hall of Parliament House was set up as a stadium, with digital imagery used to fill up the stands with people and the screen for the event integrated as if a stadium screen. We invited all the past Socceroos we could, with a special focus on the 1974 squad and their coach Rale Rasic – the first to make the World Cup.

In addition to the Prime Minister and Frank Lowy, other speakers included Opposition Leader Malcolm Turnbull, Indigenous player Harry Williams who was part of the 1974 squad, Socceroos captain Lucas Neill and senior Socceroo Mark Schwarzer, captain of the Under 17 team Jared Lum and a fan representative and 'soccer mum' from Canberra. Another former Socceroo, and SBS-TV football analyst, Craig Foster, was MC.

In the Great Hall afterwards, the guests mingled, posed for a photo on the steps holding aloft their 'Come Play!' scarves - our bid tag line. Bipartisan support was the order of the day and Kevin Rudd was tireless in giving interviews.

Ben found me amongst the throng of people, stood in front of me, put his hands on my shoulders, squeezed them and kissed me saying 'You nailed it! That was absolutely wonderful. You hit exactly the right note. Every word. Everything that happened. It was perfect. Thank you.'

He knew it hadn't been without challenges.

Only ten days beforehand when I was in Dubai to get footage of the Socceroos giving a message for use in the launch, coach Pim Verbeek bawled me out for interrupting the players' afternoon rest. The arrangement to film the players was agreed with him before heading to Dubai. It only required ten minutes of their time. But he wasn't happy. Verbeek was under pressure to qualify for the 2010 World Cup.

I felt a tap on my shoulder. Speak of the devil. It was Verbeek. He is another very tall man, quite fit looking. He was smiling apologetically at me.

'Bonita, now I know what you were doing and I just wanted to say you did a wonderful job. I am sorry I was so rude to you. What you did today really touched me,' he said. Considering his own country was also bidding, he sounded genuine.

If Ben had been eating anything, he would have choked on it, such was the rarity of Verbeek apologising to anyone - and he upset plenty in his tenure in charge of the national team.

'Thank you Pim. I appreciate you saying so.'

Lowy joined us. I received another kiss.

'Bonita. I am a very happy man today. You did a very, very good job. Wonderful, in fact. Look at this!'

He beamed as he gestured towards the crowd still laughing and happy around the Great Hall.

It led the Australian evening news bulletins on Sunday and into Monday morning and was reported on and shown around the world.

Reynald Temarii called Ben from Johannesburg where the Confederations Cup was in progress to let him know that it had been shown where the Executive Committee was meeting. The Australian bid was the subject of all the corridor talk, Temarii told us.

All of us with colleagues or friends overseas received messages to say they saw the launch from the UK, elsewhere in Europe, the US, the Middle East and Asia.

Andreas Abold, who travelled to Canberra from Munich to be with us – and who was responsible for the final presentation to FIFA in 18 months time - said nothing.

We didn't hear from Hargitay or Radmann. In their world, none of it mattered.

Sydney: June 2009

LIKE MANY PEOPLE meeting Frank Lowy for the first time, the journalist was both nervous and excited as he waited in the ante room of Lowy's Westfield office with me for an exclusive interview. It was a few days after the launch, before Lowy headed off for the European summer.

The journalist didn't normally cover football. He raised the issue of corruption in world football directly – something that most football journalists were either too scared or too sensitive to their employment to do.

Asking about a 'culture of bribes' that Andrew Jennings reported on, Lowy said:

'Corruption can be described in many ways. I don't know of any corruption. I haven't seen it. I just know these people are amenable. I'm not putting an utopian outlook on this. It's very fierce. Very competitive. But they have to make deals with each other to get where they want to be.'

'So what deals are you prepared to make with them?' the journalist asked.

'I don't know what deals I can make with them,' Lowy was reported as saying.

He added, almost to himself: 'But I'll do whatever it takes.'

Cape Town: June 2009

SOUTH AFRICA had been good to Andreas Abold. Not only could he put another winning bid on his CV after he and Fedor Radmann worked their special brand of magic for the 2010 South African bid, but he acquired a holiday home in Durban and he met two of the most famous and revered people in the world. One was Nelson Mandela; the other was Archbishop Desmond Tutu.

We were in Cape Town to select the hotel we would occupy during the World Cup Draw later that year in December. The draw would coincide with meetings of FIFA's confederations, FIFA Congress, FIFA Executive Committee as well as the first compulsory event of the bidding process - a bidders' expo for international media and football officials.

On the first afternoon in Cape Town it was Archbishop Tutu who Ben and Abold were visiting to discuss the Archbishop's support for the Australian bid.

It was successful. Ben and Abold returned to tell us that Archbishop Tutu would support the Australian bid.

We would also give Archbishop Tutu's charity $50,000. As Ben said, a small price for the PR value.

Johannesburg: June 2009

FROM CAPE TOWN we travelled to Johannesburg to select a base for the Socceroos and for the bid during the World Cup twelve months away. We were also attending a semi-final of the Confederations Cup.

On our final evening in South Africa, we hosted a function attended by more than 100 people invited by the Australian High Commission, some expats, local media, people from the South African Football Association, and FIFA staff and officials.

'Bonita, Bonita!' said a man as he made his way to me. He gave me a big bear hug with a kiss on each cheek. It was Enrique Byrom and his Australian wife, Robyn, whom I had met previously.

Between Enrique, Robyn and Enrique's business partner and brother, Jaime, they knew everything about the FIFA Executive Committee and their travel arrangements: preferred airline, class of travel, type of hotel room, details of their latest travelling companion. Their inside knowledge may explain why they had not lost a tender in more than 25 years for the ever-burgeoning set of services they provided to FIFA.

Enrique was short, dark, round with a suntanned but ruddy complexion, a continuously furrowed brow offset by a ready smile and infectious laugh, big brown eyes with a dark, greying beard. Robyn was taller, with pale skin, thin light brown hair and blue eyes. She spoke accent-free English. They were opposites in looks and also in personality: Enrique was boisterous, jolly and tactile; Robyn was quiet – so quietly spoken it was sometimes difficult to hear her – and controlled. Both were friendly.

'It is so good to see you,' said Enrique. 'We have to tell you that all anyone talked about at the beginning of this tournament was your launch. They took notice. Everyone is talking about Australia.'

The evening passed pleasantly. The Deputy High Commissioner spoke about the Government's support for the bid; Ben spoke; and we played our new promotional film.

Reynald Temarii from Oceania was to be the special guest, but he was unable to attend at the last minute. Instead, Oceania CEO Tai Nicholas attended along with former player, Christian Karembeu, twice a Champions League winner with Real Madrid and a World Cup winner in 1998 with France. Karembeu was shorter than I imagined, a little bigger than his playing days, but still with tight dreadlocks and with that unmistakeable Francophile charm.

'Anything I can do to help the Australian bid, I am happy to do,' he told me. 'I would like to see you win it because I think it will be good for Oceania. I am happy to talk with anyone. I know all the Executive Committee. You just tell me what you want me to do.'

I thought it was very nice of him to offer.

When all the guests left, Ben, Stuart Taggart, another colleague John Boultbee and I had a meeting over dinner. We debriefed on the past few days and talked about what was ahead.

I told them about my conversation with Karembeu. It may have been the beer and wine that we had consumed but their guffaws got louder and louder as I told the story. John burst into a fit of giggles.

'Bonita, he wasn't serious,' John said.

'He sounded like he was,' I said.

'Yes, he was serious. Bonita just failed to ask him the right question. For once,' said Ben.

'What question?' I asked.

They all looked at me and started laughing.

We had received representations on behalf of a number of prominent world players and coaches to be ambassadors for our bid. Pele could be devoted to us for a seven figure sum. Zinedeine Zidane, Frank de Boer, Gabriel Batistuta were amongst the many names who were seeking six figure sums. Roger Milla was by far the most modest, only seeking $50,000. Perhaps Christian Karembeu was different.

Even if Lowy agreed with the idea of ambassadors, we wouldn't have gone with any of these guys. There was nothing authentic about having 'hired hands' who had no relevance to Australia. We had numerous former players from the Craig Johnston era and younger who were not big names, but who had good contacts and networks.

Five days later Karembeu, a New Caledonian born Frenchman who spent his playing career in France, Spain, Italy and Greece, was announced as an ambassador for the Belgian-Holland bid.

CHAPTER 9
Kevin does Zurich

Dubai: July 2009

I HAD A nine-hour stopover in Dubai before travelling to Zurich. Even at 5.30am, the temperature was 34 degrees and there was a thick haze around the city. I was travelling a day before the others to meet with a photographer and film crew about our requirements for the Prime Minister's visit to FIFA headquarters.

We were also attending the first compulsory workshop for all bidders later in the week.

After Zurich, I was travelling to London to meet with Stevie Hargitay to go through the event program for the next 18 months. I was under instructions also to take Maureen Warner's pearl pendant with me so the Hargitays could give it to Jack Warner. The problem was, there wasn't one. We needed to buy another.

I decided to use up some of the long stopover time by purchasing Maureen Warner's pendant at the Australian manufacturer's boutique in an upmarket Dubai mall.

Ben was so anxious to keep Hargitay from harping-on about it, that he reminded me about the purchase via a text message on my arrival in Dubai: *'Whatever you do, don't forget the pearls!'*

The bidding guidelines were not precise on the monetary limit of gifts for the FIFA Executive Committee or their relatives. What they did say was that gifts should be of 'incidental or symbolic value'. For the Australian bid, I set an upper limit of $200 for an individual gift.

The Paspaley pearl pendant cost $2,000 in Sydney. I found the same item in Dubai for a little less than half that.

I thought we were in murky territory purchasing an expensive gift for the wife of an Executive Committee member now that we were in bidding mode, even if it was to make-up for a gift she didn't receive from one year earlier.

I sent an email to Lowy and Ben to let them know I bought the pendant. I explained that I did not intend including a note with the gift as I was 'cautious about putting something in writing about a gift when we're in bidding mode.' I added that I didn't want this to be a 'surprise to you at any time.'

Ben responded saying I was never to write something like that again. When I spoke to him about it later, he told me that someone might use what I wrote against us.

Zurich: July 2009

OF ALL THE bars in all of Zurich, Stuart Taggart and I were quietly having an end-of-the-day drink at a very un-FIFA like hotel, the Dolder Waldhaus, not far from FIFA headquarters when who should walk in but Sepp Blatter.

He didn't look around the room, but went directly to the bar. He chatted amiably with the barmaid who was tidily dressed, very efficient, had been quite friendly to us, and was probably on the other side of 60.

'We should say hello,' said Stuart.

'I don't think so. It looks like this is his local and it's somewhere to relax. He doesn't know who we are.'

The few tables in the bar were set around an 'L' shape. Stuart and I were seated at one end of the 'L', Blatter at the other.

A few minutes later, he was joined by another man.

It wasn't anyone we recognised – and if it's possible to look like a 'football type', he didn't look like one. He had dark brown hair, a beard, was middle aged, neatly but not expensively dressed. He drank a red wine, as did Blatter, and they shared a plate of hot chips. They spoke in German.

The man left. Blatter settled in for another glass, chatting again with the barmaid when she came over to refill his glass.

'We should say hello. Let him know we're here and working hard,' said Stuart.

'He won't remember us – and besides, we're not working hard. We're drinking in a bar!' I said.

It didn't deter Stuart. He got up. I followed him reluctantly.

'Mr Blatter,' he said as he approached stretching out his hand. Blatter looked up. You could see that he was whirring through his mind, wondering who we were. I felt as if we were intruding on some private time.

Stuart said our names for his benefit. 'From Australia'. I put out my hand too.

'Of course. My Aussie friends,' he said, pronouncing 'Aussie' as 'Ossie' as always. 'Welcome to Zurich. Welcome to FIFA. What are you doing here?' He gestured at the hotel, knowing it was not on the recommended FIFA list. He didn't wait for an answer. 'I am seeing you tomorrow. With your First Minister and your President.' He was referring to Kevin Rudd and Frank Lowy.

'You'll only see Bonita tomorrow, not me,' Stuart explained. 'We're also both here for the bidding workshop.'

'Ah yes, the workshop.' There was a pause. 'I am looking forward to meeting all the bidders.'

I gave Stuart a gentle nudge on the elbow.

'Likewise Mr Blatter. Enjoy your drink,' I said.

Blatter looked relieved. 'Thank you, thank you.'

Stuart and I took our seats again.

Within a minute, Blatter drained his glass, stood to leave, briefly nodded to us, had another word to the barmaid, and departed.

FIFA HEADQUARTERS is located about five kilometres to the north-east of the city precinct on the edge of a forested hillside outside of Zurich. The area is very pretty – lots of trees, pretty gardens, picturesque views back to the city and Lake Zurich. It is also exclusive.

Driving through the double security gates at the entrance to FIFA's headquarters and along the short driveway – with an unmarked football pitch on the right and a garden on the left – Ben and I were surprised by what we saw. The driveway opened up to a circular drive split by a long, thin pool. It was a squat, charcoal building, very contemporary looking, only two years old. It looked as if a very large paperweight that had been placed on the ground with a net thrown over it. 'FIFA' was emblazoned to the right of the façade of the building. At least we knew we were in the right place.

The overwhelming colour scheme inside was the same charcoal grey. At the opposite end to the entrance were a number of black leather bench-like seats overlooking an internal garden. To both sides as we walked in were chairs and sofas also upholstered in black leather. In the middle of the open space were two, very long kitchen-style benches. The one on the left had a glass display top and was the FIFA 'shop', and the one on the right appeared as if it might be the reception.

'You go and let them know we're here and I'll look out for Frank and Kevin,' Ben said as he went to the front of the room.

Sepp Blatter's personal media officer appeared from the other end of the room. She was warm and friendly. We had been corresponding by email for weeks about the visit, and had caught up the day before. We now reviewed the plan again.

Once the Prime Minister was nearby, Lowy would meet him outside the building; Blatter would meet them in the lobby; they would go upstairs to the FIFA President's reception room for VIPs; have pictures taken and exchange gifts; have their meeting; they would go outside to the adjacent football field to kick the ball around for some more pictures; then the Prime Minister would depart.

'Bonita,' she said. 'I need to raise something with you.'

My heart sank at the tone in her voice.

'Yesterday when someone from your Prime Minister's office was here, she said Mr Rudd would not kick the ball around with the President.' She paused and let this sink in before continuing. 'He must do this. The President likes this to happen.'

I saw the Prime Minister's assistant arriving out of the corner of my eye. 'Leave it with me,' I said to Blatter's assistant, walking over to the Prime Minister's staff member.

The Prime Minister was more than happy to visit Blatter on his way to the G20 but we got the feeling his staff saw it as a nuisance. I explained to his assistant why it was important for him to be seen kicking the ball around with Blatter and Lowy.

'He's never played soccer. He doesn't know what to do,' she said. Her reluctance stemmed from not wanting to see her boss look out of place, awkward or, worse, miss the ball altogether, which was understandably her concern.

'We're talking about a 74 year old and a 79 year old. It's just a few gentle kicks between the three of them so the cameras can capture the ball at their feet. Nothing more than you'd do with a three year old.'

I lowered my voice. 'Also, could you please ask him not to call it soccer while he's here?'

THE VISIT WAS a PR success, although we did receive some sobering news.

The Prime Minister arrived accompanied by his Foreign Policy Advisor, Phillip Green. Lowy and Ben met them outside, while Blatter and the FIFA CEO, Jerome Valcke, were called to the lobby area to greet them.

They met each other warmly, the TV cameras whirring and the camera shutters clicking rapidly. It was a toss-up to know who was the better showman in front of a camera and microphone between Kevin Rudd and Sepp Blatter.

Blatter walked Rudd and Lowy over to admire the World Cup that had pride of place on a pedestal towards the front corner where we had been seated. The entire time, Blatter and Rudd chatted and smiled for the cameras, Lowy silently beaming slightly behind them, followed by a trail that included Valcke, Phillip Green and Ben, the photographers, the camera crews, the Prime Minister's assistant and me. We slowly climbed the stairs at the other side of the lobby to the President's private reception room. It was located at the far end of a long corridor at the front of the building overlooking the full size football field.

The reception room was expensively furnished.

There was one long black leather sofa, three matching leather arm chairs – all contemporary in style. Another chair was brought in to the room by a male aide to Blatter, also in black leather. One wall was wood panelled with a flat screen television and framed photographs or news clippings. There was a small timber coffee table in the centre of the room. My eye was drawn to a beautiful Persian carpet in ivory, blue, fawn and light grey tones that took up most of the floor space.

And, lo and behold, there was another World Cup!

'Sepp, that's the second World Cup I've seen,' Kevin Rudd said as they took their seats – Blatter and Valcke sharing the sofa, but with enough space for another person between them; the four visitors in the armchairs.

'Oh yes, Mr Prime Minister there is more than one World Cup,' said Blatter.

'Really? How many are there?'

'Five or six.'

Blatter continued. 'There is the original trophy which is solid gold and is under lock and key. There is this World Cup which is also gold,' he gestured casually to the one on the pedestal to his left behind him, 'but not the real thing. There is the one downstairs where you had your photo taken. And there are two or three others that we use for promotions and tours. Plus the champions have a very good quality replica also.'

'Sometimes the only one that is not travelling is the real one,' added Valcke.

Making chit-chat while photographers took photos, the Prime Minister asked about transporting the original World Cup to tournaments and Valcke explained the elaborate arrangements taken to safeguard its security.

'Well I don't have anything as precious as that,' said the Prime Minister taking a package from his advisor. 'But I do have a small gift for you from Australia. It's one of our finest bottles of red wine from South Australia.' He handed over the wine that was packaged in a wooden box: Hill of Grace from Henschke.

Blatter undid the box and examined the bottle.

'Oh very nice, thank you. I always enjoy a bottle of Australian wine.' The Prime Minister also gave him a bid lapel badge.

Blatter gave the Prime Minister a FIFA pennant and one of the first of the 2010 World Cup footballs.

As this was happening, Blatter's aide brought out a bottle of wine and offered it to his guests. The wine was a dark yellow, almost, but not quite, like a sweet, dessert wine. It wasn't yet midday but in Zurich, it wasn't too early for a drink. The wine was poured.

'To Prime Minister Kevin Michael Rudd,' said Blatter in a toast. 'It is a very great pleasure to welcome you here to our most humble home of FIFA.'

The Prime Minister responded. 'To you, President Blatter, and your good health. It is a real pleasure to be here to talk to you about Australia and our bid for the World Cup.'

That was the signal for the rest of us to leave.

ALMOST AN HOUR later, the six men emerged from the meeting room. The waiting entourage – which had now grown to more FIFA staff and more media – followed them along the width of the building, down the stairs and out to the adjacent football field.

Fortunately, the Prime Minister didn't once miss the ball that was gently kicked to him. He also looked as if he knew what he was doing when he kicked it back. Blatter had a spring in his step as he showed off the perfect looking pitch lined with flags of all of FIFA's member associations. He was very proud of it.

The little kick around over, Blatter saw the Prime Minister and Lowy into their separate cars.

'I hope we'll see you in Australia again soon,' the Prime Minister said to Blatter before his car drove away.

Blatter beamed and waved farewell.

Valcke, Ben and I walked back into the building behind Blatter who returned to his office. The media pack had mostly disappeared.

Other than his French accent, Valcke was a man who was usually without charm. He had the air of always being uninterested in what he is doing.

Originally a journalist, Valcke rose to the ranks of CEO of a sports television channel in France; then moved 'upstairs' to a larger, related company as chief operating officer in Geneva; after which he joined FIFA as Head of Marketing and TV. In 2003, he was 'let go' from FIFA when a US Court found him guilty of a breach of contract with Mastercard. FIFA was fined USD$60 million.

But six months later, Blatter brought him back as CEO of FIFA, lauding him for having made FIFA so much money.

'You won't get this,' Valcke said abruptly. The three of us stopped mid-stride. 'You won't win.'

He continued in short sentences. 'You're just not competitive in the areas that count. Commercially. The broadcast rights. You can't compete.'

We didn't question who he thought we couldn't compete with.

The USA had a track record in World Cup attendance, television revenues and commercial support, as well as being World Cup ready. They hardly needed to spend a cent to host a World Cup, and had no difficulty in meeting hotel and training requirements. While the US hosted it 15 years previously, that would stretch out to 28 years by the time 2022 came along; a whole new generation of fans and players.

We had also been told by Hargitay months before that the Emir of Qatar had offered to buy the World Cup. We didn't know if that was true, but we had no doubt that Qatar could make a significant contribution to FIFA's coffers via sponsorship or broadcast deals from state-owned companies. It was already common knowledge that if Emirates did not renew its sponsorship - as rumoured - that Qatar Airways was ready to take their place.

Valcke farewelled us and retreated to his office.

I gave a soft whistle. 'Well that was honest. Do we withdraw gracefully at some stage?'

'No. He's wrong. We'll get some work done on the potential of new broadcast revenues from the Asian region,' Ben said.

'But there are four other Asian bidders, so any argument in favour of us will help the other bidders too,' I said.

'We're the only viable bidders from Asia,' said Ben.

CHAPTER 10
Meeting the other bidders

Zurich: July 2009

BEN BEGAN THE next day over breakfast by complaining about the hotel.

Abold and Hargitay had told us that we must stay in top quality accommodation on all occasions, otherwise it would look like the Australian bid is 'cheap'.

On this occasion I selected the Dolder Waldhaus, a less expensive hotel, because the budget was being cut back, and accommodation was an easy area to make savings. Ben wasn't impressed. It had to be five-star or better every time he told me.

I asked him if someone else at the office could make the hotel reservations.

Ben put down his coffee cup. 'Bonita, how many times do I have to tell you. You are working on this bid, and you will do what I want you to do.'

I couldn't understand why I had to make travel and hotel arrangements. I pointed out that it was time-consuming and took me away from my 'real' work.

'Look, I know how much work you're doing. Better than anyone, I know that. But I want you to do this. We've just got to get through the next 18 months together.'

We continued eating in silence for a few seconds.

'There are things going on this bid that I can't tell you about. You can't tell your staff what you're doing or some of the things I ask you to do. The fewer people who know what we're doing, where we're going, who we're seeing, and what's happening the better. That's why I want you to do the travel arrangements,' Ben said.

He looked out the window, and turned back to me.

'There is no one in the world I would rather have doing this job than you,' he said. He thought for a moment. 'No, absolutely no one.'

A FEW HOURS later, we were at FIFA headquarters meeting all the other bidders for the first time for the first compulsory workshop of the bidding process. It was a little like the first day at school: we were a bit nervous and apprehensive, wondering who we would meet, hoping we wouldn't look too stupid, but wanting to get on with it.

We were taken upstairs and invited to have coffee and a piece of fruit before we entered the auditorium where we would spend the day.

Each delegation stood in their own small group talking quietly amongst themselves doing exactly the same as us. Eyeing off the opposition.

The Qatari delegation stood out because one of them was in traditional dress.

We knew a couple of the English bid team and smiled and nodded to them.

We picked the Dutch/Belgian team as they were very tall and sounded like our national team manager, Pim Verbeek.

The three Americans were standing huddled in a group as if they were about to start the ninth innings of a baseball match.

There was one lone Mexican who wore his flag on the tape of his dark suit.

There were three very jolly gents, who looked more senior than most of the rest of the delegations, who were chatting loudly in Spanish.

The Russians stood in a line watching everyone else, not speaking to one another.

The Japanese were huddled in one corner.

The South Koreans were in another.

And that left one, lone, Indonesian.

'We should go and say hello,' I said, nodding my head towards the Indonesian.

'Why? We sat in a meeting with them earlier in the year and they didn't even mention they were bidding,' said Ben. He was referring to high-level Indonesian delegation that included the FA President, Nurdin Halid. 'If you want to talk to someone, talk to the Russians. You know we've got to get to know them,' said Ben.

We leaned back on our heels and checked-out the Russians again. There were three men and a woman. The woman was tall and glamorous looking, with pale skin, copper-red hair, beautifully dressed and impeccably made-up. One man stood out. He was blond, shorter than the others, had the flat face, high cheekbones and defined jawline that typified the Slavic look. His eyes were bright blue and piercing.

'Spot the FSB lookalike,' I said under my breath, turning to my companions.

My colleagues all looked at the blond Russian just as he looked at us. He gave a slight nod.

THE AUDITORIUM accommodated around 200 people and was tiered several levels upwards. Each bidder was permitted to bring four people to the workshop, and the eleven bidding nations were assigned to seats at the front of the auditorium. Observers from amongst the FIFA staff sat behind us. At the front of the room was a large bench-like main table behind which was a large screen.

We got down to business by going around the room introducing ourselves.

As it was the first of three compulsory workshops over the bidding period, all bidders had their CEO present.

Fernando from Mexico said they were not 100% certain about bidding as yet. He was attending to see whether it was in their interests to do so. Not long afterwards, they dropped out of the bidding race, when internal politics within the CONCACAF region determined the confederation would have only one bidder - the USA.

The lone Indonesian delegate was softly spoken. He said that his compatriot had not been allowed to enter Switzerland. We found this information amusing, because FIFA complained loudly when the Australian government had not given entry rights to an official from Myanmar for the FIFA Congress the year before. Here was the Swiss government not permitting entry to an Indonesian!

The day's proceedings were handled by a relative newcomer to FIFA, but an experienced hand from UEFA. He was brought in especially to handle the process and arrangements for the bids for the two tournaments, and was already well known to most of the Europeans.

His name was Juergen. He epitomised German efficiency. Things started on time; all the arrangements were right; he set the process step-by-step and, even if precise times were beyond his ambit of decision-making, he could at least point to approximate timeframes. He was politely neutral and showed very little warmth or humour. Juergen was there to get a job done. He radiated confidence that it would be done efficiently.

Jerome Valcke was the first to speak. Once again, he gave a good impression of being totally uninterested in what he was doing.

'This is a nice race,' Valcke told us. 'But remember it is about more than football. It is important to bring the flavour of your country to your bid, but you must also show us you can do something for the world and for football.'

I introduced myself to the Qatari delegation over the coffee break, and had a quick chat with the English delegation about the forthcoming international cricket series, the Ashes.

Ben told me to forget them and to speak to the Russians. 'We have to break the ice with them. You're good at that,' he said.

We now knew from the introductions that the blond Russian we all stared at was Ben's equivalent, both the CEO of the Russian FA as well as the Russian bid, Alexey Sorokin. He was accompanied by Alexander Djordjadze who was the head of the technical aspects of the Russian bid, Daniel Rupf, former FIFA head of events and competitions and a former Swiss League player. The woman's name we didn't catch, although it sounded like Ekaterina Fedyshova.

I walked over to them.

'Where are you from Bonita?' the woman asked me.

'Australia,' I replied.

'No, where are you from originally? You don't look Australian.'

I paused for a moment. Normally, I would ask someone who said that to me to explain what an Australian looked like but I thought that might sound rude so I simply said 'My name is Spanish and Greek,' which appeared to satisfy them.

We talked perfunctorily of the beautiful weather in Zurich and our comparative flight times to get here. Sorokin whistled softly through his teeth when I said it had taken around 21 hours of flying.

'That's your problem,' he said. 'You're too far away. Who would want to go to there?'

'Lots of people,' I said. 'And it's really not that far.'

I trotted-out the line we used in response to this common perception of being too far away. 'You just get on a plane, have something to eat, watch a movie or two, go to sleep – and you're there. It's easy!' I exclaimed. 'The point is,' I said, 'we have one thing in common.'

'What's that?' asked Sorokin, his eyes narrowing to slits.

'Neither of us has hosted this before. Yet both of us have hosted an Olympics, so everyone knows we can do it.'

If it was possible, his eyes narrowed even further.

I could hear Juergen letting us know we had 90 seconds left until the next session started.

'How did that go?' asked Ben as I returned to my seat in the auditorium.

'Hard work,' I said. 'You can try it next time.'

IN THE SESSION between the coffee break and lunch, there was a series of presentations on what was required of all bidders from a technical perspective. Abold had advised us not to ask any questions, but to let others do so. By asking questions, we were letting other bidders know what our concerns were and that was best left to private meetings with FIFA staff.

England and the USA raised concerns about the government guarantees – a matter of significant concern to our government also.

Australian government officials were told the previous month that if a government wanted the World Cup, they would have to sign the guarantees required of them.

The Tax Office representative had exclaimed 'But they want to be exempt from tax! Surely no government agrees to that! Certainly the Brits and Americans won't.'

'It makes it very tough for us,' said the chairperson from the Prime Minister's department. 'Some of these provisions are just unconstitutional. We know we can't sign some of them. We're not going to change the Constitution for FIFA. We can't give any ground on the indemnities. And we can't condone a form of money laundering that they seem to describe.'

But governmental concern about tax and money laundering were water off a duck's back to FIFA.

FIFA's Chief Counsel, Marco Villiger, was now telling bidders that if their government disagreed with any part of the guarantees, they would 'need to address the differences in legal opinion.'

Not that alternative legal opinion mattered to Villiger who added 'That opinion doesn't vary your obligation to deliver what we require.'

The next FIFA staff member said that there would be a limit of two stadiums per city, which was new. We were relying on including at least two, if not three, stadiums in each of Sydney and Melbourne. I wondered where that left Qatar when they only had one city.

The Argentinean head of corporate social responsibility, Federico Adiecchi, told us that our legacy proposals should focus on social development, not football development. 'It is about our people, our game, our society, our planet.' Triple bottom-line stuff.

The Chief Financial Officer, Markus Kattner, made it clear what his concern was. 'The World Cup must make a profit. The World Cup funds everything else we do for the next four years. We cannot have all these other things,' nodding politely to his colleague on social development, 'or the youth and women's tournaments, without being profitable in the World Cup.' He said that the South African World Cup was on track for a record profit of more than $420 million.

At lunchtime, we were led to the FIFA staff canteen which was across from the entrance to the building, adjacent to the main show pitch – the same one Blatter, the Prime Minister and Lowy had used the day before. It also housed their well-appointed staff 'wellness centre' that included a gym, indoor pool, steam room, massage room and related facilities.

We stood in line at the canteen, where we were joined by many of the 250 or so FIFA staff. There was a hot buffet, a salad bar, sandwiches, dessert buffet, fruit and yoghurts and soft drinks. The hot buffet was served by two or three chefs. Juergen told us that this was the type of menu available every day.

I sat with the Americans. They told me they had a 'no frills' bid, which is why only three of them travelled to Zurich. It was privately funded through donations, large and small. They were budgeting on spending no more than $10 million across the two years. There were no consultants, they had most of the infrastructure in place, they were restricting travel to the bare necessities and, if Mexico withdrew, they had at least three votes in the first round from their CONCACAF delegates which comprised American Chuck Blazer, Jack Warner from Trinidad and Tobago and Rafael Salguero from Guatemala.

I asked if they could rely on Warner and Salguero.

The US bid CEO, David Downs, said they were quietly confident Mexico would withdraw and 'there will be all hell to pay' if the US did not have three votes in round one. Eighteen months later, three votes in round 1 is precisely what the US bid had.

THERE WAS A general air of heightened anticipation when we returned to the auditorium. We were joined by more FIFA staff who sat behind the bidders. Sepp Blatter's aide arrived to check everything. Juergen was a little perturbed about not starting on time but was also strangely breathless in anticipation of the President speaking. 'He just wants to say a few words,' he told us.

When Blatter entered, there was applause. Many people stood. I was amazed. We didn't. Neither did the Americans, the English, the Dutch and Belgians or the Iberian gentlemen.

What followed was classic Blatter: alternatively expansive, discursive, dissembling, reflective, humorous and perceptive - all rolled into one.

'I couldn't miss this opportunity to speak with you, my football family from around the world,' he began. He sounded like the Pontiff about to bless us all.

'It is good to see so many of you here. When we opened up the bidding, we didn't expect there to be such strong interest. But it is good. That is competition and that's football. Our life is a competition. It is an opportunity for the World Cup to go to new lands,' he said. 'Somewhere it hasn't been before. Somewhere where it is good for the lives of the people but, more importantly' - he paused - 'it makes a difference for the world.'

'New lands' was good for us but 'making a difference for the world' was a harder one to spin our way. I wrote down what he said and wrote next to it: 'Russia/Qatar?'.

He was disdainful of the comparisons between the Olympic Games and the World Cup.

'Everyone says how successful the Olympic Games were last year. It had 5 billion spectators. We had 26 billion in 2006. In 2002, when it was held outside the sacrosanct area of Europe and North America,' – he said looking towards the South Koreans and Japanese – 'there were 25 billion.'

They bowed their heads in appreciation.

He then reeled off more statistics and said that, as long as he is President, 'the game will not become only the game of the rich. Many people ask why I haven't retired. I should spend my time with my grandchild and play that game for old footballers – golf.'

He grabbed the lectern with both hands. He raised his head before scanning our expectant faces from one side of the room to the other. He visibly breathed-in, as if about to start a meditative chant.

'There is still so much more to do.'

What he said next made us sit up in our chairs a little.

'Yesterday the Prime Minister of Australia came to see me.'

Until then, our visit had slipped under the radar of other bidders as they were all travelling to Zurich when it happened. They now turned their heads towards us.

'Kevin Michael Rudd,' Blatter explained. 'He is a wonderful man, very enthusiastic. And what he did in his country apologising to the Aboriginal people is something that is wonderful for that country.'

Just as we were beginning to feel we might have the World Cup in the bag, he went on.

'The King of Belgium is coming tomorrow.' All eyes turned to the Dutch/Belgian team who now sat even taller in their seats.

But we all should have known the Americans wouldn't be outdone.

'And President Obama has invited me to the White House,' Blatter said, beaming. 'I am going at the end of the month.' Blatter tried unsuccessfully to hide his excitement.

It was hard to compete with the charismatic American President and the White House.

He bowed his head. 'Of course, I am just a most humble servant of the game. I am happy to visit any of your countries any time.'

Applause.

'One more thing as I finish.' He looked at Juergen who smiled bleakly at his schedule in disarray. Not only was Blatter late in arriving, but he had gone 30 minutes over time.

'Enjoy the game. That's good.' Blatter paused for dramatic effect. 'Enjoy life. That's even better.'

More applause. Another standing ovation. We thought we would look churlish if we didn't join in, so we stood and farewelled our dear leader also.

In order to try to make up for lost time in Juergen's schedule, the afternoon break was truncated to 10 minutes.

One of the South Korean bidding team came up to me. 'I don't think we should be bidding,' he said. 'We had it only six years ago.' He looked back at his colleagues and lowered his voice. 'All of us would like to see Australia get it.'

South Korea's billionaire backer was the Executive Committee member, Dr Moon-Jung Chung. Unlike many other Executive Committee members who rose through the ranks of football administration predominantly through grassroots connections, Dr Chung was the scion of the worldwide Hyundai company, had a PhD in international relations from Johns Hopkins University and was a former Korean Presidential candidate.

'That's very nice of you to say so, but I don't think Dr Chung would think the same,' I said.

He smiled wanly. 'Anyway, we wish you good luck. We want to see you win.' He bowed and left.

THE LAST SESSION was concerned with broadcast operations. The scale and scope of them were enormous. There were 15,000 media representatives at the 2006 World Cup and 1,900 rooms were required for the International Broadcast Centre for the six-week duration of the tournament.

Considering all the other hotel accommodation requirements associated with the tournament, we knew that it left only two options in Australia – Sydney or Melbourne. At that stage, knowing that the Final would be in Sydney – as Lowy promised it to the Premier of that state in 2008 - Melbourne was the favourite, if not the only candidate, to host the broadcast centre.

While these presentations were progressing, Juergen had been in and out of the room a few times, head down, papers in his hand. He looked stressed. I wondered how he would be 18 months down the track.

The cause of his stress became clear when he concluded the day with what he referred to as 'some points of clarification'.

'We do not want to disadvantage bidders like Qatar with some of the requirements. For example, we said that we do not want more than two stadia per city but that is just a recommendation only. Of course, we wouldn't exclude any bidder or city because of that. And to clarify the number of stadia. We want a minimum of 12. You can go up to 18. But there must be 12. In the end, we may only need ten.'

Wow. That was quick and impressive lobbying work by Qatar.

CHAPTER 11
Special delivery

London: July 2009

I ARRIVED A few minutes early for the meeting with Stevie Hargitay at their Mayfair office. I was let in by the receptionist, with barely a nod in my direction.

Stevie bounded down the stairs to greet me warmly, and we returned upstairs to the smaller but cosy meeting room between his and his father's offices. The first thing I did was hand over the beautifully packaged pearl pendant in a sunshine yellow bag for Maureen Warner.

'Thank you,' said Stevie. 'Jack and Maureen will be so pleased. They ask about it often.'

We talked about the workshop the day before in Zurich and Kevin Rudd's visit. We discussed the issues with state governments and the other sports in Australia, the latest event plan, the functions associated with various visits, and Abold's and Ben's meeting with Archbishop Tutu.

He said that all of the bidders were stepping up a gear and we needed to do so also. I asked him what he suggested.

'We need some ambassadors,' he said.

He had told me in April that he would get Elle Macpherson as an ambassador. asked him whether that had progressed.

'Elle is no problem. As soon as she's available, she'll do anything for us. We need more,' he said.

I told him that we had tried to get ambassadors twice previously but Lowy wasn't interested.

'Why doesn't Frank want ambassadors?' he asked drawing on his cigarette.

'They won't get us any votes.'

'But FIFA loves celebrities. Can you imagine if you had Elle Macpherson, Kylie Minogue, Nicole Kidman and Cate Blanchett all in the same room saying 'Come Play'?' He drew on his cigarette again. 'The old guys would love it. They might even have heart attacks!'

Stevie drew on his cigarette again and continued. 'I'll have my father talk to the others about it and they can raise it with Frank. We must also be at Leaders in Football.' He was referring to an annual conference run by close associates of the Hargitays. 'I think we should do something extra special at this year's Leaders in Football. Some ambush marketing. Take England by surprise.'

England again. The Hargitays were apparently obsessed with the England bid because of the handling of their departure once Lord Triesman became head of the English FA.

'Why England? They're not our competition.'

'Why not?' he asked. 'We're in their backyard. They think they can own this conference. I've spoken with the guy who runs it, and a very good friend who looks after all the event arrangements. I think we can do something extra special.'

'Such as?'

'Such as sponsor a part of it. Something that will be a big surprise and get lots of PR.' He added that neither of the people involved with Leaders in Football 'could stand Triesman or the English bid' and best of all, from his perspective, it was being held at Stamford Bridge, the home of Chelsea Football Club. 'Right in enemy territory,' Stevie said.

I wasn't certain whether he meant the England and Russia bids as enemies of one another, or the people associated with the bids and Chelsea Football Club.

He paused. 'There's two more things, Bonita. I think we should have a regular catch-up with you, me, my father, Fedor, Andreas and Ben of course.'

We had been thinking the same thing. I saw the need for it as just common sense but also as a means of relieving Ben of some of the pressure of having to remember everything between the consultants and the rest of us – especially me, as I had the most work arising from the 'A' team meetings. Ben liked to be in control and be the conduit for everything; he also liked to be copied on all communications, but the workload was getting to him. I also knew that some of my colleagues in Australia not involved with the bid were becoming increasingly frustrated at the lack of decisions in some of their areas of responsibility.

'Done. Let's start in the next two weeks. What's the second thing?'

Stevie lowered his voice. I wondered who might hear us. 'Russia. My father tells me the Russians are ready to cut a deal.'

I told him we had briefed the Prime Minister to speak to Medvedev at the G20 meeting.

'My father is in Russia now. He is finding out more and will tell us. Of course, he knows Markus Siegler and Andreas Herren.'

Sydney: July 2009

A FEW DAYS later I was in the office meeting with Ben.

We agreed to give the concept of ambassadors another try with Lowy. The 'A' team were due to meet and Ben asked me to prepare a status update on the bid – what we had done, what we've achieved, the key themes and the political focus. He flicked through his notebook to their previous meeting.

He read from his notebook. 'One, unite Asia behind our bid. Two, foster competition in Europe. Three, secure support from the African delegates. Four, foster South American support. Five, make sure FIFA management understands the commercial and other value Australia brings to the World Cup.'

'How are we going to unite Asia behind our bid when there are four other bidders?' I asked.

'Indonesia will drop away.'

'OK, three then.'

'Japan and South Korea won't get it. And Qatar can't possibly win it.'

I took a long, slow breath in. 'I reckon dismissing Qatar is a mistake. They have unlimited resources. To them, this is much bigger than just the World Cup. It's about their country being more significant geopolitically. And the whole idea of a World Cup in the Middle East would be very appealing to Blatter. He will think it will help him get a Nobel Peace Prize.'

'But they can't play a World Cup in June in Qatar.'

'I agree that's the biggest thing against them. I agree. But who said the World Cup has to be in June?'

'It's always in June,' he replied. 'That's what the bidding documents say.'

'Have you read them? The bidding documents also say FIFA can change any of the details any time they like before, during or after. And we've all got to accept it.'

He bit on his pencil, thinking. I continued.

'We also run the risk of sounding arrogant. Publicly we're saying *'Asia is where it's all at'*, but we're privately saying to the other Asian bidders *'Get behind us because we're the best in Asia.'*

'That's why I'm telling you. So you can get the message right,' he said.

'How are we securing Africa's support?' I asked.

'We're finding out what they want.'

'Who is?'

'I've told you before. Fedor is looking after Africa.'

'And South America?'

'We're talking to them.'

I was about to say that his responses were not helpful when he added that Lowy wanted a letter the same day to Vitaly Mutko inviting him to join him on Lowy's boat in the South of France.

He added that Mohamed Bin Hammam had been in touch with Lowy to let him know that three Australians had been appointed to chair Asian Football Confederation committees: Ben to Pro Leagues, Board member Moya Dodd to Legal, and Executive Chairman of one of the A-League teams to the Clubs Committee.

Why was our star on the rise at the AFC?

THERE WERE GUFFAWS around the table.

Ben put up his hand to silence us. Five of us were seated around the table in his office. Ben, Stuart, me, my colleague responsible for national teams and international issues, John Boultbee, and another responsible for the Asian Cup bid, Rob Abernethy.

Ben had just told us that our under-20 team was to play Trinidad, USA and England in Cyprus in a mini-tournament ahead of the under-20 World Cup in Egypt later in the year. We all laughed. Jack Warner managed to get three bidding nations vying for his attention in one pre-tournament training camp. The mood was jolly, light-hearted.

'We're paying for Trinidad and Tobago to go there and for their accommodation for a week. It's no more expensive than us going to Trinidad, and we were on a promise to Jack.'

Ben continued. 'We've got Oceania sorted. We've cut a deal with Vision Asia.' He turned to me. 'Bonita, it's time to get us some more money. We need $5 million for Asia. And then there's Africa.'

Here we go again. 'What are we trying to achieve with this money?' I asked.

I looked around the table at the other three who were still sniggering quietly about Jack Warner.

'Just think of it as more material for your book Bonita,' said Rob Abernethy, the colleague looking after the Asian Cup bid.

'You do realise we'll all be in this book?' asked Stuart.

'Yeah, I can't wait,' said Rob. 'I've got to think about who can play me in the TV series or the film.'

'Well we know Ben will be played by George Clooney,' John said. We all laughed uproariously.

Ben had been literally mobbed at a function of inebriated expats in Doha 12 months beforehand where the women decided he was the spitting image of the actor.

'That's enough!' said Ben crossly, cutting off the conversation. 'You can all figure out who's going to play you in the film of Bonita's book another day. In the meantime, just get the money from your government friends Bonita.'

'Okay Ben, but I still don't know what I'm supposed to tell them.'

He sighed. 'Just do it for me. Please.'

I stayed behind after the others had left.

'I don't understand why we're giving the Asian Football Confederation $5 million.'

'It will help us get AFC's support.'

'There are four voters in Asia, three of whom are from bidding nations, and one of whom Hargitay tells us does whatever Mohamed tells him.' I was referring to Thailand's Worawi Makudi. 'You're telling me that even though they're from the same confederation, the only way we can convince them to vote for us rather than the US is by giving our own confederation $5 million.'

'That's it.'

'What if we're not in it at the end?' I asked. 'Do we get our money back?'

'Peter, Fedor and Andreas are extremely confident we will be.'

Cairns: August 2009

WE WERE INSTRUCTED by the Prime Minister's Office to be at the venue for the Pacific Leaders' Forum three hours before the signing ceremony for the $4 million deal with the Oceania confederation.

'Reynald is very happy, you know, Bonita,' said the CEO of the Oceania Confederation, Tai Nicholas. 'Very happy. We didn't think this was going to happen at one stage. It's very good for him politically.'

'In FIFA?' I said.

'No, in the Pacific. In Tahiti. He wants to run for President eventually. This is very helpful to him.'

With a seasoned media performer at the helm in the Prime Minister, the signing ceremony went off without a hitch. The photo opportunities were picture perfect.

The three speeches were brief but clear. Australia gave Oceania Football Confederation $4 million over three years to help the communities, villages and churches of the Pacific. Oceania would be voting for Australia in the World Cup race.

I looked at the 16 other Prime Ministers and Presidents from the Pacific. A few of them were engaged and interested, but most of them looked as if they were wondering what this had to do with them.

Before boarding the flight back to Sydney that afternoon, the photos and media material were sent to Hargitay, Radmann and Abold to distribute to all Executive Committee members.

CHAPTER 12
'This is my town'

Zurich: August 2009

IT WAS THE height of summer and very warm in Zurich.

There were six of us, accompanied by our consultant Andreas Abold, for the second of the compulsory workshops for all bidders. We were required to attend group sessions on technical bid issues related to stadiums, accommodation and venue precincts, as well as one-on-one sessions with FIFA staff discussing legal, accounting and commercial matters, broadcast arrangements, media relations and public relations.

The opening meeting at FIFA headquarters on the Monday morning was with Juergen, who looked even more worried than when we had seen him at the first workshop six weeks previously. It was our opportunity to ask any questions we had about process, timeframes, requirements and expectations.

He was able to answer almost everything with ease, rattling off answers to our questions.

'The inspection tours will start in July and end in September this year. You will have an exhibition booth at the FIFA Congress in 2010 at the time of the World Cup. In December, for the Final Presentation and vote, we'll expect you to be here in Zurich for at least three days – two days for the presentations and then the final day. You will be permitted 30 minutes for your final presentation. No more, no less. The technical inspection for you will take place at the end of July.'

He finally drew breath.

July? We were expecting September for the technical inspection. Hargitay told us in February he would make sure it happened at a time to suit us. All we had to do was let him know, and he would arrange it though his FIFA connections.

I could see that Stuart and his team on the technical operations were trying hard to mask their amazement with the July date.

'Are you sure that's right? July?' asked Stuart.

Juergen didn't even look at his notes. 'Of course,' he said giving a faint smile, surprised that his accuracy was in question. 'Why wouldn't it be right? You'll be one of the first.'

He told us that the technical inspection should include the venues for the opening match and the final, some base camps for the teams, the location for the draw and anything else we wished to include. The same five people would be involved in the inspection with rotation of note takers and report writers.

'The report will be published about one week before the final decision,' Juergen continued. 'The report outlines the country's strengths and weaknesses. It makes no recommendations.'

THE AFTERNOON WAS free. Abold travelled to Teufen, near St Gallen, to visit Radmann. He told us they had papers to sign.

Hargitay was in Zurich for a few days and we had arranged to meet to talk about a visit by international journalists to Australia as our guests. He had been on holiday in the south of France, and was heading to Russia again on bid business.

I waited under the portico at the entrance to the hotel, as arranged. I heard the soft purr of the black Porsche before I saw the vehicle or Hargitay at the driver's seat.

From the way he drove around the winding roads of the Zurich hills it was obvious the car gave him great pleasure.

We drove for about 15 minutes down the hill and through tree-lined back streets to a parking lay-by on a pretty street with a view to Lake Zurich. The area appeared mostly residential with double or triple storey Swiss style buildings on one side and new construction and buildings hidden by higher fences and trees on the other. Hargitay's light grey, vine clad building looked like older-style apartments.

There was no sign pointing to Hargitay's current company name, ECN. There was a sign pointing to ABI Investigations.

When I was first informed of Hargitay's engagement nine months earlier, he was named as one of the principals of ABI on the company website. According to the website, ABI specialised in 'looking after' the needs of high net worth individuals - such as Frank Lowy. It boasted of the capacity to conduct surveillance, hacking, phone tapping, bank account interrogation, and other activities that sounded like something out of a James Bond movie or, in the case of Hargitay, a Swiss Secret Service manual.

Not long after Hargitay's involvement with us was known, his name disappeared from the ABI website. It left only his business partner, Fausto Bonvini. By the time of my visit, the ABI website disappeared all together.

We proceeded to the second level and came to a landing with an open door on either side. A man appeared. Hargitay introduced us. He told me it was his business partner. They spoke briefly in German.

He led me to the opposite side of the landing to a meeting room with windows on three sides with a view down to the lake. He showed me in, told me to sit down, and said he had to have a word to his business partner. He asked if I wanted anything. I asked for a glass of water.

I looked around the room, and wondered why such formality was needed for a meeting to discuss the international journalists visit. We could have met at the lounge at the hotel or a coffee shop in the city. I was tempted to get up and look around the room more closely, but I didn't know when Hargitay would return and thought that he would probably disapprove if he thought I was being too inquisitive. Instead, I got out my notebook and waited for him.

After several minutes Hargitay brought me the glass of water, then closed the door of the meeting room behind him. He didn't sit down. What was already a quiet location became almost oppressive with silence because of the thickness of the walls. No sound could be heard either incoming or outgoing and it did flit through my mind that one could be lost forever in this room. Despite the warmth outside, none of the windows were open.

I drank the glass of water.

He looked at my open notebook; sniffed and cleared his throat, raising his eyebrows. He told me I wouldn't need the notebook.

'But Peter, you know I always take notes.' I made a joke of it.

'This is not a meeting for notes, Bonita.'

I put my pen down and closed the notebook. He took out a cigarette and lit it, continuing to stand across the table from me. He sucked on the cigarette, turned slightly and looked at me.

'You know, this is my town and my game and I've been doing this for 35 years. You should just butt out.'

I asked him for another glass of water. While he was out of the room, I wrote down his words verbatim.

He returned a few moments later with the water and some papers. He sat across the table from me.

His manner had changed. He was almost friendly. Expansive. Wanting to share information.

'I am putting the list together of journalists you should invite. I think you should have the visit at the end of November. They can visit Australia and then go on to South Africa for the World Cup draw all in one trip.'

I thought that sounded expensive.

'The expense will be worth it, Bonita. They'll be so grateful to Australia for picking up their tab to go to South Africa. They'll never forget Australia for that. The people I am thinking about are Paul Kelso, Charlie Sale, Martyn Ziegler, Matt Scott, Tariq Panja ...'

'That's an awful lot of people from England,' I said. 'We were hoping for others as well.'

'Bonita! What did I tell you earlier? I know what I am doing. Look!'

He pushed a printed email over the table to me. It was from Jack Warner. Hargitay had written to him asking for his suggestions for a journalist from Trinidad and Tobago.

'See! Jack answers me in less than two minutes after sending that e-mail. Two minutes! That is how close we are. That is how helpful he is to me and our bid.'

I had got that by now. I wondered what more we possibly needed to do to influence Jack Warner.

'It would be good to have some people from Africa and South America also if possible,' I said.

'Leave it with me. Now,' he put his big hands on the desk and closed his eyes momentarily as if he was thinking, 'what else is there?'

'You tell me. You're the boss.'

I thought that would be the end of the meeting. Telephone discussions with him were short; and in the reams of emails he sent through, they were generally one-liners forwarding negative press about the England bid or an acerbic comment about Lord Triesman. Today, for some reason, he wanted to talk. Perhaps it was because he was so rude to me earlier.

'America are finished,' he said abruptly.

'I beg your pardon?'

'The US. They're finished. They have no hope.'

'Why?'

'Chuck Blazer is an active supporter of McCain. And Gulati and Blazer don't get on.'

'Why does that mean the US is finished?'

'Blazer couldn't care less about the US bid.'

'Really?' I asked. 'That's surprising.'

'I've talked to the old man' – he meant Sepp Blatter – 'and asked him what could we do to help get him over the line. As you know, we will set up an office in Zurich if we win to make it easier for FIFA.'

We decided to incorporate this suggestion into our bid proposal as a means of mitigating against the tyranny of distance for meetings with FIFA. We thought it was better for Australia's Local Organising Committee to travel to Zurich, rather than have FIFA staff in Zurich travel to Australia.

Hargitay continued. 'He thought it would be a nice idea if the Australian LOC could offer his daughter a job. As an extension of the previous relationship in the days before Frank.'

'And if we do this, Sepp Blatter will vote for us?'

'Of course. All he wants in life is his daughter to be happy.'

He sniffed and looked out the window towards the lake. 'We are talking to the Russians about what we can do together. And we are working on Lefkaritis, Erzik, Grondona, Teixeira and the Africans.'

'Erzik told Frank last year that he wouldn't vote for us.'

'We think that can change. Andreas is doing work there for the Turkish FA. He and Fedor are talking to them.'

He held out his fingers and counted. 'So that gives us Temarii, Franz, the other four, Russia, the old man and hopefully three out of four Africans. Plus Jack.'

'When the US drops out,' I said.

'Now all of this will be achieved without paying any bribes of course,' he said. 'One. We don't have the money to pay bribes. Two. It's government money. We can't use government money. Three. We don't want to go to gaol. And four, of course, it's not right.'

I sat silent, wondering why he felt it necessary to say this, and wondering how much money was necessary for bribes if $50 million, and potentially $55 million if we also got money for the Asian confederation, wasn't enough.

'One last thing,' he said. 'I am talking to the Standard Chartered Bank about sponsorship.'

'Why would they want to sponsor us?'

'I am talking to them in London. They are a FIFA sponsor and I know them very well. I am very close to getting the money.'

'But what for? What do we need extra money for?' I asked.

'We need extra capital for special events and activities with ExCo members.'

'What special events and activities?' I asked.

'Nothing you need to worry about,' he said.

Hargitay was as evasive as Ben Buckley when it came to providing answers.

We drove back through the streets of Zurich in the Porsche up the hill to the hotel. Hargitay gave me a bear hug when we bade farewell. I felt physically ill about all that I heard. It was one thing to try to endure it by working with Ben, it was another to hear Peter Hargitay talk in those terms.

It was clear to me that Franz Beckenbauer was being paid via Andreas Abold and Fedor Radmann; we gave $4 million - perhaps for worthwhile reasons - to Oceania in exchange for a vote; we were giving $5 million to the Asian Football Confederation to supposedly secure the four Asian voters once their own country's dropped out to be spent at Mohamed Bin Hammam's discretion; and there was still the question of our support for Africa for which I had been directed to get money.

'Remember, what I have told you today is confidential. You speak to no-one about it. No-one. Ever. That includes your colleagues who are here.'

I told him I understood and thanked him for his time.

I SAW MY colleagues through the full-length windows behind the reception to the outdoor terrace with the picture postcard view of Zurich laid out in front. I joined them briefly. They asked me how I had survived the meeting with Hargitay. The rest of them had nothing to do with him but his difficult reputation was legendary. Andreas Abold was with them, returned from his trip to St Gallen. I didn't want to say anything about Hargitay in front of him, so I told them I would see them for dinner.

Upstairs in my room, I finished my notes of the meeting and text messaged Ben. It was getting quite late in Australia but I knew if Ben was awake and felt like talking, he'd get back to me. He did.

'You cannot believe what Peter said to me today.'

He sighed. 'Tell me,' he said with a note of dread in his voice.

I told him about Peter's opening comments. He laughed. 'You should know by now with this job that you've just got to lie back and think of Australia,' he said laughing again.

'I don't think that's funny, Ben.'

'Lighten up. It was a joke. A bad one maybe. You – we,' he emphasised, 'have less than 16 months to go before this is all over. What else did he say?'

I went through the detail of the discussion.

'He said all that?'

'Yes. I knew about Russia. I didn't know about Corinne Blatter. The stuff about Blazer sounds far-fetched to me. But tell me, what's this about sponsorship from the

Standard Chartered Bank and what are these events with ExCo members?'

'I don't know.'

'How much is he seeking?'

'I don't know.'

'What do you mean you 'don't know'? Shouldn't you know if he's seeking money on our behalf? And why did he make a point of giving me that rehearsed spiel about bribes?'

As always, when it got too tough, Ben shut down the conversation. 'It's very late here. It must be getting on for dinner time there. Why don't you have a nice drink, a dinner, be nice to your colleagues and relax? How's Andreas by the way?'

'Andreas is Andreas. He went to St Gallen this afternoon to see Fedor to have some papers signed. They're probably setting up a Swiss bank account,' I said darkly.

Ben told me to buy a nice bottle of champagne for the rest of the gang and hung-up.

Dinner was still a few hours away in Zurich but when I joined my colleagues later, I said nothing to them about either conversation. I also didn't buy the champagne.

THE SEVEN OF us strolled down to FIFA headquarters together the next morning for more one-on-one meetings with FIFA staff. It was much the same as the day before with Juergen; an opportunity to ask questions without the other bidders present as well as get information about specific activities.

Most of the first meeting was concerned with the expo to be held in Cape Town in December in conjunction with the draw for the 2010 World Cup. We had been given very precise instructions on what was required and permitted – the word limit for the booklets, the languages, how many photos we could use, the time limit on the promotional film. All of it had to be checked by FIFA for approval two months prior to the Expo.

FIFA gave us some good news at the next meeting, informing us that they wouldn't require the other winter football codes to stop for the World Cup. It gave us scope for negotiation with them.

This good news was offset when they talked to us about the technology requirements of a World Cup. They told us they were not sure if Australian telecommunications infrastructure was up to the task, based on their experience in Sydney at the FIFA Congress. Ouch.

The following day all the bidders met together in the auditorium at FIFA House. This time, the day started with Blatter. He strolled in after a short film on the Confederations Cup played in June. Everyone stood. Blatter beamed at us and beckoned us to be seated.

'Do I look like a happy President?'

I tried not to laugh out loud.

'That film,' he said. 'It is emotion. It is pure. It is passion.' He looked around the room. 'It is football.'

Applause.

'They loved it in South Africa,' he said. 'They are going to love it even more next year. And don't forget that South Africa are world champions in rugby also. We must let the game be played the way it is played.'

I could tell he was just warming-up to one of his familiar themes.

'The difference is this. The Olympics is one city for 18 days and 6 billion people watch it. In football,' he shifted at the lectern, 'in football, it is national; it is 64 days; and 26.3 billion people watch it. 26.3 billion,' he repeated. 'With football, you get a better country, because you have to build better stadia, better facilities, better roads, better hotels.'

'I have been 41 years working in FIFA,' he said. 'I know that it is the universal language. It is the language of discipline and respect. And it has an important social and cultural aspect.' He paused and held his hands to either side of his head, gesticulating as he spoke.

'You fight, but there is fair play. You are in a group, but you must also play to your best. You learn to win, and you learn to lose.'

He was on a roll.

'And there is an economic dimension to the World Cup,' he said. 'It is FIFA's only source of revenue. Now, to finish … I just want to say to you all. You must bid within the boundaries of fair play. I must protect the game. I must insist you do this.'

'I had a very nice time last night with the Indonesians,' he said. 'They had a function with me and some other local Zurich officials. I am very pleased they are bidding.'

We looked around. We wondered whether the Swiss had demurred on the Indonesian who had not been allowed in from July, or he had been replaced.

'Now I must go. But remember one thing,' he said smiling at us again.

Here we go again, I thought.

'Enjoy football, that is good. Enjoy your life, that is better.'

Applause.

Juergen jumped up and accompanied Blatter from the auditorium before hurriedly reappearing to introduce Jerome Valcke.

Valcke gave a big sigh as he reached the lectern, unenthusiastic as usual. I wondered whether perhaps he was simply burdened by managing Blatter and the Executive Committee. Or maybe he didn't like having his time cut short every time by Blatter running over time. But he always looked as if he wanted to be somewhere else.

The final session of the workshop was on accommodation and was led by the jovial Enrique Byrom. We were led to the Executive Committee meeting room on the third level underground.

Enrique greeted us as we took our places around the generous table arranged around a hollow rectangle to resemble a football field.

The Executive Committee spared no expense in the decor and furnishing of their meeting room. The floor was lapus lazuli stone. Above the hollowed out area was a large cylindrical crystal chandelier that was shaped to depict a stadium roof. There were 25 seats around the table, a small bank of around five or six chairs with a bench table behind one side and a larger number of chairs, also with a table, on the other side of the room. The walls were made of brushed aluminium. There were large, fresh and elaborate floral arrangements around the room. On the table before us, we had FIFA pads, FIFA pens, FIFA mints and Swiss-branded water. The whole effect looked opulent and expensive.

The room was also dark and windowless – supposedly a feature required by Blatter so the Executive Committee wouldn't be distracted by the everyday world when they made important decisions of the football state. With no-one from the outside able to look in on their proceedings, I thought it was an appropriate metaphor for the way they governed themselves.

'Welcome, welcome,' said Enrique smiling broadly, his big teeth sparkling in his suntanned face. He lowered his voice. 'This is it ladies and gentlemen. This is where the decision will be made in a little over 15 months. This is where your fate will be decided.'

Everyone looked around at each other in silence. 'There's a meditation room next door so the ExCo can adjourn to there if they have something they need to think about carefully or need a break.'

I suppressed a giggle. I couldn't imagine anyone on the Executive Committee needing to meditate about anything.

Juergen, who was sitting in on the seminar, piped-up. 'In the centre of the room is the foundation stone which has dirt from every member country of FIFA.' There was no explanation as to how they got more than 200 samples of dirt through quarantine.

'Now,' said Juergen looking at his watch, 'that is enough of the tour. We must get on with this otherwise we'll run out of time.'

Enrique and one of his staff gave us some facts and figures, emphasised the scale of the event and what they required: for example, access to an airport which operated 24/7 and could handle aircraft large enough for 100 people, within one hour of the FIFA hotel and team hotels. I sat there thinking about the curfews applying in Australian airports that had the capacity to take large aircraft.

Just like stadiums, accommodation was another area of concern for us. There were insufficient hotel rooms of the required five-star rating in the country. The only Australian cities that could, at that time in 2009, meet what was required of them were Sydney and Melbourne. For the Final alone, between 8,000 and 10,000 five-star hotel rooms were required. FIFA's financial demands also included requiring hotels to sign-up to providing rooms in 2018 or 2022 at 2010 rack rates.

We sat silent letting the others ask questions as instructed.

Towards the end of the session, I saw the Qataris' to the right of me confer with one another. 'Could we use hotels in Dubai?' one of them asked.

'Of course,' said Enrique. 'Why not? Dubai is one hour away by air. That is nothing compared with some of the other bidders.' Enrique looked in turn at the three geographically large countries bidding – Russia, USA and Australia.

'What you must realise,' said Enrique, 'is that accommodation is a very, very important part of your bid. Very important. It is a key experience factor for visitors and it has to be right for the teams, FIFA and for visitors. I cannot stress this enough. But don't worry, I am here to help you.'

CHAPTER 13
Getting on with business

Munich: August 2009

ANDREAS ABOLD DROVE Stuart Taggart, two of his staff and me from Munich airport directly to his office in his Audi Q7. I was staying for the day and returning home that evening out of Frankfurt. The others were staying for the rest of the week.

The office was in a charming location on the eastern side of the Isar, and not far from Munich's English Garden. The building was a former house located in what looked like predominantly a residential area. It was large and at least two or three stories high.

Abold showed us some of his past bid books. Munich 2002 for the Olympics. Germany 2006. South Africa 2010. Abu Dhabi 2009 and 2010. Women's World Cup 2011. Leipzig 2012. A concept for the Euro 2016 bid for Turkey. The books were large, elaborate and heavy. We made complimentary noises.

'So these are the bid books no-one reads?' I asked fingering the opulent motif on the Abu Dhabi book.

We again sat through the same presentation Abold had given us twice before.

I took him through what we planned. My team and I had developed a calendar which kicked-off in December in Cape Town and was a balance between garnering and building domestic support for the bid at the same time as promoting it internationally, all within the ever-diminishing budget allocation.

'That is excellent, Bonita, and very comprehensive,' said Abold. 'There is one thing missing. What about some ambassadors?' Not again.

'We identified ambassadors from all areas of the community some time ago,'

I took out one of my many pieces of paper and handed him and the others the list.

'So why not have them?'

'Frank doesn't want them. He says they won't win us a vote.'

'But you must have ambassadors to help you with the domestic audience,' said Sonja Abold.

I turned to her. 'We know. Ben and I have tried a couple of times but Frank doesn't agree.'

'We should try again,' said Abold. 'Leave it with me. I will talk to Fedor and we will talk to Frank. What about international ambassadors?'

I told him who had approached us so far offering to be our ambassadors.

'You don't want any of those?'

'For one, we can't afford them – except maybe Roger Milla. But it doesn't fit. We can't say we're genuine and authentic and then have Pele or Roger Milla or Zinedine Zidane speaking for us.'

'How much does Pele want?' Abold asked. I told him.

'No, you are right. You don't need Pele when you have Franz already. But you must have the domestic ambassadors,' Abold said.

'Especially if we don't win,' I said.

'Bonita,' Abold exclaimed. 'Don't say that!'

'I'm planning on three scenarios Andreas: winning – no problems, except how we're going to pay for it. Losing, but only just – that's fine, it's an honourable loss. Or losing badly – in the first or second round.'

'That won't happen. We won't lose and we especially won't lose in the first or second round. You are being too negative,' he said.

'I'm not negative. I'm just being prepared. Don't forget we've so far used $50 million of taxpayers' money.'

'That's okay. We move on,' he said. 'There's one thing to add in,' he said, making sure we were all attentive. 'Don't forget Tutu. That is confirmed for December when we are in Cape Town. Frank must visit the children's hospital and hand over money to Tutu's charity.'

AFTER LUNCH AT the Abolds' favourite business restaurant, I bade farewell to my colleagues and hopped back into the Q7 with Abold who was taking me to the airport. It was a quick trip on the autobahn.

Abold pulled up in the car park and turned to me. 'You don't like working on the bid, Bonita'. It was a statement, not a question. He asked me why not.

I hesitated only briefly. I knew that whatever I said would be relayed back to Ben, Radmann and Hargitay before I arrived home 24 hours later. It was a time either to say nothing or lay it out bare.

'You said it yourself, Andreas, when you visited us in January. It doesn't matter what we do, how well we do it, or what we offer, that is not how this World Cup bid will be won. It will be won because of what goes on behind closed doors, whatever it is that you and Peter and Fedor do, and which I do not know about.'

I paused slightly.

'You forget. Unlike my colleagues, I've been around FIFA and the confederations before. I know how it works. It's about whose palms are greased and what favours can be sought and given. Frank even said as much to a journalist a few months ago but the journalist didn't realise what he was saying. Winning the bid is about making a series of deals with people who want things. You find out what they want.'

I looked up.

'When I met with Peter in Zurich, he told me some of the things we're doing. It worries me. I think we're close to breaching bidding guidelines if we haven't already. We've got extra money for Oceania. My budget has been cut back for no reason. I am guessing it's so we can fund whatever it is we're doing in Asia and Africa if the government doesn't give us any more money. I'm embarrassed to ask the government for it.'

He raised his eyebrows. 'If that is how you feel, Bonita, you should tell Ben.'

Ben knew how I felt. What I didn't say was that Ben also didn't want to be left alone to deal with the international consulting trio of Hargitay, Radmann and Abold.

A little over 24 hours later when I was back in the office Ben asked me why I talked with Abold in Munich.

'Don't tell those three anything about what you think or what you feel or anything we're doing that I haven't told them. And before you ask me 'why' it's because I said so.'

Seoul: September 2009

BEN AND I were meeting in the coffee lounge of yet another five-star hotel - this time in Seoul. It was another standard and nondescript large, polished marble lobby, with sofas strewn around. It was a Sunday morning – the day after a friendly match between South Korea and Australia that we lost 3-0. We were seated around a coffee table having breakfast.

The idea was that we would meet with the South Korean Executive Committee member, Dr Moon-Jung Chung. Hargitay told us that Chung wasn't interested in bidding and it was all about his national Presidential aspirations. Dr Chung ignored our overtures.

Ben had travelled to Seoul from London where he had another meeting of the 'A team', and he was briefing me on the work I was required to do.

'We need an invitation to Salguero to come to Australia as Frank's guest. All expenses paid.' Rafael Salguero was the FIFA Executive Committee member from Guatemala. This personal invitation to visit was in addition to the letter to Salguero inviting a Guatemala team to matches with Australia, Jamaica and Trinidad and Tobago.

'That's against the bidding guidelines,' I said.

'Well find a form of words so it isn't,' Ben replied sarcastically.

'Why are we inviting him?' I asked.

He looked at me and rolled his eyes.

'No, really,' I said. 'We have to have a rationale. I can't just write *'Dear Rafael, come to Australia as my guest, love Frank.'*

'It's his birthday. We're inviting him for his birthday.' He crossed off the item. 'We have to get the women's under-17 team playing in Trinidad and Tobago.'

'More for Jack?' I exclaimed, emphasising the 'more'.

He ignored me. Instead, he said that our Sports Minister needed to be in Egypt and Angola. 'And talk to the Prime Minister's office about getting Anouma, Adamu,

Hayatou and Thompson an honorary consul position each.'

'We can't just go around appointing FIFA ExCo members as honorary consuls.'

'For fuck's sake, Bonita, just do it.'

Ben seldom swore in front of women.

'Okay, okay, I will. But I'm just saying. It's going to be difficult.'

'Peter says it's essential. They all want to be an honorary consul.' He paused. 'Now. You are not allowed to laugh with what I am about to say,' Ben continued.

'Oh?'

'It seems Tutu wants more money.' I started to give a short laugh, almost a snigger, and Ben held his hand up. 'I told you. Don't start. I know what you said.'

'It was always going to happen. If we thought of it, someone else would have too. How much is it now?'

'$100,000.'

'How much are we prepared to pay? Is this coming from the bid budget?'

He slammed down his notebook. 'I am sick of your questions. I'm just not going to answer any more of them. Why can't you just do something because I tell you to?'

I sat there stunned and said nothing. 'Ben, what's wrong?'

He was wearing a pale pink polo shirt. His face was a deep red. He looked like a person who was unhealthy with high blood pressure.

'You – and I - have got a job to do. You don't need to know why. You don't need to know the answer to everything.'

I looked at him. 'But that's where we're different. I do.'

We ordered another coffee and sat in silent contemplation for a few moments.

'Fedor and Franz are going to Qatar.'

'What for?'

'To convince the Emir he doesn't have a hope of winning the World Cup but he has a great chance of winning the World Expo or the Olympics. They will tell him that Australia and Germany will support a World Expo or Olympics Bid and he should concentrate on that.'

'Good luck.'

'You don't think the Emir will take notice of Franz Beckenbauer?'

'Franz will probably come back being an ambassador for them,' I smiled.

'That's not funny,' said Ben. He continued. 'We want Kylie Minogue to come in December,' referring to the events taking place in Cape Town.

'Not Elle?' I joked.

'They think Kylie would be better. We'll leave Elle for next year.'

'What do we want Kylie to do?'

'Sing and be nice to FIFA ExCo members.'

'And that's going to win us the World Cup?'

'It all helps. Why do you think we want Kate Ellis everywhere?'

'Because she's the Sports Minister?'

'Bonita, I know you're not stupid. You know what these men are like.'

'I just find the whole notion of having to pander to these men by having good looking young women around them obnoxious.'

'Peter, Andreas and Fedor are telling us we have to get Kylie, Nicole, Elle and the Sports Minister before the ExCo somehow in the next twelve months. Is that so terrible?'

I sat silent for a moment, looking at him steadily. 'No comment.' He stared back at me, pursed his lips as if he was about to say something and thought better of it.

He took a deep breath. 'And one more thing,' he said softly. He tore off a piece of paper from his notebook and wrote: *No arguing with Ben.*

As he put it on the table between us, he said 'We're in this together.'

I picked it up, dated it and stapled it to my notebook.

Canberra: September 2009

A FEW DAYS later, Ben and I were meeting with the deputy head of the Foreign Affairs department, accompanied by some advisors.

'Some dates for you,' said the senior diplomat, reading from a paper. 'Rudd will see Medvedev at the G20 meeting in Pittsburgh at the end of the month. Smith will meet Lavrov at the UN in New York at the end of the month.' He was referring to the foreign ministers of Australia and Russia, Stephen Smith and Sergey Lavrov.

'Smith may also visit Moscow in February. We're expecting Lavrov to invite him. But that's a big 'may'. Rudd's also going to the UN soon, and he can see Medvedev there. So tell us exactly what you want in writing.'

He continued.

'There's also going to be a meeting of African Foreign Ministers in January in Addis Ababa and Smith is going to that. In terms of Brazil and Argentina, our Ambassadors will call you and have a chat. There's a chance that Rudd may be going there some time. But it's just talk. In respect of Nigeria, we're aware that they're keen to host a Commonwealth Games some time. They tried for 2014 but lost. We should offer to help them put together another bid,' he continued.

'But Adamu is on the outer in Nigeria,' I said. 'He lost his job.'

'Yes we know. We think it might help him rehabilitate himself politically and he'll be grateful for that.'

Adamu lost his job as Director-General of the Nigerian National Sports Commission because he was accused of leading a corrupt group of bureaucrats. It was an odd thing for us to be helping to rehabilitate him.

The deputy head asked if there was anything further.

'One thing,' said Ben. 'Franz Beckenbauer,' he looked at their faces to make sure they knew who Franz Beckenbauer was.

He continued. 'Franz Beckenbauer is going to Qatar for us to convince the Emir to withdraw their bid and concentrate on the Olympics or the World Expo. We also need the Prime Minister to write to the Emir inviting him to Australia.'

'No problem,' they said. 'Just send us a draft and we'll see to it.'

Sydney: September 2009

IT WAS LATE. About 8.30pm. I was sitting in Ben's office at the white meeting table with my back to the door. He was sitting in his customary position at the head of the table. He had pushed his chair back from the table a little, with one foot crossed at right angles over the other leg.

I had been in his office for well over an hour. It was an amiable meeting, going through the calendar for the next 15 months until 'D-Day' as we referred to Decision Day on 2 December 2010. The discussion over, I stood to leave.

'There's one more thing,' he said. 'Have a seat.' I sat back down. 'There's one thing I've got to say to you. No-one likes you.'

I wasn't expecting that. 'That's a big statement. No-one. My family does. There's bound to be some others ...' I said trailing off, trying to make light of it.

'You know what I mean.'

'No, not really.'

'It's not me. I like you. I like you a lot. I've never met anyone like you. I've never met anyone with half as much integrity as you. And I want to be working with you in ten or 20 years time if possible. You are the best communications person I've ever worked with.'

I looked at him. 'But?' I said prompting him.

'Peter, Andreas and Fedor don't like you.'

I laughed. 'Is that all?'

'They want me to get rid of you.'

'The consultants? So what are you going to do? Sack me?' I asked. 'That's okay as long as you give me twelve months full pay.'

'No, I would never sack you. I told you. You're the best work colleague I've ever had. More than that, you're my favourite work colleague. But I've got to do something.'

'That's okay. You know I never wanted to work on the bid anyway.'

'But I want you to.'

'Well you're the CEO,' I said. 'Not them. They're consultants. Either tell them to get on with their jobs and live with it. Or just let me do another job.'

'They want you completely out of the way,' he said.

'Why? What difference is it to them if I'm working on the A-League, or the Socceroos? What business is it of theirs?'

'They say you're a risk to the bid. They say you will lose us the bid.'

'What? Me? If they're doing their jobs in getting us the bid, how can I lose it for them?'

'I've got to figure out what I can do.' His eyes started to well up with tears. He was emotional and, like the rest of us, tired. 'Can you try being nice to them?' he asked quietly.

I thought about how to answer that. 'Ben, I am professional with them. I think that's as much as you can ask of me.'

The tears started. I got up and handed him the tissues.

'Don't worry Ben. I'm not worried. Just let me know what you want me to do.'

'But I don't want you to do anything other than what you're doing,' he said, his eyes tearing up again, as he wiped his eyes.

I took a deep breath.

'Ben, you know I will do this job because you asked. I'll even try very hard to be nice to the consultants. But I'm not going to pretend everything is fine. We both know one of them is crazy. One is an overpaid show pony. And the other. Well, there's no way in this world that Fedor Radmann is worth $3.7 million. Seriously. Where is that money going? I think they're up to something – or we're up to something – that we shouldn't be.'

I waited for him to tell me I was wrong. He said nothing. He blew his nose.

I got up to go. 'See you tomorrow.'

BEN AND I continued the next day almost as if the conversation had never taken place.

We had scheduled the first of our new, regular teleconferences with the two Hargitays, Radmann and Abold for later in the week. I asked him whether he still wanted to go ahead with it.

He looked at me. 'We are going to make the time to do this. I want them to understand how much you do and how important you are. And I don't want them to have any excuses. They don't do anything they say they're going to do and it's either you or me who cops the blame from them every time. You get it on these issues, I get it on the other things. So I want you to take very good notes and then send out a record to them. Also get a list together of people we could possibly take to Cape Town with us.'

'You mean like Craig Johnston and Mark Viduka and others?'

'No, I mean like Kylie Minogue, Nicole Kidman, Dwight Yorke and Batistuta.'

More overseas footballers, but at least both Yorke and Batistuta had an Australian connection. Yorke captained Sydney FC in the A-League's inaugural season. Batistuta lived in Perth.

'You really think Dwight Yorke would support our bid over England's?'

'Peter says he will because he's close to Jack, and Jack will ask him to do it.'

MONTHS AFTER IT was first discussed, Hargitay sent through his recommendations for the visiting journalists program.

Unlike most of his other communications, which were either short and via email or by telephone, this one was a formal letter. It contained twelve names and an explanation as to why each of them should be invited. The journalists were from Nigeria, Cameroon, Egypt, France, England, Germany, Cyprus, Switzerland, Trinidad and Tobago and South Korea - all Executive Committee member countries.

Hargitay wrote that the recommendation for the French journalist had not only come from Jerome Valcke but that Valcke had spoken with the journalist first.

One of the German suggestions came from 'a very close buddy' of Radmann – which meant from Franz Beckenbauer.

Jack Warner recommended a political correspondent 'who is important to him at this time'.

And, Hargitay wrote, it was a 'must' to invite a prominent South Korean football writer along with his translator.

His other two suggestions were courtesy of Andreas Herren, a consultant to the Russian bid with whom we were apparently now 'coordinating our efforts', according to Hargitay's letter.

Soon after writing, Hargitay was in Beijing seeing the Chinese FA on behalf of the Australian bid. In 2008, we were concerned that China would bid themselves, but they didn't. The fear now was that the US bid would ask the Chinese FA to support them for 2022 and, in return, lend their support to China for a tilt in 2026.

Europe in 2018 followed by the USA in 2022 and China in 2026 would have been commercially attractive for FIFA, so Hargitay's task was to convince the Chinese to support the Australian bid publicly first.

Three days later he returned to Europe and told us it was important to invite a Chinese journalist whom he described as a *'strong ally of FIFA, the AFC and ours'*. His recommended journalist was John Yan. He couldn't make it to Australia because of visa issues, but he was in touch and said he would say nice things about Australia.

Yan later became a regular correspondent for the website *Inside World Football.*

IT WAS THE first of our weekly catch-ups with the Hargitays, Radmann and Abold.

Abold kicked-off by telling us we needed ambassadors. Ben and I looked across the speaker phone at each other and rolled our eyes.

Not waiting for our response, we heard Hargitay agree at his end of the teleconference. There was a faint grunt from Radmann. He just wasn't interested in such frippery.

'Yeah, we've tried that guys but it just hasn't been able to happen,' said Ben.

'What do you mean it hasn't been able to happen?' thundered Hargitay. 'Are you people too stupid, too thick or too lazy? You have to have ambassadors.'

Ben and I looked at one another again. Sometimes Hargitay drove us crazy; other times we just rolled with the punches. Ben took a deep breath.

'Peter, Andreas .... we had a list of ambassadors drawn up last year. It was even included in our submission to government for the money.'

'So what's the problem, man? What are you waiting for?' Hargitay demanded.

'Frank doesn't think ambassadors are necessary. They're not going to win us any votes.'

More silence.

'But if nothing else, you need ambassadors for internal purposes,' Abold said.

I put our end of the teleconference on mute for a moment. 'I can't believe this. This is exactly what I talked about with Stevie in July and Andreas last month,' I said to Ben.

Hargitay coughed. 'I'll talk to him,' he said. 'He will listen to me.'

Ben and I looked at one another and smiled. In Hargitay's mind, we were small-fry. Frank Lowy wouldn't listen to us, but he would to Peter Hargitay.

Abold encouraged him. 'Good idea, Peter. When we had Claudia Schiffer for Germany, it was the icing on the cake for the ExCo. I walked through the streets of Zurich with her and it was just fantastic,' said Abold.

We had heard the Claudia Schiffer story at least ten times before.

Still Radmann said nothing.

'But you have to have big names,' Hargitay went on.

'The key thing is keep it Australian,' I said. 'We can't compete with David Beckham, and we can't afford to pay people like Qatar are, but we can stay genuine. That's why we've got kids coming to South Africa with us in December. It reinforces how genuine we are.'

'Usain Bolt.'

Hargitay hadn't listened to a word I said.

'What was that Peter?' asked Ben.

'Usain Bolt. He is a close family friend of ours. He will do anything I ask him to. He owes me big time anyway. He can be our number one ambassador. Wouldn't that be fantastic? That would blow their minds out on the ExCo. The fastest man on earth, the most famous sportsman in the world, supporting Australia's bid.' He added: 'And Jack loves him.'

Anything Jack loves, we loved too.

Another pause. 'See what I can do for you.' It was a statement, not a question.

'Fantastic, Peter,' Abold exclaimed excitedly.

Ben sighed. I sighed.

Australia still awaits Usain Bolt's endorsement for our bid.

CHAPTER 14
The world's most expensive computer bags

Sydney: October 2009

TWO DAYS LATER I circulated the notes and action plans from the teleconference. Hargitay responded almost immediately - although not on any of the substantive issues discussed. He was more concerned with security of information.

> 'Never again mention the full names of attendees on a written document. Never again send such a document unprotected. Always add a password to open the PDF. Ideally, do not send such a document AT ALL but upload it to the Intranet group which has password protection instead. You, we all, are dealing with a hugely dishonest, false and backhanded competitive world out there. To jeopardise our collective effort by not taking appropriate proactive protective measures is not advisable.'

One week later, we had the next teleconference. They hadn't done a thing.

Initially all they were asked to do was tell us where we could encounter Executive Committee members in the months to come. Our consultants said they were the only ones with the expertise to make that decision.

It was silly – and inefficient. Instead of simply contacting FIFA staff, or Enrique Byrom who booked Executive Committee travel, we had to wait for the consultants to tell us. Rather than have Australian diplomatic missions make appointments to catch-up with foreign government officials or Executive Committee members, we had to wait for the consultants to give us information or make the appointment time. Rather than issue an invitation to a foreign VIP, we had to wait for Hargitay to invite them personally.

Ben wrote on his notebook as we listened to the teleconference: '*He is so full of shit.*'

We were less than a week from travelling to Cairo for the under-20 World Cup, but neither Hargitay nor Radmann had come up with a date for the Executive Committee event.

In the meantime, Embassy staff were getting anxious. 'Bonita, we just can't wait any longer to know what we're doing,' they said. 'We've got to order food, alcohol, extra staff. This is Cairo, not downtown Canberra.'

I let the consultants know I gave the go-ahead to a barbecue at the Ambassador's residence.

'You did this without consulting us, Bonita,' Hargitay said over the phone.

'Peter, that's not fair,' Ben replied. 'We talked about this last week. Bonita leaves here in four days, me in six. We need to know what we're doing. We have to manage the relationship with our government.'

For Ben, that was quite some push back. We heard an indrawn breath. I could imagine Hargitay putting his finger around his collar and cricking his neck. The sniff would be next. It was. He said nothing.

'So we have a barbecue at the Ambassador's residence,' said Ben. 'Now all we need is a day from you guys.'

'Friday lunchtime. It can be a brunch style barbecue,' came the crisp response from Radmann. A decision at last.

'Friday it is,' said Ben. 'What's next? Nigeria. We need to settle Nigeria too because the High Commission is getting anxious and it's even harder for them to order things in.'

'When do you arrive?' asked Hargitay.

This was discussed a week ago also. They were sent schedules many times. A copy even existed on the new cloud facility we had installed for bid documents. I gave him the details again.

'So we must have it on the 13th,' he said.

'But you and Fedor said the official dinner was on that night,' I pointed out. The official dinner was the highlight of the social calendar at any tournament and seen as an essential event to attend.

'Well the 12th then,' he said.

'But the semi-finals are on in Lagos on the 12th,' I said. They had all this information in a calendar that had been regularly updated all year. 'We were thinking of a cocktail reception on the 14th at the High Commissioner's residence.'

'No that's no good,' said Radmann.

'What's no good Fedor?' asked Ben.

'Both. It needs to be another date and not a cocktail reception.'

Ben and I rolled our eyes. It was exactly the same discussion from the previous week.

'Peter, Fedor, Andreas,' Ben said. 'We need to know what your recommendation is. We need to have this when we meet in Cairo next week. You must also tell us which ExCo members will be there, so we can make sure they're invited.'

'Have you got the ExCo gifts for Cairo, Bonita?' asked Abold.

'A leather wallet from RM Williams,' I said.

We heard Abold clasp his hands together in approval. 'Oh, that is perfect,' he said. 'Perfect. Does it say that they're leather?'

'Kangaroo leather,' I replied.

'Perfect. Perfect,' said Abold again. 'It is Australian. Everyone knows RM Williams. It is kangaroo. It is leather, so highest quality. Perfect. Are you putting some money in them?' he asked.

'I hadn't thought about that,' I said.

'You must include a gold coin. Next time,' Abold said a little breathlessly 'you can buy them RM Williams boots.'

The 24 wallets already cost us more than $3,500. There was no way I was including a gold coin as well. I also wondered how much would it cost to transport 24 pairs of boots around the world and how we would get the shoe size of 24 ExCo members? Perhaps our consultants could help us with that.

But there was more.

'There's one very important thing.' It was Radmann.

He seldom said much, so Ben and I looked at one another wondering what on earth it could be.

'When you order all the accreditation, make sure they give you VIP car passes,' he said.

'Oh yes, Fedor,' Hargitay rejoined. 'That's critical. In fact, you must get two, Bonita. Two!' he emphasised. 'We will need two chauffeured limousines. It is very important we have these.'

'Just ask the people you're dealing with over the accreditation. They can give them to you,' Radmann said. 'If you have any trouble, let me know straight away. And let them know you're letting me know.'

Our highly paid consultants were really focussed on the big issues.

London: October 2009

PETER AND STEVIE Hargitay were ecstatic.

They convinced Frank Lowy that we should pull a stunt at the Leaders in Football conference at Stamford Bridge. The conference boasted of *'bringing together the most important football leaders in the world'*. We didn't attend but all other bidding nations were represented.

Instead, the Australian bid sponsored the conference computer bags to be distributed by locally engaged archetypal Aussie 'chicks' as Stevie referred to them – the more blonde, buxom and what they imagined to be Bondi Beach-like, the better.

After telling us earlier in the year that it was essential to be there, Hargitay took a 180-degree turn and told Lowy and Ben that speaking at the conference, and presenting on the merits of Australia's bid, was a waste of time and 'uncreative'.

The conference began with Jack Warner loudly criticising the English bid for giving £230 Mulberry handbags for the partners of Executive Committee members. He said the gifts were extravagant and outside bidding guidelines. He ostentatiously returned his wife's handbag claiming it was 'tainted' and declared his vote couldn't be bought.

We smiled.

'Let's not mentions the pearls,' Ben said to me as we read the report.

The next step was for Warner to lavishly praise the Australian bid and its consultants, commenting that 'everyone' was taking notice of it and our $40 computer bags. No mention of his criticism earlier in the year.

Despite what Hargitay and Stevie said was their stunning work, it was obvious that the only person commenting was Jack Warner.

Hargitay and Stevie sent multiple emails with photos, online reports and notes from journalists thanking him for the scoop. Hargitay was keen to make sure we understood this was a PR coup he had orchestrated from go-to-woe. He wrote to Lowy:

> *'PS: If you believe that I am entirely innocent for Jack's statements, I may disagree. Sky News crew, BBC Radio and PA were hand-fed and led to the troph (sic), i.e. Jack's hotel.*

For the privilege of providing the computer bags, the Australian bid paid £15,000 in sponsorship via the Hargitays' 'dear friend' working on the conference, who also later worked for the Australian bid. The cost of the computer bags and their shipment to England - twice, because the first shipment was stuck between UK Customs and the Hargitays' office - cost another £40,000 - so £55,000 in total.

The England bid team's infamous Mulberry handbags for the partners of the 24 Executive Committee members – that Jack Warner was so affronted by and made a huge display of returning - cost around £5,500 in total.

CHAPTER 15
Lobbying in Cairo

Cairo: October 2009

I WAS MEETING with the Australian Ambassador and her staff in their offices at the World Trade Centre adjacent to the FIFA hotel in Cairo.

We were here for the final week of the under-20 World Cup, in which the Australian team was taking part. We were knocked-out in the first stage, but all of the Executive Committee were expected to be in town for the semi-finals and final.

'We have all these invitations ready to go,' said the First Officer as the Ambassador, two of her staff and I were having coffee in her office. They showed me the standard Australian crest embossed official white card invitation.

'We delivered the first list that you gave us last week but we're still waiting for the rest,' she said.

I apologised and explained that we were still waiting for the final list from the consultants. I extracted a paper from my folder. Enrique and Robyn Byrom had helpfully given me a list of FIFA officials who were in Cairo. 'However, here is an additional list based on who's here. Perhaps we could deliver invitations to these people and once I hear from the consultants, we can add any more they have.'

'That's all we can do,' the Ambassador said matter-of-factly. 'These consultants of yours don't sound very helpful,' she said.

'They're not really typical consultants.'

'I've arranged for you and Ben to meet the Egyptian Sports Minister on Thursday. What about Hany Abo Rida?' she asked, referring to the local Executive Committee member.

'The consultants said they were arranging that meeting.'

'If you have a problem, just call me,' she said.

A LITTLE WHILE later, Ben and I were in the hotel lobby. I watched other people talking, smoking sheesha, huddled over blueprints, drinking coffee.

Ben wanted to know if any other bidders were in Cairo. I had so far only seen Andy Anson from England.

'Peter says it's good if we're the only ones here,' Ben said over coffee.

'It's good if we get access to the Executive Committee I guess. But it seems pretty pointless if not.'

He asked whether we had a meeting time with Abo Rida. I said that the Ambassador had offered to arrange it for us, if the consultants failed to do so.

'They're going to be the death of me. They're all talk. That's why I asked you to take detailed notes of the meeting,' he said.

'I'm not sure they'll even read meeting notes, let alone take any notice of them.'

'No, I know. But they will if Frank says something to them.'

We both saw Abold and Radmann making their way to us. Ben stood to greet the two men warmly, shaking their hand and giving each a one-arm man hug.

It was the first time I had met Radmann. He was in his early 60s. He was tanned, but with a ruddy complexion. His hair was receding but still thick, cropped close. He had a grey moustache, thick eyebrows and cold, light blue-grey eyes.

'Ahh, the famous Miss Bonita Mersiades,' he said, pronouncing my family name the Greek way and taking my outstretched hand as if he were about to kiss it. Instead, he held it briefly, gave a little bow and clicked his heels together. 'It is a pleasure to meet you at last.'

'This is where your World Cup bid really starts,' he said. 'Here, then in Nigeria, then Abu Dhabi, Luanda and so on. You will spend a lot of time over the next 14 months in hotel lobbies and stadiums. Make sure the Executive Committee know you're here. Everytime.'

CAIRO INTERNATIONAL STADIUM is only 12 kilometres from the hotel but it took more than an hour to get there, most of it on a freeway that ran above the building line.

The VIP area of the stadium had an elaborate gated entrance. It led immediately into the building which was a 'T' shape, opening into a large lobby off which there was a large number of rooms. There was signage elaborately displayed outside each room. The air-conditioning kept the area cold despite the heat outside.

Radmann excused himself and headed for a door that was marked 'VVIP' for very very important persons. Ben followed, but Abold put his hand on his arm to stop him, shaking his head indicating he shouldn't go there.

We walked out to the stadium and found our seats.

To our left was the area put aside for the Executive Committee and other VVIPs. The seats were larger than the standard stadium seating where we were located. They were cushioned, and had small tables between them for food and drinks.

We returned inside out of the heat, wondering what we should do. Abold's hand on Ben's arm made it clear that we were not permitted to mingle with the Executive Committee - yet that was the reason for being here.

An usher showed us upstairs to a hospitality room that took up almost half of the floor space of the building. It was a large, impersonal room with a bar, a tea and coffee station, and some self-serve finger food. There was a smattering of people around.

The three of us found a table and chairs by a corner and sat down.

'What are we supposed to do, Andreas?' I asked.

'We wait. We wait. Soon some more people will come and we will talk to them.'

We waited until 15 minutes before kick-off in the first semi-final. Absolutely no-one else came.

At half-time, the three of us were ushered upstairs to the same cavernous room again. I noticed England bid chief, Andy Anson, disappear into another room downstairs - not the VVIP room - where there seemed to be a lot of men in suits. We sat in the same seats at the same table. I asked Abold again whether we should be doing anything rather than sitting around.

'This is all you need to do. The main thing is that the Australian bid is here and Ben and you are seen.'

It didn't make a lot of sense.

Towards the end of the match, Hargitay arrived. He was waiting for us in the air-conditioned lobby when the game was over. His eyes were shining. He seemed excited. He greeted us warmly.

'I've been checking this out,' he said. 'These passes,' he pulled out the one around his neck which was the same as ours, 'only gets you upstairs. The real action is here and here.' He pointed first to the door on the other side of the lobby with the VVIP sign where Radmann had gone - never to be seen again, it seems - and then to the door nearest to us that Andy Anson entered.

'The old man will get me into the VVIP room. I will try to get you into this room. You go upstairs and I will fix it,' Hargitay told us.

We did as we were told and made our way to the same table and chairs yet again. With 90 minutes until kick-off in the second game, there was a buffet set out for the guests of whom there were more since the first game. After the meal, I stood up.

'Where are you going?' asked Ben.

'I don't see what use this is doing anyone. I'm at least going to talk to someone.'

I marched over to someone I recognised: Bora Milutinovic, most recently the national coach of Iraq but previously of many other national and domestic league teams. Milutinovic was standing by himself. He had thick salt and pepper hair and looked slightly dishevelled even though he was wearing an expensive suit. I greeted him in Serbian.

He was very happy to chat. 'You have some good players,' he said. 'Schwarzer, Cahill, Kewell, Viduka, before that Farina, Okon. I wanted to coach your national team, but they didn't want me.'

What could I say?

'You think you can win this bid?' He peered at me intently through his thick, black-rimmed glasses.

I didn't flinch. 'Yes.'

'Well I think you need ambassadors. Someone like me who can speak on your behalf.'

Here we go again.

'Is that your boss over there?' he said flicking his head towards Ben. 'You tell him Bora Milutinovic will be an ambassador for the Australian bid.'

'He'll ask me how much?' I asked. Not only had I learned my lesson from the episode with Christian Karembeu, but we had received many proposals from high profile international players and coaches willing to be bid ambassadors.

He shook his hands in front of him. 'Later, later. We talk about that later.'

I told Ben, Abold and Hargitay – who had now joined them - of the offer. They laughed.

'No-one takes Bora seriously,' said Hargitay.

'That's a bit unfair Peter. He wouldn't be suitable for us as an ambassador, but he has coached five teams at a World Cup. I think the football world takes him a seriously.'

'Big fucking deal,' said Peter. 'That's not going to win you the World Cup,' he said.

Neither is sitting around in this room I thought.

Less than three months later, Milutinovic was named as another one of Qatar's bid ambassadors.

Much later, Qatar received criticism for their bid ambassadors and the expense they represented. However, except for their final ambassador named in September 2010 – Zinedine Zidane – all had played or coached in Qatar at some stage in their career. Milutinovic had coached Al Sadd, the favoured club of many of Qatar's elites, including the CEO of the 2022 Bid, Hassan Al-Thawadi.

At half-time in the next game, Hargitay decided he needed to be pleasant to me for a while. As we entered the lobby again, he pulled me aside.

'Bonita, you can come with me into this room.'

I really didn't want to. 'I'll get Ben and Andreas,' I said.

'No, no. Leave them. They've gone upstairs. Come in here and get yourself a drink.'

We entered the room where I had seen Andy Anson go. Hargitay being pleasant was disconcerting and unusual.

The room reminded me of a small and modest airport lounge with a drinks cabinet and bar down one end, a few tub chairs and a table in the centre of the room with some hot and cold food. The food and drink were better quality than upstairs.

I poured myself another sparkling water and waved to Andy Anson over the shoulder of the person with whom he was speaking. I remained standing and made small talk with the person nearest me.

Then I heard Hargitay's voice across the room. He was making sure he was heard. 'Andy Anson, what are you doing here?'

'Hello Peter.' There was some quiet and polite chit-chat from Anson, until Hargitay decided to give the England bid some free advice.

'You know what?' he asked. 'You have a very strong bid. Very strong. You should win this easily. But you won't if you don't do what I told you to do.' He was making reference to the strategy he prepared for the England bid that was not taken-up by them once Lord Triesman arrived as the FA and England bid chief. Triesman later said that the proposal from ECN, which then included Hargitay and Markus Siegler, now with the Russian bid, involved spending lots of money on events for the Executive Committee.

I didn't hear what Anson replied, but Hargitay was speaking loudly enough to make sure everyone heard him.

'Yes, you need to be out at these events, pressing the flesh, being seen, getting to know Executive Committee people, talking to them. And you need to ditch that fuckwit Chairman of yours and take Jane Bateman along instead. No-one listens to Triesman. He's an arrogant prick. You should do what I say and then you'll win.'

I looked around the room to see who else was listening. Almost everyone.

I was embarrassed. Here was a consultant for the Australian bid publicly speaking in disparaging terms of another bid's Chairman to the CEO of that bid, and in front of a senior executive of his employer. I wanted to sneak out of the room, but Hargitay made his way back to me. He put his finger around his collar, lifted his neck and sniffed.

'See if the idiot takes any notice,' he muttered in a stage whisper.

'Shall we go Peter?' I walked out of the room, mouthing 'I'm sorry' to Anson as I did so.

WE WERE IN an even more luxurious hotel where we used the video conference facilities for a meeting to link-up with the rest of the 'A' team in Australia.

'Come on,' said Ben to me quietly when the video conference was finished. 'We're going to have some fun now.' He sounded quite upbeat.

We made our way to a lounge just off the lobby of the hotel. It was opulent and lush with a circular stained glass window as its feature, soft cream sofas and chairs, occasional tables and corner tables adorned with vases and artefacts and a grand piano. We managed to find a sofa and three seats for the five of us. We ordered some coffee and pastries.

Ben and I took out our meeting papers. It was the notes of our previous two teleconferences and the action items. Even though they had received them already, I handed around copies to each of them.

'So gents, have you got that information for us on Nigeria yet?' Ben asked.

Hargitay spread his hands, palms facing up. 'Ben, we've had no time since last week. We've been so busy.'

'We need to know. When's the latest we can tell them?' turning to me.

'The end of the month,' I said.

'Plenty of time to sort it out,' said Ben. 'That's what? More than two weeks away. Please let Bonita know. Now Dubai,' he continued reading from the list of action items.

It was a long meeting. The three of them became increasingly uncomfortable as we made our way through the action list from the previous meetings. Not one item which they committed to was completed. I could tell from the tone of his voice that Ben was feeling quite pleased.

'Now. Last item. What are we doing here in Cairo?' he said putting his cup back in its saucer. The three consultants laughed nervously. 'Bonita and I have a meeting with the Egyptian Sports Minister tomorrow.'

'What for? Who arranged that?' asked Hargitay.

'The Australian Ambassador.'

'Well I must come too,' said Abold, affronted that he wasn't included. 'I know these people because I am currently working with them on a bid for the 2017 Mediterranean Games. I have met all of them.'

'Hany Abo Rida. Do we have a meeting arranged with him yet?' Ben asked.

Silence. He ostentatiously looked at the two sets of action items from our two previous teleconferences. 'Yes, it definitely says here that you would organise a meeting with Hany Abo Rida.'

The FIFA Executive Committee member from Egypt, Abo Rida was chairman of the local organising committee for the under-20 World Cup.

'Can you give him a call now, explain that we've come all the way from Australia, and we'd like 30 minutes of his time?' Ben asked.

The three of them looked at one another.

'I don't think I have his number on me,' Hargitay said.

Ben turned to me and asked me to call the Ambassador to arrange the meeting.

Hargitay and Radmann spoke with one another in German as I made the call.

'That's too funny,' she said to me. 'They haven't come through. They've got to be the funniest consultants.'

Hargitay turned towards Ben a little more. 'Ben, I think we should check out the Ambassador's residence.'

'Why Peter?'

'Well only Bonita has seen it. We don't know what it's like. I need to check that it is suitable for Executive Committee members.'

I saw Ben look down and count to ten before he replied. 'I'm sure we can arrange it.'

'And I want to raise the problem with the invitations,' he said.

We didn't say anything.

'The invitations only arrived yesterday, some today.' He turned to me. 'What have you been doing Bonita? They should have been with them long before this.'

I said that the first lot of invitations were delivered to the hotel by the Embassy last Friday. 'We're still waiting for your invitation list, Peter, but that's no matter. I gave the Embassy another list based on what Enrique told me on Monday about who's here, and those people received the invitations on Monday evening.'

My phone rang. Radmann and Abold turned to one another and talked further in German.

I told them that the Ambassador said we would meet with Hany Abo Rida in two day's time.

'Terrific,' said Ben. 'That's what we're here for.'

HARGITAY WAS REALLY angry.

He had got out of his limousine and I could see him talking to the driver. Our driver, in the second car I had shared with Radmann and Abold, had gone over to join them.

Radmann and Abold stayed outside still conversing. I walked into the hotel. Ben caught up with me.

'He was already upset with us,' Ben said. 'But something seemed to upset him more all of a sudden. He started swearing and muttering.'

Ben and I lingered in the entrance of the lower ground floor of the hotel, waiting for the others.

'Are you an idiot?' Hargitay thundered as the double doors parted for him.

Ben and I looked at each other.

'Bonita. Are. You. An. Idiot. I asked.' Hargitay said slowly, emphasising each word.

'I beg your pardon?'

'Did you tell those two fuckwit drivers to come this way?'

'Yes,' I said, wondering what the problem was.

'You never do that. Do you understand? Never.'

'Peter, he asked if it was okay as it was easier to drop us at this door rather than have to go two kilometres up the road to turn around and come in the main door.'

This seemed to anger him more. His bulbous face was getting redder by the moment and the thinning wisps of hair on the side of his head appeared to stand out on a 90-degree angle.

'Are you crazy? You're an idiot,' he said again.

'I'm sorry, Peter, I don't know what the problem is. I don't think you should talk to me like that.'

'My job is to win this bid and I'll talk to you any way I want,' Hargitay spat at me.

'I don't think so,' I said 'but I still don't know what the problem is.'

It was clear from the look on his face that he really did think I was an idiot.

'Never, never come in the back way,' he said.

'What?'

'Never come in the back way. This,' gesturing to where we were standing, 'is the back way. This. Is. Not. The. Main. Door.'

'I explained why it was simpler for the drivers.'

'I don't care about the fucking drivers! They are paid to do what we fucking well tell them. Do you realise how stupid it looks to come in the lower ground floor?'

I looked at the shopping arcade behind us, the double glass door entry, the people milling about at a variety of shops and the grand stairs up to the ground floor a few metres away.

'As a matter of fact, no.'

'Important people do not come in the lower ground floor,' he thundered. 'They come in the main door. They get noticed. And we do that in case there's anyone important sitting in the lounge upstairs when we come in.'

I thought I was going to burst out laughing, but I turned and walked towards the lift. The lift doors closed. By this time tears had welled in my eyes. Laughter? Frustration? Anger? Injustice? Absurdity? All of them.

My phone rang as soon as I walked in the room. It was one of the two drivers assigned to us for the week.

'Miss Bonita, I am very sorry.'

'What for?'

'Mr Peter. He was very angry with us and said we would lose our jobs.'

'You will not lose your jobs. I agreed for you to go the short way. For us, it is not a problem, but we'll go the long way from now on. It's simpler.'

'Thank you, thank you Miss Bonita. Sorry to cause trouble.'

'Truly, no trouble. We'll see you later this evening. Thank you.'

ABOUT 15 MINUTES later, Ben called and asked me to join him for lunch. He asked me how I was. I said I was fine.

'I am just so sick of them,' he said. 'They drive me up the wall. They do nothing. You don't know half of it.'

'I can only imagine,' I said.

'Believe me, it's probably worse than you imagine.'

He said the office in Sydney phoned to say no progress had been made with the state governments about stadium venues. He said Stuart was at his wits end after another discussion with the Sports Minister's office.

We discussed whether it was time to put our concerns in writing; the government always had to react to something when it's in writing. So far, all the back and forth with the Sports Minister, the rest of the Federal government and the state governments was by telephone or in meetings. We thought it was possible it wasn't the Minister's office that was the problem.

'Could we be upsetting the Prime Minister if we write a tough letter?' Ben clarified.

'Either the Prime Minister, the Sports Minister or the bureaucracy, yes,' I said.

'I don't care about the bureaucracy.'

'On the plus side, it will spur them into action. On the down side, they're likely to be annoyed. It means it's forever on the record.'

The problem was that the signed bidding agreement was due in Zurich in less than seven weeks. Stuart and his team thought that if we didn't have certainty around stadiums soon we should consider pulling out of the bid altogether.

'Write a letter. Put at the end that I'd like to see her when I get back from Cairo. And make sure it's really strongly worded. Make sure she understands that we can't go on much more like this.'

We also agreed to set-up meetings with key government Ministers ahead of the Cabinet Submission about the government guarantees. Not only did we know from our discussions with public servants that there was a lot of nervousness around the government guarantees, but we heard that Ministers had expressed concern about them in 'corridor talk'.

FIFA's government guarantees essentially required host governments to sign away their rights to FIFA for the duration of the World Cup and a period before and after it. The ones that were of most concern to our government - and, we assumed, countries such as England, the USA, Japan, Holland/Belgium, Spain/Portugal and South Korea - concerned right of entry of everyone connected with the World Cup, indemnification, employment provisions, the broad scope of tax exemptions, and the establishment of restricted trading zones within a two kilometre radius of stadiums. There was also concern that it was unconstitutional for one government to bind a future government to such onerous arrangements.

'Check whether Rudd has spoken to Medvedev or Putin yet. The Russian bid won't go any further with us until they have a signal from their government to do so. They haven't got one yet. Also make sure the letter to the Emir has gone. And do a brief on Anouma and Adamu.'

'A brief for whom about what?' I asked.

'I don't know! Just a brief.' He paused. 'Let's move on. We want a letter to every member of ExCo asking them to visit.'

I raised my eyebrows.

'What's wrong?' he asked.

'That's not permitted according to the bidding guidelines.'

'There's nothing wrong with inviting them.'

I asked him who was paying.

'I'm sure you'll write the perfect letter so it doesn't appear like we are.'

'Is it for their birthdays?' I asked. 'Like Salguero?'

He ignored my barb. 'Now – wait for it.' He paused. 'Peter is inviting Usain Bolt to Angola.'

I guffawed.

'And they want us to invite Cathy Freeman.'

'Not an Indigenous footballer also?' I asked.

'No, they all say it has to be the biggest name possible and no-one's heard of our Indigenous footballers. One more thing,' he said. 'We're visiting every ExCo country next year. Frank, you, me, and sometimes Brian. And Andreas. And either Peter and Fedor.'

'Great,' I muttered.

'Don't worry. It will be okay. They'll be on their best behaviour with Frank there.'

CHAPTER 16

'If Qatar wants it, Blatter is in a tough spot'

Cairo: October 2009

'BY THE WAY, we have to thank you for arranging the meeting with Abo Rida,' said Ben to the Ambassador as we rode in her chauffeured car to the meeting with Hassan Sakr, the Egyptian Sports Minister.

'No problem. It's what we do.'

'I know. But it was brilliant when it was done so quickly. You don't know how good it was.'

'Consultants saying it was too difficult?' she asked. We both nodded. 'Think you need new consultants.'

We met Andreas Abold at the Hassan Sakr's offices in a nondescript looking building in the Giza district.

After passing through security, we were met in the lobby, taken up two flights of stairs in silence, led into an office suite with a long corridor that led to a reception room. It was ornately decorated - some time ago. Every step of the way, more silent people tagged on to the delegation.

By the time Hassan Sakr appeared from behind large sliding double doors, there were ten Egyptian officials to we three Australians and Abold. The Minister was a big man. Tall – even taller than Ben – with a long face, thinning grey hair, deep set eyes with dark circles, craggy features, wearing a well-cut suit.

He ushered us through the doors to his private office that had the same interior decorator. Ornate, lots of timber, leather, velvet brocade, and dated. It was large. The Ambassador, Ben and I were shown to an 'inner circle' of chairs and sofas, along with the Minister, the head of his department and the equivalent of his chief of staff, while the rest of the group pulled up meeting chairs in an outer circle.

We were offered some sweet tea or Arabic coffee – I chose the coffee. The Ambassador had already instructed us to drink what was on offer, along with the sampling of anything to eat which, on this occasion, included baklava and dates. The refreshments arrived over small talk.

After we were served, the Ambassador got straight to the point.

'Minister, we're here because Australia is bidding for the World Cup in 2018 or 2022. The Australian Government fully supports the bid. Hany Abo Rida is a member of the Executive Committee who votes. We want his vote, and we want your help in getting his vote.'

He gave one nod of his head in acknowledgment.

'I want to visit your country,' he said. 'I want you to invite me. I am very impressed with Australian sport and your sports institute.'

The Ambassador smiled. She looked at the head of the department. 'That can be arranged Minister.'

He looked at Ben then me. 'And, of course, I would like you to show me something of what you offer in football.'

'We'd be delighted to Minister,' said Ben.

The real business was over in a matter of minutes in those few sentences, but we spent another 45 minutes or so learning of the challenges of organised sport in Egypt and of getting children to play sport. Minister Sakr and his officials appeared genuinely interested in looking at something such as the Australian Institute of Sport to consider whether it would work for them.

We said farewell, promising that Minister Sakr would have his letter of invitation from the Australian Sports Minister within the coming weeks. We exited the building in the same silence with which we entered.

WE WERE BACK in the busy hotel lobby. This time we returned via the front door. The Ambassador, Ben and me waiting for Hany Abo Rida. We found a small round table with four chairs set away from others.

Abo Rida was right on time. Medium height, medium build, immaculately tailored light grey suit, receding hair, broad forehead, dark brown eyes, strong jawline, light olive skin. He shook our hands: first the Ambassador, then me and then Ben, and asked us to call him Hany.

As soon as he sat, a waiter appeared to take our order. 'This is on me,' he said. I ordered my fourth coffee of the day. 'Is this your first visit to Cairo?' he asked Ben and me. 'Have you seen anything of it?'

'Unfortunately, no,' said Ben.

'That is a shame. I was in Sydney last year for the Congress and I know it is a very beautiful city. I had the opportunity to look around. We have a much different country but it is also beautiful. You will have to come back one day.'

'I would like to,' I said.

'Where would you like to go?' he asked politely.

'Here, Cairo. Luxor, Aswan, Alexandria, Port Said.' The under-20 Australian team had been based at Port Said for the tournament. It was where Abo Rida was born and grew up. His factory was located there.

'Ahh,' he said. 'You are interested in Alexandria because you are Greek. It is certainly worthwhile visiting. But why Port Said?'

'Family history. My mother-in-law made her way to Australia via Port Said,' I answered. 'We have a photo of her boarding the boat there.'

'A genuine reason. I thought you were being polite because you were well-briefed and knew Port Said is my home.' He smiled.

'No, I wouldn't be polite just for that reason.' I smiled back.

The coffee arrived.

'That's good. I'm pleased. So,' he said. 'What would you like to tell me?'

The Ambassador gave a similar introduction to the morning meeting. She added that we met with Hassan Sakr, the Sports Minister, and that he would be invited to Australia.

'I know quite a bit about the Australian bid. I have read about it,' he said. 'Let me tell you what I think your shortcomings are.'

'Please do,' said Ben.

'Distance. You are too far away. And money. Why would ExCo make the decision to have the World Cup in Australia when the TV money elsewhere will be much, much more?'

Abo Rida was well-briefed.

'We don't accept that the TV money will be so much more elsewhere, Hany. We're in the Asian time zone. Three-quarters of the world's population lives in Asia. The biggest growth for FIFA is going to come from Asia, not anywhere else. We're doing some work to show the Executive Committee this,' Ben said.

'I'd be interested in seeing the work, but there are other bidders from Asia to which that applies,' said Hany.

'Yes, but we think we have a stronger case overall than the other four.'

'You certainly have the experience to host it,' he said. 'And I have no doubt you would do a good job.'

'In terms of distance, we don't think that's an issue for the World Cup. It's five weeks long,' said Ben.

'That's true for players and teams. What about fans? Not all fans can go for five weeks. They may only get one week's holiday and two days of that is taken up in travel. It's just so far away, it takes so long and it is so expensive.'

'A small proportion of people may have one week's holiday. Most, if they know they're travelling to Australia, would probably plan a longer holiday,' I said. 'The average length of stay of inbound visitors to Australia is 10 to 12 days.'

'Why should FIFA care about Australia when you have all those other football codes?'

Ben indicated for me to answer.

'It's precisely because we do have the other football codes that FIFA should care about Australia,' I said. 'This would help us build football, push it to a more prominent place.'

'But you only have 20 million people,' he said. 'The same as Cairo. What difference will it make?'

'If FIFA wants a global footprint, it can't leave out 23 million people in Australia and another 8 million in Oceania,' I said.

'Or 300 million in the United States,' Abo Rida said.

'They had it only 15 years ago,' Ben said.

'By the time 2022 comes around, it will be 28 years,' he said.

Abo Rida was well-informed. He was an engineer and self-made businessman, but he certainly wasn't uninterested as Hargitay led us to believe.

He looked at his watch and leaned forward in his chair. It was time to go.

'I'm sorry, I must go as I have things to do here,' he said. 'I have found it very interesting to meet you and talk with you. It has been good. I will just say this. I am happy to listen to anyone. I am happy to hear your arguments. But Mohamed and I are very close and I will do whatever my brother tells me to do.'

We exchanged gifts and he departed. The Ambassador stood to leave also.

'I didn't think he'd be so well-informed,' she said. 'How do you read that?'

'I don't think we did either,' said Ben. 'At least he didn't say 'no'. He effectively told us where we need to do some work.'

'It shows he's interested,' said the Ambassador. 'As you said, it gave you some feedback. Together with Sakr visiting Australia, hopefully it will help. I'll see you tomorrow.'

We said farewell, expressed our gratitude to her, and sat down again.

'But you heard what he said at the end?' I asked. 'He'll do what Mohamed tells him.'

'Peter says Mohamed doesn't support Qatar,' Ben said.

'I think that's a load of crap. Bin Hammam may have been surprised by their bid, and may not have supported it from the beginning, but sooner rather than later, he's going to support his own country. He's duty bound to. How can he not? How can we expect him not to?'

'That's precisely why we're trying to get them to withdraw their bid. Franz is going there. We're inviting the Emir to Australia. If Qatar is no longer in the race, who's Mohamed going to support? Not Japan or South Korea.'

'Indonesia?'

'They'll drop out soon,' he said confidently. 'And even if they don't, he'll support us over them.'

ABOUT AN HOUR later, Ben, Hargitay and I were returning - via the front door this time - from Hargitay's inspection of the Ambassador's residence. He declared it was good enough for the Executive Committee. I wondered what he had been expecting. A tent?

I was stopped by someone whose face was familiar.

'Bonita, I'm Davidde Corran.' Corran was a young journalist from Australia. He was in Egypt at his own expense covering the under-20 tournament for SBS-TV and other outlets.

I shook his hand. 'Hi Davidde, it's wonderful to meet you at last. I enjoy reading what you write.'

He shuffled his feet a little and acknowledged the compliment. 'Thank you. I'm wondering if I could interview Peter Hargitay?'

Under continuing instruction not to, we still hadn't announced that Hargitay was working with us, but I could hardly deny it when he was now standing a few feet away talking with Ben as they waited for me. I walked over to them.

'Peter, this is Davidde Corran,' I gestured to Corran who remained where we had been talking. 'He works for SBS and others and is interested in interviewing you. He knows you're here and working with us so we can't really say no.'

Hargitay and Ben looked over at him. They would have seen a young man, casually dressed, a bit anxious and looking slightly out of place in a hotel lobby dripping with FIFA extravagance and expense.

'He works for SBS you say? So Les will see what he writes first, and clear it? No problem. I'll do it now.' Hargitay proceeded with the interview because he knew that his friend, Les Murray, the FIFA Ethics Committee member and SBS-TV commentator, would make sure Corran's interview wasn't critical.

He followed me. I introduced them, and left.

THE OFFICIAL BANQUET for the tournament was held that evening at a large open air restaurant complex across the Corniche from the hotel and overlooking the Nile. The five of us walked over together – Ben, Hargitay, Radmann, Abold and me.

Once we arrived, we were given a wristband as identity and ushered to pre-dinner drinks. There were probably 400 or more people packed into an area that included some outdoor decks and a large indoor room. Hargitay disappeared, Abold stuck with Ben, and Radmann told me to stick with him.

Without exaggeration, Radmann knew everyone and everyone knew him. He introduced me to so many people. We talked, we drank, and more than an hour later someone announced we should take our seats. Hargitay found us amongst the throng as we began to make our away from the drinks to the tables.

There were at least 50 tables tightly packed into a large outdoor area, facing the Nile, with a stage in front of the tables with a large canopy over it. A band was playing.

'Where do we sit?' Ben asked.

'Anywhere,' came the reply from Hargitay. 'Only the VVIPs have specific seating. I'm with them. Sitting with the old man. Making sure he knows about the Australian bid, of course,' he said. 'But keep me a seat with you too in case I can escape.' Radmann also made his way to the VVIP tables.

'He's so full of it,' Ben whispered to me, referring to Hargitay, as we made our way to the top tier of tables at the back of the dining area.

We found a table at the back, looking out over everyone else. Ben and I sat together, Abold on his left and a spare seat for Hargitay on Abold's left.

On my right was a woman from Nigeria outfitted in national dress. We talked the entire evening. Alhaja Ayo Omidiran owned her own football team, the Omidiran Babes, and was a member of FIFA's Women's Committee as well as being on the organising committee for the younger women's tournaments. She was a Nigerian FA Board member.

'So you must know Amos Adamu?' I asked.

'Very well,' she said. 'Would you like me to introduce you?'

'He's here?'

She peered around the area and focussed in on a table. 'Yes, there he is over there,' she said discreetly pointing.

I quickly conferred with Ben. 'Ayo is offering to introduce me to Adamu,' I said.

'No.'

'What do you mean 'no'?'

'Leave it to Fedor and Peter.'

I looked at him and turned back to Ayo, who shrugged her shoulders. She lowered her voice and said 'Men. They like to keep the power games to themselves. Doesn't matter if they are young or old, black or white, rich or poor. They're all the same. Are you coming to Nigeria next month for the Under 17s?'

'Yes.'

'That's good. We'll see one another there and we will make some time to talk more and you can tell me more about the women's league in Australia. I would love to see the Nigerian women's team play the Matildas.'

'I'll let our head of women's football know,' I said. 'I'm sure that could be arranged.'

She continued to regale me with stories of horror of what it was like to be the woman owner of a women's football team in Nigeria.

'Yet you're here,' I said.

'Only because I have so much money they can't ignore me,' she laughed uproariously. 'It's what counts. In Nigeria. And in FIFA.'

We sat through the speeches. Blatter ended with his usual line: *'Remember this. Enjoy your football. This is good. Enjoy your life. This is better,'* to thunderous applause.

'Do you know how many times I've heard that?' asked Ayo.

'I can guess,' I said.

The live entertainment started again. It was too much for Ben to bear: a cross between a Pat Boone, Dean Martin and Perry Como-style crooner.

Ayo laughed. 'He's Blatter's favourite,' she said. 'He turns up nearly everywhere.'

Ben grimaced. 'Come on Bonita, let's go,' he said.

As Ben, Abold and I made our way to the Corniche, Radmann materialised also, chatting with Abold in German. Despite keeping a seat for him, as requested, we didn't see Hargitay all night.

'Why didn't you want me to meet Adamu?' I asked Ben as we waited on the median strip.

'You don't need to worry about Adamu. Fedor will take care of that.'

IT WAS ANOTHER fine, sunny and humid day for the barbecue.

People were slowly starting to arrive, mostly Australians living in Cairo who were known to the Embassy and some of the FIFA invitees, including Jack Warner's aides. There was no more than about ten guests when Sepp Blatter and Jerome Valcke turned up – unfashionably early.

Why would they do this? Were they avoiding other Executive Committee members?

There was nothing we could do except offer some small talk and meet and greet the guests. Blatter looked as if he enjoyed it. He's a politician. He likes pressing the flesh, getting his photo taken with people. There was even a baby to kiss! Valcke stood about awkwardly in the background, looking as if he'd rather be anywhere else but here.

Although not everyone had arrived, the Ambassador judged the time right to welcome her guests officially. Standing on the terrace, with the small group around her, she gave a welcoming address again reinforcing the government's support for the bid. Blatter responded as he always does in these situations: politely but not really saying anything.

'Thank you, Madam Ambassador. It is always wonderful to be in the company of Australians and to enjoy your wine.' People laughed. I noticed he was only drinking ginger beer. 'You are such friendly people. I always enjoy my visits to Australia. And who knows? You might host the World Cup. I am sure you could host the World Cup. But there are 24 people. I am only one. Who knows what is going to happen?'

'Might?' He was noticeably less effusive than he had been in May the year before.

Some more photos were taken, more greeting of guests and, in just under one hour, Blatter and Valcke were gone.

The Ambassador gave the instructions for the cooking to start when the next special guest arrived, around 15 minutes after Blatter and Valcke departed.

Jack and Maureen Warner looked like any other well-heeled couple in their late 60s. They looked fit and healthy; Jack was wearing his FIFA blue blazer over a yellow, white and navy striped polo shirt; Maureen was wearing black trousers and top with a lime green Jackie O style jacket, trimmed with black. We were disappointed to see she wasn't wearing her pearl pendant.

This time we were seated at the tables, with the Ambassador, the Warners, Hargitay, Ben and I seated together, as well as Radmann for a short time. Abold sat elsewhere. The Ambassador and Ben made similar speeches again and we showed our short promotional film. Warner didn't stop smiling.

'Great film, beautiful scenery,' said Maureen Warner to me. She told me she visited Australia for the Sydney 2000 Olympics, but did not travel further than the Blue Mountains. 'We very much like Australian red wine. We always try to buy some if we can.' The waiter appeared on cue to pour another glass.

Other than the presentations, there was no talk of the bid. Unlike Abo Rida the day before, Warner had no questions or points to raise.

When I mentioned this to Hargitay, he said that this was because Warner was already so well-informed of the Australian bid by him that there was nothing more he needed to know. The Warners were generous with their time. They stayed for a couple of hours and were amongst the last of the guests to leave, happily posing for photos, signing autographs and talking with anyone who talked with him.

Even the Byrom's – Enrique and Robyn who, as ever, also attended – commented on it.

BEN AND I had one more meeting: the Egyptian FA President, Samir Zaher. We met him in a reception centre on the way to the airport over a coffee. He was a big man like the Sports Minister; tall, a little older – maybe late 60s, thinning grey hair, thick glasses. He was exceedingly frank.

'I'm here because I have the support of President Mubarak and his two sons,' he said. 'If I didn't, I wouldn't be here. This is the third time I've been President of the football federation and if we don't qualify for the World Cup, I probably won't be President again,' he laughed.

He continued. 'You know that what Abo Rida does will depend on what Bin Hammam tells him? And we don't know yet what Bin Hammam is thinking in relation to Qatar. He hasn't said. I think their bid took him by surprise as much as everyone else. What you need to do is talk to the Arab Football Federation.'

He then reeled off the 26 countries that were members of the Arab Football Federation with its eight Executive Committee members, and waited while I wrote them down in rusty shorthand and longhand. I asked him when the Arab Football Federation was established.

'1998. Bin Hammam started it with Prince Faisal of Saudi Arabia to get together Arab support for Blatter when he ran for the President. Blatter owes Bin Hammam and this part of the world. So if Bin Hammam wants it, if Qatar wants it, Blatter is in a tough spot. A very tough spot.'

He paused briefly.

'I've spoken to Sakr. We want a cooperation agreement with you,' said Zaher. 'I will come with him to Australia and we can sign it together.'

'We'd like it if Australia and Egypt could play a match too,' Ben finally got a word in.

'That would be good. We'll have it here.' He smiled broadly. 'This bidding business. It's wonderful. All of a sudden, people from everywhere want to play us. But we don't have much availability because we have African Nations Cup qualifiers. But definitely we will play Australia here in Cairo.' He wrote it down.

We asked him which other bidders approached him for a game.

'Oh, let's see,' he flicked through his book. 'England. Japan. South Korea. Russia. Qatar. America. It's really wonderful,' he said happily.

CHAPTER 17
'International Man of Mystery' no more

Abu Dhabi: October 2009

BEN'S AND MY flight landed in Abu Dhabi around 8pm local time after the short flight from Cairo. We had about two hours for a stopover. It was 3am in Sydney so the first thing I did was check the Australian Sunday papers online.

I saw a photograph of Peter Hargitay with the headline 'International Man of Mystery' in *The Sun Herald*.

Matthew Hall had told me he was writing about Peter Hargitay and had been back and forth in correspondence with him for some on-the-record comments. Hargitay emailed his proposed response to Lowy who sent them to Ben and me for comment. We suggested, via Lowy, toning down some of the pompous language and implicit arrogance. We had not seen what Hargitay sent to Hall in their final form, and Lowy did not let Hargitay know he had asked us to comment.

Hall also asked for comment from us for the piece. We acknowledged - finally - that Hargitay had been engaged as a consultant since January.

Hall's article didn't contain anything about Hargitay that wasn't already publicly known - other than the crucial fact that he was working for Australia, the issue both Lowy and Hargitay didn't want us to announce. It duly noted his acquittal from drug charges in Jamaica as well as his closeness with Blatter, Bin Hammam and Warner.

The damning part was that it took us so long to admit he worked for us. It was capped-off by a particularly unattractive set of photos of Hargitay. I showed it to Ben.

'You better ring him,' he said.

'Who? Peter? I should ring Ellis' office also. We haven't yet told them that we've employed him either.' I was referring to our Sports Minister.

Ben looked at me across the coffee table. He sighed heavily. 'I know, I know. You said this day was going to come.'

I checked the time in London before dialling Hartigay. He answered quickly. 'How does it feel to be an 'international man of mystery'?' I greeted him cheerily.

'Are you an idiot, Bonita?'

Here we go again.

'Are you an idiot?' he yelled down the phone line. I held it away from my ear. Ben looked at me as he read the Australian Rules footy reports in the Melbourne papers and raised his glass of red wine silently.

'This man, this friend of yours,' he spat out, 'has ruined everything.'

'Really, Peter? How is that?' I was tired of being bullied by him.

'You're in charge of media, aren't you?'

'That's one of my roles, yes Peter.'

'Well, it's your fault that he wrote this article. He's a friend of yours and you probably got him to write it. You should be able to control what people write.'

I told him that was an insult to Matthew Hall and to me. 'He approached you and asked you for responses on the record. I'm not going to tell him what he can or can't write.'

I told Hargitay we would contact the Minister's office to suggest they let us respond to any follow-up inquiries if there were any, and to let them know Ben and I would be uncontactable for 14 hours.

Hargitay said he was going to sue the newspaper and Hall. There was more thunder down the line. 'We cannot win the World Cup when there are media reports around like this.'

'Peter, if this is what stops us from winning the World Cup bid, then I would suggest we were never going to win it.'

Ben beckoned me to hand the phone over.

'Peter,' he started. He then fell silent. He was copping an earful too.

'Peter …' Silence. 'Uh huh. Peter ….' More silence. 'Peter, I really don't think Matthew Hall is working for the Americans.' Ben had more wine. 'Yes, I know he lives in New York but that doesn't mean he is working for the Americans.' More from Hargitay. 'Sure Peter, you do that. I'll call you tomorrow. Bye.'

Ben handed back the phone. 'Peter says Matthew Hall is working for the US bid, he's got the evidence and he's going to expose it. He's also going to call Les and get him to write something on the World Game website to counter what Matt wrote.'

Les Murray, FIFA Ethics Committee member, coming to the rescue of his mate Peter Hargitay yet again wasn't a good idea. I said so.

Ben continued to flick through the newspaper from the day before, finishing his wine.

'Matt is a journalist with a story that was always going to be written,' I said. 'The simple fact is, we were wrong in not being upfront about it. We were never going to hide him. Or Radmann. And, by the way, Matt is not working for the US bid.'

'Yep I know all of that. We told Frank,' Ben said. 'Which reminds me, I'd better call him.'

I got hold of the Minister's advisor. He was not concerned because it was our decision and they were not aware of it. It was the truth. He lowered his voice as he spoke. 'By the way, who did make the decision?'

'Frank.'

Sydney, October 2009

A FEW DAYS later Hargitay became even more incensed when Davidde Corran's article appeared. It didn't appear on the site for which Corran usually wrote, and which was overseen by Les Murray, but another general sports site.

Corran wrote that *'the corridors of global sport politics are messy and few walk away from them with clean consciences and pure reputations.'* He added that we would be paying with more than dollars and cents. Ben called me into his office.

'Peter's blaming you for Davidde Corran's article now.'

'You're kidding. You were there. Davidde asked could he interview Peter. I asked Peter if he was happy to be interviewed. He said yes. Davidde interviewed him. End of story.'

'Well, now he's done a TV interview with Les Murray.'

It was my turn to roll my eyes. 'You're kidding. That just draws attention to him. He's a paid consultant for God's sake. He's not the be-all and end-all of our bid and if we had owned up to him in the first place, we wouldn't even be having this conversation now.'

'Frank told Les that he is not to broadcast it. Has anyone else asked about it?

'John Stensholt from the *Fin Review*.' I explained that he wanted to do a piece on the bid for his paper's magazine that would be published at the end of January. I thought we should do it.

'Is it going to be negative?'

'He's asked for a complete list of consultants. We must give it. Peter's out of the bag. It's only a matter of time until Fedor is. We may as well just get it out there and get it over and done with. I think you and Frank should be interviewed.'

'Frank won't like me being interviewed.'

'He just has to. He chose you to be the CEO. If we win, you'll be the continuity between the bid and actually organising it. You can't be ignored.'

'You tell Frank that,' he said.

CHAPTER 18

'Harvey Weinstein and Peter Hargitay are like that'

Sydney: November 2009

WE SAT IN Ben's office staring at the spreadsheet setting out the internal budget for the bid. It was the fourth or fifth time we had seen it and it had not changed. But, as always, we were not permitted to take it out of the room.

With 13 months to go, there wasn't a lot of money left that was not committed. My budget was being cut again and reallocated for unspecified international activity.

I had made no progress in getting more money from government for Asia and Africa.

The federal and state governments were still arguing about FIFA's onerous guarantees.

We didn't have 12 stadiums that met FIFA standards on which we could rely.

Five-star hotels were not willing to sign-up to a deal that saw them hold 2010 rates until 2022.

If we won, we were facing a $100 million bill to deal with the other football codes because their winter football competitions would be disrupted by the World Cup. Unless government paid that bill, it would cut any profit from hosting the event.

But on the plus side, we had two votes. Reynald Temarii and Franz Beckenbauer.

I AWOKE TO find an email Hargitay had forwarded from 'brother Jack' Warner saying who would be in Abuja, Nigeria, for the final of the under-17 World Cup.

The email was prefaced by the usual sarcastic tone, directed at me. He thought the Cairo event was a waste of his time and effort essentially because we did not publicise it around the world. Hargitay's view was that a function was a waste of time unless the world knew about it. Ben's and my view was that it was an official function, hosted by an Ambassador, to reinforce the Australian Government's commitment to the bid. Fifteen months out from the vote, it was better to fly under the radar rather than let other bidders know what we were doing.

Hargitay also went into detail about how the invitations should be issued – irrespective of whether the Australian Government had protocols around official diplomatic events.

It was Saturday morning. Ben called me. 'Don't take any notice of Peter's email.'

'No, Ben, it's fine. I read it aloud over breakfast at home and we laughed.' It was always easier to deal with Hargitay's pomposity when you could share it with someone. 'I've also kept a copy of it for my book!' I added.

It was many hours later when I was working, that I decided to clean up my email folders. There was another email from Hargitay, also written overnight, which had gone through to the spam box.

It had been written after the previous one – and it was obviously the one to which Ben was referring in his morning phone call.

It was almost as if Hargitay forgot he sent the earlier one and felt compelled to up the ante on sarcasm and finger-pointing. He expressed amazement that a cocktail reception was being planned in Abuja by the High Commissioner. He referred to the consultants 'masterful effort to position the bid in Cairo'. He lamented the lack of publicity. And for good measure referred to invitations to the Cairo event that he presented as going 'AWOL'.

Hargitay also complained about the Australian High Commissioner to Nigeria organising a meeting with FIFA Executive Committee member, Amos Adamu.

The meeting with Adamu arose from a meeting Ben and I had in Canberra with all Australian heads of mission working on the African continent to talk about the bid. We specifically talked about the four FIFA Executive Committee members from Africa: Adamu, Hayatou, Anouma and Abu Rida. Knowing we were travelling to Abuja, the High Commissioner to Nigeria used his initiative and organised a meeting with Adamu for Ben's and my time in Abuja.

Hargitay wrote that he *'and F are in charge of strategy. It is not the way we should do things'.* In Hargitay's world, it was an unwelcome intervention for Australian diplomatic staff to organise a meeting with Executive Committee members.

I wondered why the consultants were so anxious to exclude Australian government officials? The bid was publicly funded and was a high priority of the government. The officials were doing what was expected of them.

I laughed. I forwarded part of the email to the Department of Foreign Affairs. I thought they'd be amused that our consultants were not at all happy that Australia's diplomats were doing their job.

BEN CAME BY my office. We were flying to Abuja via London the next day.

'Keep the luncheon meeting with Adamu. Peter and Fedor are arranging a separate meeting with him. But don't tell the High Commissioner that.'

Why would we need two meetings with Amos Adamu? Because they had things to say to Amos Adamu that couldn't be said with the High Commissioner present?

He also told me I didn't have to travel to Nigeria. I was relieved, but asked why there was a change of plan.

'I want you to stay here. It's just better this way. You don't need to meet Adamu. And I also want to sort out this business between you and Peter once and for all. You've both got to stop it.'

I opened my mouth to protest. He put his hand up to stop me.

'I know, I know. You didn't start it last weekend. In fact, I thought you were absolutely professional, measured and appropriate in your response to him. He was totally out of line. I've told him that. So has Frank. I don't understand why he doesn't like you.'

'That's easy Ben. Because (a) I'm a woman, (b) I get things done, (c) and I'm awake to the scam he's perpetrating on us with his mates.'

'YOUR BOSS IS delightful,' the Second Secretary at the Abuja High Commission told me over the phone. 'Your consultants are weirdo - like, really weirdo - but Ben is just wonderful. It was a great night. Small but good crowd. They all enjoyed themselves. I love the promo film. And thank you so much for the peppercorns.'

'No problem. Glad to hear it went well. Who turned up?

'Oh, lots of locals. Some media which the High Commissioner arranged.'

I laughed. 'I'll be in trouble.'

'Why?'

'One of our consultants doesn't like our Foreign Affairs department doing things like that.' I laughed again.

'Oh. That would be that man with the wispy beard?'

I didn't respond, but asked again who attended.

'I don't really know. But Jack Warner was there.'

'Good old Jack,' I said. 'Not Amos Adamu?'

'No, but some of his people were. They met with him separately. I'm not really in that loop.'

Ben confirmed in a phone call on his way home that two meetings took place with Amos Adamu: once with the High Commissioner and Ben only; the other with Ben and the consultants but no High Commissioner.

'OH FOR FUCK'S sake. Is this guy for real?' Ben was back in Sydney and reading an email both of us had just received from Hargitay. He looked at me and laughed. 'Excuse the language,' he said as an afterthought.

Dear friends

I contacted Hollywood producer Harvey Weinstein through a close friend, Oscar winning producer of all Quentin Tarantino films, Lawrence Bender, with whom we - ecn motion pictures - co-produced a few movies in the past.My personal letter to Harvey was couriered over to him by Lawrence yesterday afternoon.Can't go any higher than that: Harvey calls all the shots. If he says no, it is no. But it was worth a try. Please do not use any other parallel avenues: they are all useless at this stage.

Warm regards

Peter

'How many times did you ask Nicole?' Ben asked.

The consultants said we needed some star power in Cape Town in December for the international launch of the bid.

'We need big stars there for them to sit up and take notice,' Abold told Ben and me. 'It is very important. Vital.'

The consultants' first preference was Kylie Minogue, but her manager said she was not available. Hugh Jackman declined the invitation because he was playing at the West End in London. Elle Macpherson again informed the Hargitays she wasn't available, even though they had said repeatedly she would do anything, anytime for them.

So the consultants returned to Nicole Kidman. It made sense to ask her because she narrated the bid promotional film to be shown for the first time in Cape Town.

When they determined that Kidman should be there, I twice asked her personal assistant whether the actress was able to join us for the launch. The first time I asked, her personal assistant was polite, kind but also firm in saying Kidman had both film and personal commitments to attend to in that week. Despite this, I was instructed to ask a second time - this time offering Kidman the use of Lowy's personal aircraft for the return trip. Kidman's personal assistant was insistent on this occasion.

'I know you're acting under instructions but please pass on to your bosses that Nicole just can't do it. She has other commitments. It's as simple as that. If it wasn't that she was occupied, she'd happily do it.'

Instead, we agreed to pencil her in for the following December in Zurich.

Ben was looking at the email again.

'Hargitay actually rang and told me he was going to call Harvey Weinstein but I didn't believe him. He told me he and Harvey are like that' – he crossed his index and middle finger - 'and he'd let Harvey know how important this is.'

All I could think was that Nicole Kidman and her PA would be annoyed with us. I didn't want her to be so annoyed that she would also turn down the Zurich appearance next December. I rang to let her personal assistant know what happened, and to apologise. It wasn't a pleasant conversation.

I WAS WAITING in the arrivals hall of Sydney International Airport for four visiting international journalists, individuals recommended by Hargitay in August.

Fanis Makrides from *Politis* newspaper was a young, Greek Cypriot who looked like almost any journalist of his age the world over. Shabby but cool in a Gen Y way. A five o'clock shadow. He considered himself fortunate to be in Australia.

Hargitay told us that *Politis* is a conservative paper. He included it because *'everybody forgets Cyprus but being a Cyprus registered company ourselves we don't'*. FIFA Executive

Committee member, Marios Lefkaritis, was also from Cyprus.

Inas Mazhar – a woman Sports Editor of the English language newspaper *Al Ahram* in Cairo – was not what I expected. She was about the same age as me, very short, dragging an enormous suitcase, plus hand luggage and a giant Prada handbag. Hargitay told us she was *'keen to come along' and that 'she is personally known to the Egyptian ExCo member (!)'* - he included the exclamation mark - Hany Abo Rida.

The third person was Osasu Obayiuwana from Nigeria. He was tall, big, with a round, kind face. Hargitay had told us he used to head the Africa Desk for the BBC World Service and now ran the *New African* magazine and had committed to *'placing stories in numerous Nigerian papers'*. He arrived with an oversized suitcase, a computer bag and a backpack.

The three of us made small talk while we waited for the fourth arrival – Kang Young Kim and his interpreter who arrived on a separate flight. He was Sports Editor of the largest newspaper in Seoul. The two of them could have been any father and son combination as they exited the customs hall. Both were dressed in shorts and polo shirt and strangely matching carry-on luggage only. It seemed to be very light travelling for an eight-day visit. Kim was assured but happy to leave the greetings and small talk to his young assistant.

After a few hours settling into their five-star hotel in the city, the group made its way to meet Lowy and Ben for lunch on Lowy's super yacht. Jill Margo, Frank's biographer and a health industry journalist, accompanied us.

Less than 36 hours later our South Korean friends left us. Kang and the interpreter were waiting for me in the hotel lobby when I arrived on Monday morning. They expressed their regret but Kang had been called back 'urgently' to the office. I noticed they now had two shopping bags each, as well as their carry-on luggage. We knew they had been at the casino since we returned from lunch on Lowy's super yacht.

'I think that's the only reason they came,' Fanis Makrides said to me. 'He didn't even bring a computer. What journalist travels for a week away without a computer?'

Charlie Sale from the *Daily Mail* joined us in Brisbane. I knew that Hargitay regarded him highly from our first meeting with him in February, but he reminded us that to get Sale for the trip was a 'major coup'. I was prepared for someone unpleasant, but Sale was the opposite. Pleasant, friendly, a walking encyclopaedia on sport, direct. As with Inas Mazhar, he had visited Australia before.

'I don't think you have a chance in hell of getting it,' he said, 'but that doesn't mean you couldn't do it. They're two entirely different things.'

'So who do you think will?' I asked.

'Well, we're only talking about 2022. 2018 will go to Europe, yeah?' he said in that English way of checking we understood what he was saying. I nodded. 'So USA has to be favourite for 2022. Or watch Qatar.'

He continued. 'Blatter wants to make his mark and this is his chance. I would like to see England get it of course, but watch Russia and Qatar.'

As well as a busy travelling schedule, the journalists got a taste for what the Australian bid was up against domestically also.

We were meeting with a phalange of officials from the Foreign Affairs department, about 20 in total.

Several officials made presentations on one aspect or another of Australian life, the economy, culture and politics. It was routine stuff.

Unusually, the meeting chairman - the same official who knew of the Beckenbauer and Radmann visit to the Emir of Qatar - asked the officials if they had anything to add. One woman, a middle-ranking officer, stepped straight into it.

'I just want to say that it's important you people realise we're not really into soccer in this country. We're more into AFL,' she said. 'That's our national sport. Soccer is not very popular and it's been associated with ethnic violence in the past. The only thing going for it is that kids like playing it.'

There was shocked silence around the room. Her superiors looked on aghast. I wondered how she passed the various tests and interviews to be a member of the diplomatic service.

Osasu Obayuiwana, who had trouble staying awake in the darkened room, was suddenly alert. Charlie Sale wrote furiously in his note pad in shorthand. Inas Mazhar and Fanis Makrides shifted uncomfortably in their seats, each pouring themselves another glass of water.

It was a comment that couldn't go unchallenged. This was a commonly held attitude football faced in Australia. This was why I wanted to work in football in the first place. This was precisely the reason why hosting the World Cup would be so valuable.

'That's not true, of course,' I said. 'Not only is it the most popular participation sport amongst children aged 5-14 years, it's also the most played team sport amongst adult men and women and it's the fastest growing sport for girls and women in the country,' I said looking directly at her.

She opened her mouth to say something, but I cut her off.

'At a professional level, we are the only football code with a truly national footprint. As communication technology makes the world relatively smaller and more accessible, more and more children will grow up understanding that this is truly the only sport that has global reach. In fact, most diplomats around the world understand that football is truly the number one global language.'

I was on a roll. This was my bread-and-butter stuff for work - if not my entire life.

'It's good for individuals, it's good for education, it's good for business, and it's good for government. There will always be a place for the other football codes, and the other sports, in Australia as they're part of our culture,' I said, turning to our visiting journalists.

'But football will always be the number one sport in the world; it has always been a part of the culture of the 42% of Australians who have at least one parent born overseas; and it is why the Government is supporting this bid. They know it's good for Australia and good for the region.'

I looked around the table. The diplomats kept quiet.

'That was fantastic,' said Charlie Sale as we got into our mini-van to take us back to the hotel. 'It was the highlight of the day.'

'It certainly livened up proceedings,' said Osasu Obayuiwana. 'Do you have this trouble with everyone in government?' he asked.

I told them it was a viewpoint held by many in the community.

'We're still seen as a sport of people who are foreign to this country. Football has been built on, grown and developed on the back of our migrant populations over the years, and the sport has allowed itself to be marginalised. It is why Frank Lowy was important for the game. Yes, he is a migrant but he is a successful one, and he gave the game instant credibility when we needed it.'

'I see,' said Obayuiwana thoughtfully. 'Fascinating.'

'I also think it's the number one argument in Australia's favour,' said Sale. 'You're such a leading sporting nation, so you should be a leader in football too.'

WHILE THE JOURNALISTS continued their tour of Australia, the Prime Minister was getting ready to visit Trinidad and Tobago for the Commonwealth Heads of Government Meeting (CHOGM).

A week beforehand the Prime Minister's Office had asked for a gift suggestion for Warner. Remembering that Maureen Warner said they liked Australian red wine, that's what I suggested.

Hargitay was not impressed. He said it was 'very cheesy/cheap.' He said he was embarrassed. He thought a case of wine was more fitting for his friend. We sent his email to the Prime Minister's office so they could change the gift if they wanted to. They didn't.

Although he only received one bottle of wine from Australia, the one person to do well out of the CHOGM meeting was Jack Warner.

The preference for the Prime Minister's staff was for him to have a tete-a-tete with Warner at the official CHOGM breakfast, rather than a separate meeting. The Australian High Commissioner was trying to ensure that Warner and the Prime Minister would be seated next to one another.

It turned out England had got in beforehand. Gordon Brown was placed next to Warner at the official breakfast. That meant that a one-on-one meeting was definitely on.

At the time, Warner was the co-leader of the Opposition in Trinidad and Tobago and chairman of his political party. He ended up meeting with two of the leading Prime Ministers in the Commonwealth in Gordon Brown and Kevin Rudd, with the meetings reported around the world.

Warner told Kevin Rudd in front of media that Australia had a 'good chance of succeeding'. In the same breath, Warner reminded Rudd of the importance of football, social responsibility and commitment to football. He identified his own region of the Caribbean and Africa as especially needy of Australian generosity.

CHAPTER 19
Doing something good

Cape Town: December 2009

CAPE TOWN LOOKED splendid. There were cloudless, early summer skies. The temperature was mild. Even if your business wasn't associated with football, it was impossible in that week not to be infected by it. There was a carnival atmosphere in the streets, and the city looked spruced-up.

There was a large number of us in Cape Town for the big week. There was a tour for the technical operations people from each bid, the international launches of each bid at the official expo, the FIFA Congress, Confederation meetings, the FIFA Executive Committee meeting, the official banquet and the draw for the 2010 World Cup.

Lowy, Jill Margo, Hargitay, Radmann and Lowy's personal assistant were staying at the same hotel as the FIFA Executive Committee. Hargitay claimed this as a coup for Lowy to be 'close' to the Executive Committee.

TYGERBERG HOSPITAL IS a large, sprawling hospital to the east of the city centre, not far from a rail yard, amongst a quiet, leafy, ordinary suburb. There was a larger building which was clearly much more recent than other parts of the complex.

It was our first morning in Cape Town. We were directed to a smaller and older block towards the back of the new building. It was two stories high, grey, looked as if it was built in the 1950s, and was linked via a series of walkways to other buildings. We were headed to a part of the hospital of which Archbishop Tutu and his wife were patrons, comprising both a school and 24-hour care service for children with complex disabilities.

It was one of the all-too-few moments in life – let alone the unreal year that had been 2009 so far – that reminds you of everything that is good and pure in life.

All the children had been affected by HIV in-utero. Their disabilities were significant and several, mostly physical, some intellectual.

The money we were donating would go towards improving some of their facilities that were adequate, but dated. Meeting some of the students with Professor Mariana Kruger, who was Head of Paediatrics, there was no question that this was a worthwhile cause - whatever the reason we were doing it.

We were brought back to reality by the Archbishop's PR manager who explained there would be a large media contingent, in addition to the journalists who were in Cape Town for football purposes.

Ten minutes later, I waited outside the hospital school entrance with Professor Kruger and the Archbishop's staff to form a welcoming committee. Ben was the first to spring out of the car and bounded over to me before the others could manage to get out of their car.

'Peter's on the warpath,' he muttered in my ear.

'What for?'

'I have no idea. But evidently you've done something else wrong,' he said. He peeled away to greet the professor and PR manager who moved forward.

Hargitay ignored the welcoming committee altogether and made a beeline for me.

'Are you an idiot, Bonita?'

'What's wrong, Peter?'

'Why did you make the cheque out in Australian dollars?' he asked.

'Well, technically, it's just dollars,' I said, 'so it could be anyone's dollars. But it is our currency.'

'You didn't think to put it in Rand?'

'No, as a matter of fact. Did you before today?' I asked. 'It's really not such a big deal, Peter. It's easy enough to make the change. It won't be noticed in pictures and it's not the real cheque you know.'

He wasn't sure if I was serious and looked at me sharply. Lowy came up to us.

Hargitay turned. His face turned from a scowl to a smile in one movement.

I told Lowy the Archbishop hadn't arrived yet, but suggested he see some of the facilities and meet the children.

Hargitay followed, but as the others disappeared upstairs to look at some of the rooms, he pulled me aside again.

'Have you changed it to Rand?'

'I haven't finished yet.'

'What have you been doing? You've been here for how long? An hour? Have you been doing nothing?' He kept his voice low but threatening.

'I've been meeting people, talking, and helping to move furniture, Peter.'

'You're just wasting time. You should have got this right in the first place. And you need to change the media release for the new amount.'

Ben had turned back and was coming towards us. Hargitay turned to him and shifted from scowl to smile again.

'Is Peter telling you the amount's changed again?' he asked.

'I was just about to tell her, Ben.'

'It's now 1 million Rand,' Ben said.

Ben stared at me, willing me not to say anything. In June, the amount was $50,000. In September, it increased to $100,000. Now it was $150,000.

'I feel we need to make a statement,' said Hargitay. 'It needs to be a big figure. To make sure everyone takes notice that we are serious. Do you think you can manage those changes Bonita?'

'I'll give it a go Peter,' I said.

I made my way to the administration office to make the further changes to the media release and cheque.

I sat at the school administrator's desk logging-on to the computer waiting to change the media release. The giant cheque was next to me with the white-out drying on the amount and the currency sign.

'Who was that funny looking man, Bonita?' asked the PR manager, as she brought me a coffee.

'That's one of our consultants.'

'I heard the way he spoke to you. You shouldn't let him speak to you like that.'

'Unfortunately, he does most of the time.'

'That is shocking. I feel so sad for you. The Arch would never let anyone speak to one of us like that. It is a terrible work environment when you have someone like that around.'

We heard a noise behind her from the adjoining office.

Archbishop Desmond Tutu walked in, accompanied by his personal assistant.

We stood. The PR manager introduced us.

I was blown away. Archbishop Tutu was the most eminent person I had ever met – and probably ever will meet. He was small, round, with a cheeky and ready smile and big round eyes. He was dressed casually in trousers and a loud batik style shirt. A very loud batik style shirt.

I put out my hand to shake his and he clasped it with both of his. 'Ah, Australia,' he said. 'Bless you my child. It is lovely to meet you.'

'Thank you Your Grace. It is an honour to meet you.'

We had a few moments talking about who was visiting from Australia, the children at the hospital, and what the hospital would be doing with the donation.

'Now take me to meet your big boss, the one donating the money to our facility,' he said as he gestured with his arm. I didn't mention that it was actually a donation via the taxpayers of Australia, not Frank Lowy personally.

He followed me out into the corridor where Lowy and the others were returning from their tour upstairs. I made the introductions.

Abold stepped forward. 'Archbishop Tutu,' he said. 'I am Andreas Abold. Do you remember me? We met several years ago for the South African World Cup bid and again in June. And this is Ben Buckley whom you met in June.'

Tutu looked Abold and Ben up and down, both immaculately dressed – Abold in a light grey suit, Ben in a dark suit. 'The Arch', as his staff affectionately called him, was much too experienced to let on whether he remembered them or not.

'Of course, of course.' He held out his hand to greet both of them.

'Now, Archbishop,' said his assistant, 'Mr Lowy wants to meet with you privately.' She beckoned them to a small room with just a table and a few chairs. They went in alone.

The plan was for Lowy to invite the Archbishop to be the face of the Australian bid in Africa.

Apart from the donation to the hospital, and the schools programs funded separately by government, it still wasn't clear what we were doing in Africa. There was $4 million put aside for development in Africa in our bid budget, and I had also been asked to get more money from the government aid agency - which had not progressed. I was told Radmann was 'looking after' Africa but that was all anyone seemed to know, or wanted to share.

THE LARGE ROOM on the ground floor that we prepared earlier in the morning was buzzing with anticipation.

As part of our promotion for the bid domestically, we ran a competition for a junior football player from each state and territory in Australia to join us, accompanied by one parent. The eight children, who ranged from 8-12 years, were now intermingled with the children from the hospital; the Australian, other football media and South African media were setting up; a big banner was in place; and the gifts we brought of balls and shirts were on a front table ready to distribute. You couldn't notice the giant cheque had been altered from dollars to Rand and increased, unless you were up close to it.

The Arch and Lowy walked in, and a human corridor formed like the Red Sea parting.

Archbishop Tutu walked directly to his Tygerberg children and high-fived those who could, and kissed others. He emanated joy and love. Lowy walked behind him and did the same. It wasn't his milieu.

Tutu had an unmistakeable aura. The next hour was like no other. There was singing, dancing, clapping, laughter. It was like a large, joyous, bountiful children's party. Archbishop Tutu included the Tygerberg children in everything. He included the Australian children in everything also; their parents were snapping away along with the professional photographers. Everyone sang 'happy birthday' to Lowy on the Archbishop's instructions – no matter that his birthday is in October.

I was standing next to Ben who was leaning on a weight-bearing post in the middle of the room. 'Well done,' he whispered. 'This is fantastic.'

I was taken aback. 'It's nothing to do with me. It's him. He is just wonderful. I have to pinch myself that I'm here.'

'It's like that,' he looked down at me. 'But don't ever doubt this would have happened like this without you. You've thought of everything. Whatever Peter or the others say.'

The room fell silent as Lowy handed over the giant cheque.

'Archbishop, I hope you will support our World Cup bid and join us in Zurich this time next year,' said Lowy.

The Archbishop looked at Lowy for a few moments. I wondered what he was thinking. They were a year apart in age – Lowy was older – about the same height; Lowy neat and trim in a dark suit and open neck white shirt; the Archbishop round and soft in a slightly too small bright yellow 'Come Play!' jersey he was now wearing.

Archbishop Tutu looked around the room at all the reporters and turned back to Lowy.

'It depends how much more you give us!' he exclaimed. There was a brief silence. If it had gone any longer, it would have been really awkward.

Archbishop Tutu broke the ice with a high-pitched giggle. Lowy looked on and guffawed awkwardly. Others joined in.

'You've got to get them not to report that,' Ben said referring to the journalists.

I looked at the room packed with about 100 media representatives from around the world.

'I think it's a bit too late for that,' I whispered.

Cape Town: December 2009

THERE WAS NOTHING special about the function room we were assigned by the hotel for the government-hosted function later that same evening.

It had a wall of windows overlooking a small, courtyard-style garden. A large screen was up one end of the room, adjacent to a lectern, Australian Government signage and our life size banner of Nicole Kidman inviting people to 'Come Play!'. There were bar tables set around the room, the music was non-intrusive, the canapés were plentiful and delicious, the beer, wine, champagne and other drinks were flowing.

There were small gifts for every attendee as well as a large bag of gifts for every FIFA Executive Committee member. The main gift this time was an RM Williams belt. It was fun picking the sizes.

Jack Warner was the first to arrive. He cheerfully inquired whether there was any Australian wine available.

'We do have some, but not much because the hotel wouldn't let us bring any in,' I replied.

'That is a shame. Any in the gifts?' He had spotted the large yellow 'Come Play!' gift bags that were for Executive Committee members. I laughed – as I assumed he was joking, but he walked to the bags and had a look. He would have been disappointed; there was no wine.

Angel Maria Villar Llona, the Spanish Executive Committee member and former national team defender, put in a surprise appearance. Hargitay told us from the outset that Villar Llona would never support us. I watched him. He mingled easily and appeared relaxed.

Mohamed Bin Hammam looked dapper, dressed in a high collar navy shirt with a houndstooth style blue and black jacket.

He told me he wasn't staying long. 'I just came to say hello because it is Australia. I have to leave soon.'

Reynald Temarii arrived with his CEO, Tai Nicholas, and another companion. He greeted me warmly.

'Everything is going very well,' he said to me in French. 'Everyone is talking about the Tutu visit. And this,' he looked around the room, 'looks very good.'

'Thank you. That is good to hear. It is a marathon and not a sprint. There is a long way to go.'

Stevie Hargitay arrived with England's Executive Committee member, Geoff Thompson and his wife, Anne. Stevie reminded me that the Thompsons were 'very old and dear friends of ours.'

They looked like regular people, probably from a small town, with grandchildren, who had somehow managed to get themselves on to the FIFA Executive Committee and were enjoying the ride with everything it had to offer. Thompson was short – shorter than Lowy – bright blue eyes behind thick glasses and was wearing a rather odd linen-style navy suit.

I was chatting to the Thompsons when Radmann pushed past me. I had never seen him move so fast. 'Franz is coming. He's here,' he cried, rushing up the stairs to the hotel lobby.

Thompson smiled and the couple moved on.

A few minutes later Franz Beckenbauer came down the stairs talking amiably with Radmann in German.

'So this is football royalty,' I thought. He was tall, still trim, fit looking, receding silver hair. He walked and carried himself like an athlete. Radmann introduced us.

'Franz, this is Bonita Mersiades. She is looking after all the non-technical side of Australia's bid.'

'And doing a very good job too,' he said to me.

'Thank you. It's an honour to meet you,' I said. 'I'm old enough to remember you captaining West Germany when you met us in the 1974 World Cup.'

He laughed. 'That's good. I'm pleased to hear. Someone working in football who knows something of football.'

When Beckenbauer entered, the function turned up another notch. He had a commanding presence, and was at ease with the many people wanting to chat with him and get their photograph taken with him.

'Bonita, we meet again,' said Enrique Byrom who was also in attendance with Robyn.

'It's lovely of you to come again, both of you. You must be getting sick of these things.'

He smiled broadly. 'No, no, never. We will always support the Australian bid.'

ALL WAS GOING well until the speeches started.

After Lowy said a few words of welcome, the plan was that the Australian High Commissioner would talk for around five minutes, once again emphasising the government's support, and launch our new promotional film with Nicole Kidman.

The High Commissioner didn't adhere to the plan.

She wasn't new to the role but perhaps the star power of Franz Beckenbauer affected her; or maybe she didn't give a toss what an audience of football people thought. She went way over her allotted time. What she had to say was interesting if it was an audience of trade representatives, but it was an audience of the FIFA Executive Committee, FIFA employees, football officials and football journalists.

I was standing at the back of the room, worrying. It was clear that people were restless. They were shifting from one leg to another, looking around for somewhere to lean on, starting to have private conversations out of the corner of their mouth, glancing at their watch. One or two people near the door left quietly. Radmann turned around to me, glass of white wine in hand, rolling his eyes several times.

Now he walked over to me.

'She's ruining the evening. People are completely switching off. Tell her to stop.'

By the look on his face, he wasn't joking. 'You know I can't do that Fedor.'

'Well think of something. You have this wonderful film to show and no-one will be here. Franz is getting very bored.'

We stood in silence for a few more moments. She continued speaking. Radmann looked at the audio operator, who also looked bored. 'Can you take down the microphone sound?' Radmann asked him.

'Yes sir,' said the man.

I put my hand up. 'Don't do it.'

'Bonita, we have to do something. This woman is never going to stop.'

'Fedor, she's the Australian High Commissioner. She has to be able to talk. We can't just pull the sound on her.'

'I have managed to get all these Executive Committee members here. You have made this wonderful film. If she's not finished in two minutes, we're pulling the sound otherwise the evening is a waste,' he said.

I looked around the room. More people had left. Others were openly talking to one another.

The audio operator thought this was the most exciting thing that had happened all evening and counted down the two minutes on a stop watch.

With 17 seconds to spare, the High Commissioner stopped talking. I sighed with relief. Radmann raised his glass. She gave the cue for the film to roll. The AV operator turned down the lights, turned up the volume and played our film in public for the first time: in a little over five minutes, it set out the rationale, the credentials and the emotion behind Australia's bid to host the World Cup.

The film was received warmly and enthusiastically. Bin Hammam and Villar Llona left immediately after its viewing, but the other Executive Committee members stayed behind.

Even Hargitay praised the film extravagantly. After he first saw it in September, he wrote to Lowy:

'I have just downloaded the promotional film presented by Nicole Kidman. I have been around in this business for a bit and have seen many failed attempts at glory - and very few exceptional products that touch the heart, convince the rational thinking, convince the viewer of the message and deliver all of that in an informative yet entertaining way. Without hesitation, without even the slightest criticism and with maximum pride to be involved with such an incredibly powerful message, country and people, I want to spontaneously offer you my respect first, my congratulations second and my professional compliments of the highest order. What you guys have 'manufactured' here, ticks all the ExCo boxes - as we discussed so many times in the past. You managed to deliver a product that is convincing, a message that screams 'let's go to Australia - it's the best' and an approach which is completely professional by being credible in every respect. Whoever was the father of this baby, deserves a very massive compliment. This is a product we can and will and must use. And this is a product that I'll be proud to show off to all and sundry: nobody will escape. Now to the viral campaign and let's shoot this thing into cyber space for all to see.'

At the time, Ben sent an email pointing out that the 'father' of the baby was actually a 'mother' and that was me. Hargitay never said another word about it.

WARNER AND BECKENBAUER were generous with their interviews. By now, Warner's praise for our bid - or specifically, our consultants - was no longer new, but Beckenbauer's support for the Australia bid was big news. No-one bothered to speak with Oceania's Reynald Temarii or England's Geoff Thompson.

Some time later, Ben, Board member Brian Schwartz and I were sitting in a corner of the large lobby lounge bar of the hotel. Ben had a beer, Schwartz and I a glass of wine. There was a plate of tapas-style food to share.

Lowy, Jill Margo, Hargitay, Radmann and Lowy's personal assistant returned to their hotel.

'It's been a great day for us. A big day. Well done Bonita,' Ben said.

'I don't think Hargitay was happy,' I said.

'Why do you say that?' asked Brian.

'He didn't say a word to me out at Tygerberg after he told me off, and he didn't say a word tonight.'

Ben's phone rang. It was Lowy. He excused himself.

'I think you should just learn to ignore him,' said Schwartz quietly. 'Don't let him bully you. He needs to stick to what he's supposed to be doing for us. He's getting a large amount of money from us and he needs to perform.'

Ben returned and took his seat. 'Frank's happy,' he said. That meant Ben was happy too.

THE NEXT MORNING a convoy which included the Australian Sports Minister, the High Commissioner, Lowy and Ben as well as the eight Australian children, visited a school to the south east of Cape Town. The VIP group was to present 1,700 lap desks, as well as 'Come Play!' footballs and other resources, to children at the school.

Lap desks, as their name suggest, are a portable blackboard-style surface that can be used in the classroom or at home to help children do their school work. It was part of a broader Australian international aid project focussing on practical measures to help African children with their education.

The school was located in a township area – a large, flat dustbowl, almost in the middle of nowhere. It looked a little like a scene from a movie where someone might be dumped if you were trying to make it hard for them to return. There was some basic housing around but not much. The roads were good and there were signs of construction and development around the area.

The school complex was large. There were two long buildings and two smaller buildings set around a concrete quadrangle. The school was surrounded by a barbed wire fence. A teacher told me that most of the children came from disadvantaged family situations with inter-generational poverty, and little history of access to education.

The entire school was out to greet their Australian visitors. Rows and rows and rows of them sitting attentively on the hot concrete while they listened to speeches from the school principal, the Australian Sports Minister, Lowy and national coach, Pim Verbeek. Of all of the visitors, Verbeek was the most natural with the children.

A few hours later I was sitting in the lobby of the Westin Hotel with Ben. We were waiting for Lowy. Hargitay was nowhere to be seen. Radmann made a brief appearance. 'If you see any ExCo, go over to them and say hello,' he told us.

Bin Hammam walked by, saw us and stopped to say hello. He congratulated us on the night before.

Marios Lefkaritis from Cyprus walked in and paused at the end of the sofa where I was sitting. I greeted him in Greek. He smiled and replied in Greek, sitting on the arm of the sofa. 'How is the Australian bid going?' he asked.

'Perhaps you could tell me,' I said.

'I received the gift, thank you. It was delivered last night. It is very nice,' he said in stilted English. He looked down at his nails. 'It is a funny business you know.'

'What do you mean?' I asked.

'This,' he gestured around the L-shaped lobby and lounge which looked out to an outdoor café that was packed and buzzing. 'All this. It is too much. The draw, two bids. Never again.'

IT WAS FRIDAY – the really big day for all bidding teams. It was the first and only one of three times that we would be up against each other for a direct comparison.

The expo was for international media, of whom there were approximately 2,500 in Cape Town for the World Cup draw the same evening. FIFA said we could only have nine accredited attendees.

This caused us a problem. By the time we included in our accreditation those of us who were working, we were left with five spots for 17 others: the Sports Minister, her chief of staff, the eight prize-winning children not to mention the six members of the 'A' team - seven if the junior Hargitay was included.

Hargitay and Abold were livid. Even when presented with inarguable logic, they saw themselves as more deserving of accreditation than almost everyone else on the list. Radmann quietly arranged his own accreditation without a fuss.

We wanted the children there because they were our best hope of getting some cut-through with the international media. Other bidding teams had the likes of David Beckham, Ruud Guillit, Luis Figo, Christian Karembeu.

We had the children. And they worked well. Dressed casually and colourfully in specially made 'Come Play!' t-shirts, they mingled amongst the huge throng of people, played football on the lawn where the expo was being held and had their photograph taken with almost everyone including Sepp Blatter, Dr Chung from South Korea, Marios Lefkaritis from Cyprus and others.

By the time the rest of our delegation arrived, the FIFA staff controlling the head count of accredited people knew it would look churlish to turf out the children, and they could hardly deny entry of the Sports Minister or Lowy, the President of the FA, so we managed to get everybody in.

The Nigerian journalist Osasu Obayuiwana came up to me. 'I've been watching you,' he said. 'You've managed to get twice as many people in here as everyone else.'

Just as we hoped, even when David Beckham arrived, the eight Aussie kids were in the photos.

With their 'Come Play!' books in hand, the children formed a mini guard of honour for Beckham. The Sports Minister stood near the children, called Beckham's name as he walked by, and asked him to sign autographs. Beckham being the sports star that he is, obliged. He signed his name on a 'Come Play!' book while our photographer snapped away. Gold!

Lord Triesman, who was standing nearby, looked on aghast. He knew we had ambushed their star's entrance. 'Bloody Australians!' he said to Andy Anson.

We were delighted. And even more so after the four-minute films from the nine bidders were shown.

You could have heard a pin drop for a split second when ours finished. It was followed by loud and sustained applause. It was by far the most compelling story told that day. We knew it. Everyone else in the room knew it too.

Afterwards, the children walked around giving out packs comprising the full-length film and the cut down booklet to journalists and other visitors, while there was a queue of journalists from around the world at our exhibition booth. They wanted to interview the Sports Minister, Lowy and Ben – and pass on their compliments.

'That was incredible,' they said. 'I didn't think you guys had a hope in hell until I saw that.'

'That blew me away. It was superb. Well done. You really are serious contenders for this.'

'That was superb. Really, really good.'

'If a vote was held today, you would have won hands down. No-one else came close.'

CHAPTER 20
Gone!

Sydney: December 2009

'I JUST WANT to let you know that I sense that there are forces moving against you.' It was the late Michael Cockerill, then one of Australia's highest-profile and most respected football journalists.

'Oh, why?'

'Well I think it's good old-fashioned chauvinism, actually. Just watch your back. There are three things coming to play. It's politics. It's gender politics. And then there's the people you work with, especially after last week.'

'In Cape Town?' I said. 'What was wrong with that?'

'Nothing. It was superb. That's the problem.' He paused. 'That slime ball consultant hates you and wants you gone.'

'How do you know that?'

'One, a Board member told me. And two, you can see by the way he looks at you and treats you.'

Dubai: December 2009

IT WAS NEARING Christmas. Ben and I were having coffee in yet another hotel lobby, this time in Dubai on our way to the last event for the year - the Club World Cup in Abu Dhabi. We were to meet Russian bid officials. But now he was telling me I didn't need to attend. I couldn't believe it. It was the reason I was in Dubai.

He said that Hargitay was bringing with him the close friend involved with the Leaders in Football Conference. She was also a producer on the trilogy of films called Goal! made by the Hargitays with the support of FIFA.

Ben looked out the large picture windows onto a lush garden. He was glum.

'What's wrong?' I asked.

'Everything,' he said. 'I will be glad when it's this time next year. I've got to put up with this lot over the next few days.

'The problem is the consultants don't understand our environment,' I said.

'What do you mean?' he asked.

I ticked the answers off on the fingers of one hand. 'One. We have to respect the other sports domestically. They don't. Two. We can't just control the media and tell them to 'shut up' as Hargitay thinks we should. Three. It's public money and we have to be accountable – I actually think we've been pretty lucky on this aspect so far. That also means we have to work with the government and their officials. And four, we're dealing with up to nine governments in Australia, not just one. The consultants probably don't realise we can't even agree on one driver's license in our country – let alone spending billions on football stadiums.'

I folded my arms on the table.

'I've absolutely had it with Peter's continuous bullying. You're lucky I don't complain officially about it,' I continued.

Ben said nothing.

'Putting aside Andreas and the Bid Book, maybe, can you put your hand on your heart and say they are worth the money they're being paid?'

He looked at me with sad, tired eyes. He shook his head.

Sydney: January 2010

IT WAS THE first day back at the office after the Christmas break. Ben asked to see me. Unusually for him, he got straight to the point.

'Look, Bonita, this isn't easy for me. But I've got to let you go.'

I looked at him. 'Leave?'

'Not leave altogether. I just have to let you go from the bid.'

I was happy about it. 'What do you want me to do?'

'There's so much work to be done. You can work on all the things I'm not getting done. There's so much.'

'Why? Hargitay?'

'Yes,' said Ben. 'He doesn't like you. They don't like you. It's only for six months.'

'Six months? Why? That makes even less sense.'

'It's just the way it's got to be.'

'What does it matter if it's six months? The bid goes for the rest of the year.'

'Well, I want you to be in South Africa. And I want you involved in all the arrangements for the end of the year.'

'What if I said 'You give me twelve months pay and I'm out of here?''

'I wouldn't accept it.'

'But what if I said to you that's what I want and it would make me happier that way?' I asked.

'I would think about it, of course, but I would plead with you not to go. I don't want you to go.'

Not long after I left Ben's office, Lowy was on the phone. He was in New York.

'How are you?' he asked, again with an upward inflection.

'I'm okay.'

'I know what Ben said to you. And I just want to say, please don't go Bonita. I don't want you to go.'

'Thanks. I said to Ben I'll think about it.'

'Of course.' There was silence.

'Promise me something,' he said.

'What?'

'Please do not make up your mind to go without speaking to me again first. I do not want you to go. Ben doesn't want you to go.'

'OK. I promise.'

I thought little of the conversations throughout the rest of the day, because there was a mountain of work to get on with.

We had just heard that the Qatar bid was sponsoring the African Football Confederation (CAF) Congress in Angola the following week. Ben and I were due to attend and present our bid to CAF.

A local journalist called wanting to know if we were still travelling to Angola in light of Qatar's sponsorship of the Congress.

Ben was sitting with his head in his hands when I walked to his office to ask him. He said he didn't know. He would talk to Hargitay and Lowy.

Later in the morning Ben said at a management team meeting that we wouldn't be going to Angola because of the Qatari sponsorship. He asked me to write a letter to CAF expressing concern about their acceptance of the sponsorship.

Only a few hours had gone by when he called me into his office again pointing at his computer screen. It was the journalist's report that Australia was not attending the Angola CAF Congress.

'Did you tell him we were not going?'

'Yes.'

He looked at it. 'Shit,' he said. 'Shit. Shit. Shit. Well I'm going to blame you for it. We're going now. Ask the journo to take the story down or change it or something. But I'm going to blame you and you are to take the blame.'

I thought it simplest just to tell the truth to the journalist. I told him I was being made the fall guy, but in reality, something changed in the period between what Ben had said earlier in the morning, and his calls with Hargitay and Lowy. Whatever that was, the fact is Ben was now going to Angola along with Hargitay, Radmann and Abold.

AFTER DISCUSSION AT home, I decided to take the new role. I walked into Ben's office the next morning to let him know.

There was a big sigh of relief from him when I told him.

'That's fantastic, I'm so pleased.'

'So what is it you want me to do exactly?' I asked. 'Here's my list of what I think needs to be worked on.'

I handed him a copy of a list I had made the night before of non-bid issues that needed addressing or that had fallen behind in the past twelve months. He read it.

'That looks good. Your new title will be Chief Strategy Advisor to the Chairman and CEO. There's one other thing. I also want you to work from home,' he said quietly.

'What?'

'I can't have you in here.'

'You can't have me in here? Why?'

This wasn't making sense. Just prior to Christmas he had given me a hefty annual bonus for a job well done. Then he didn't want me to work on the bid; now he didn't want me in the office.

'It's just better if you're not in the office for six months. If you need facilities at home for an office, we'll pay for it,' he said. 'We'll pay for what you need.'

I looked at him and laughed.

'This is getting even more ridiculous. You don't want me working on the bid because Hargitay and the consultants said so. Now you tell me you want me to work from home and you give me no reason. Plus you're prepared to pay for, what exactly – a new room, so I have a home office?'

'Obviously you'll need a proper work space.'

'I don't understand why.'

He sighed. 'Believe me, it's the best thing. I want you to leave now. This morning. Andreas will be here soon. I don't want you here when he gets here.'

He looked down at the piece of paper I had given him, twisting his pen.

I walked out of his office. The phone was ringing in mine as I returned.

'Bonita.'

'Mr Lowy.'

'How are you?'

'I'm okay.'

'I rang to see if you're taking the new job.'

I told him I was.

'I'm so happy Bonita. I'm so relieved. That is the best decision for you and for us.'

I told him that Ben wanted me to work from home and wanted me to leave the office this morning.

'I'll call you back,' he said. True to his word, Lowy rang me back later in the day. All he did was state facts, not reasons.

Ben handed me a position description for my new role as Chief Strategy Advisor. I read it briefly: on paper, it sounded terrific – a dream job for a corporate affairs professional who loved football. It more or less gave me free rein to look into anything and everything on the domestic football scene, formalised some of the ad hoc work I had been doing outside of the bid, and broadened some of my existing non-bid responsibility around communications and government relations. There wasn't much not to like, from my perspective, especially as it provided the opportunity to address some of the issues that had been allowed to fall by the wayside because of Ben's absences and focus on the bid.

Despite the fact that Ben said he wanted me out of the office before Abold arrived, I stayed at work for my usual long working day and started packing up my office. Abold walked past my office several times, his head turned the other way, as if distracted.

Later in the evening, my husband had a phone call to say that there were two deaths in the family. We needed to travel interstate for their funerals more than 1,200 kilometres away, which were scheduled for Thursday and Friday.

I rang Ben to let him know I would be away for the rest of the week.

'That's okay,' he said. 'Can you draft me something to send around to everyone about your new job so I can send it out this week? I'd like to get it out by Thursday at the latest.'

IT WAS SUNDAY evening and we were back home.

There was still nothing official from Ben about my new role. He never changed anything I wrote, so I wondered what the hold-up was. I rang him.

'I still haven't had a chance to talk to a few people I need to talk to but it's all fine. I'll send it out first thing in the morning. Don't bother coming in.

'OK, but what do I do? What will I tell my staff?' I was used to working 80-90 hours a week. The prospect of being idle was both horrifying and novel.

'I'll be in early and I'll talk to them first thing,' he said.

Soon after 9 the next morning, my staff rang me to ask where I was. Ben hadn't spoken with them.

After the fourth 'phone call or text message, I sent an email to them. In letting them know about my new role, I also added that I would be working from home; that I didn't know why but pondered whether it had something to do with 'this man' - meaning Hargitay - with a link to Matthew Hall's article about Hargitay from October. Within seconds, I received some return emails saying it was a shock 'but I can think of no one better to have responsibility for the future strategic direction of football.'

The phone rang. It was Ben.

'Bonita, I told you I would let people know.'

'I know Ben, but that was last Tuesday. This is Monday. My staff were wondering where I was, what was going on. What was I supposed to do? Lie to them?'

An hour later, I had a call from two of my staff on a conference phone.

'Ben told us you have a promotion, that's fantastic!' they enthused. 'But what will we do without you?'

'You'll be fine without me. We have our work program for the year, we know what we're doing, just do as we planned, and make sure you look after each other.'

There had been many occasions throughout 2009 when the frustrations of the bid had made an impact on all of us. My small team working on the bid were shielded from dealing with Hargitay, Radmann and Abold, but they had to deal with the practical impact of the consultants' haphazard advice. This meant we couldn't always plan ahead as well as we would like, and there would be many last minute changes of direction in matters that I knew would not make a difference to the vote, simply to satisfy the consultants' latest whim.

Ben called again late in the evening. I hadn't heard from him for more than 30 hours. He asked me to meet him the next day. I put the phone down. I told my husband I would lose my job tomorrow.

The next morning Ben and I sat across the table from one another. Ben's friend, the new Chief Financial Officer, was seated to one side. I took out my notebook and pen, and wrote while Ben read from a prepared script. He was nervous.

'I have decided not to go down the path of your new role and I am terminating your employment. I am disappointed in the communication that went to your staff. Those actions have brought about this decision.'

I looked at him. I laughed. 'Ben, that's not a reason to terminate employment.'

'It is if I say so. I'm the CEO and I can do what I want.' He just went off script.

Technically, legally, he couldn't. My contract of employment did not allow him to terminate it simply because I wrote an email he didn't like. However, I also knew it also wasn't worth arguing when things had got to this state.

He pointed out that I was not permitted to talk about the bid or the consultants. Ever. I was not permitted to return to my office to pack it up or collect my personal items.

We looked at one another across the table. His whole body was tense. His hands rested flat on the table. His face was beetroot red. I thought his head might burst. I wondered whether he might be dead before the bid is over.

Four hours later, Lowy was on the phone.

'You must be upset. I just wanted to call to ease the pain. I want to urge you to look to the future. I want to keep our good relationship. I don't want this to come between us. I wish it could have been different. But I don't want to interfere. It is Ben's decision. I understand how you feel.'

I was silent for a few moments. Lowy was keen to absolve himself from any role in the decision-making, yet it was well known that not much happened in football in Australia without him agreeing to it first.

'I don't think you do understand how I feel. It's disappointing, yes. I totally accept that a CEO can do what he likes with staff. What I don't understand is why the consultants are being allowed to run FFA like this.'

'I didn't think Ben would do this. I know he wanted to keep you. I know he didn't want to let you go.'

'Let's just hope the consultants deliver for you. Then this won't matter, will it?'

IT WAS DISAPPOINTING a few days later to see FFA had briefed their favourite journalist for his gossip column in the Sunday paper. A man who was known for hating football wrote a short piece saying there would be 'no tears' for my departure and describing me as 'bombastic'. We had never met.

More disappointing was a few days afterwards when one of the journalists from a Melbourne newspaper who had made it his job to follow the bid wrote that I was to blame for the poor relationship with state governments, the venues and the other sports, particularly the AFL. He knew this was wrong. I wasn't responsible for the relationship with state governments or the venues. Other than being in the same room at a summit on binge drinking called by the Prime Minister in early 2008, I had not even met Andrew Demetriou, David Gallop or John O'Neill, Ben's counterparts in AFL, Rugby League or Rugby Union. Those three matters were clearly in Ben's and Stuart Taggart's bailiwick.

He had not even given me the professional courtesy of responding.

Charlie Sale from the UK *Daily Mail* called me early one evening and asked me what happened.

'But you were the heart and soul of the Australian bid,' he said. 'They have just shot themselves in the foot and lost the bid as far as I'm concerned. It's one thing to have expert consultants like Hargitay, but any bid needs passion for football and you were it for Australia. Anyone could see that after just a few minutes in the company of you and your colleagues. In fact, I interviewed your boss last month and he was like an empty shell. He left me cold.'

Sale wrote about my departure in the *Daily Mail*. He referred to an 'Australian insider' - his contact, Hargitay - who claimed I made unspecified 'strategic errors.' Sale also made the point that I had more 'passion and knowledge about football than anyone else connected with the Australian bid' and was supported by Australian and Everton player, Tim Cahill.

Successive staff at FFA kept themselves busy defaming and disparaging me, in breach of their duty, for years.

MEANWHILE, ON THE other side of the world, Sepp Blatter repeated what he said 19 months beforehand at the FIFA Congress in Sydney. The 2018 World Cup should be held in Europe.

Blatter's comments were enough to prompt Lowy to make a rare live television appearance with his and Hargitay's old friend and FIFA Ethics Committee member, Les Murray.

'Did you have any inkling that the FIFA President would say this?' Murray asked.

'We know about the push by the Europeans to host 2018. This is all a storm in a tea cup. Nothing has changed. Blatter gave his opinion. I am not concerned about the President. He can't exclude us from bidding for 2018. This issue is blown out of proportion and I want to put it to bed.'

Frank Lowy might command many things, including some football journalists in Australia; he couldn't command the FIFA President or FIFA. In the eyes of the public, his stubbornness regarding 2018 was hard to fathom.

The launch of the bid at Parliament House, Canberra, in 2009. Ben Buckley (left),
Frank Lowy and Prime Minister Kevin Rudd in centre foreground

Blatter's disdain with the Qatar decision
is clearly etched on his face
[REUTERS/CHRISTIAN HARTMANN]

The author speaking about whistleblowers
as the fifth pillar of democracy, Aarhus,
October 2015

Qatar 2022 World Cup chief, Sheikh Mohammed Al-Thani with Sepp Blatter in Doha, November 2013 [REUTERS/FADI AL-ASSAAD]

Franz Beckenbauer and Frank Lowy, Cape Town, 2009

David Beckham signs Australia's 'Come Play' booklet surrounded by Aussie kids, Cape Town, 2009

Prime Minister Kevin Rudd, Sepp Blatter and Frank Lowy admiring one of the World Cup trophies, FIFA HQ, 2009

Reynald Temarii, Prime Minister Kevin Rudd and Ben Buckley sign the agreement to give Oceania $4 million, 2009

Archbishop Desmond Tutu and Frank Lowy, Tygerberg Hospital, Cape Town, 2009

Fedor Radmann and Mohamed Bin Hammam, Cape Town, 2009

Frank Lowy with the Dream Asia Award, 2010

Rupert Murdoch with Sepp Blatter, FIFA HQ, January 2012

Fedor Radmann, Maureen Warner, Peter Hargitay and Jack Warner, Cairo, 2009

Prime Minister Kevin Rudd meets Sepp Blatter, FIFA HQ, July 2009

Mohamed Bin Hammam and Jack Warner, Cape Town, 2009

Frank Lowy and Mohamed Bin Hammam in happier times, Athens 2004

Franz Beckenbauer, Frank Lowy and former FFA CEO John O'Neill, Germany 2006

Not happy. Frank Lowy and Mohamed Bin Hammam, Doha, January 2011

Franz Beckenbauer being shown around the Aspire Academy, Doha, by Andreas Bleicher with Fedor Radmann, October 2009

Sepp Blatter and the author, Zurich, November 2017

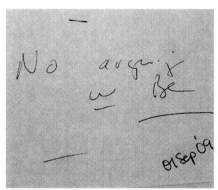

Ben Buckley's note telling the author not to argue with him, September 2009

Markus Harm (left) and the crew from ZDF Television with the author in Sydney, November 2015

Sepp Blatter greets a guest with Andreas Abold looking on, Cairo, October 2009

Manhattan skyline from Mike Garcia's office, November 2013

CHAPTER 21
What a waste of a kangaroo!

Sydney: February 2010

A FEW WEEKS later I was sitting in Lowy's office over morning coffee. He was telling me about FFA's troubles with the bid.

'The other sports are trying to make it as difficult as possible. And the state governments are being difficult. The AFL is terrible. Terrible. The biggest problem is getting a bid together. It's the governments, the other sports – except rugby – and some of the stadiums.'

'They were the same issues this time last month, this time last year and this time two years ago,' I said, wondering why I was here.

'I don't know why it's come to this,' he said wearily. He put down his coffee and reached for a paper on his desk.

'Did you see this article by Andrew Jennings?' he asked, waving a recent piece from Jennings' website. It posed the question whether Australia's bid was the dirty bid.

'The recent one? Yes.'

'How did you know about it?'

'I read it. Lots of people read Andrew Jennings.'

'He's an idiot,' Lowy said.

'That's certainly Peter's and Les' view. That doesn't mean he's an idiot.' The FIFA machine, Hargitay, and people associated with them, such as Les Murray, hated Jennings.

He grunted. 'Where did he get the information from about Radmann?'

'He writes in there that he picked it up from a newspaper article because he mentions an interview Ben gave to Charlie Sale in December.'

'I don't know this Charlie Sale.'

'He was one of the visiting journalists who came here last November, recommended by Hargitay.'

'How did Jennings know about the meeting in Zurich? In 2009?' He was referring to the report which revealed a meeting between Lowy, Ben and Radmann in Zurich.

'I have no idea. I didn't know about the meeting until I read the article. Who did? You? Ben? Hargitay? Radmann? Les Murray? Perhaps someone saw you. Hotel lobbies are not the best places for secret meetings.'

He thought for a moment. 'I just don't know why Jennings has it in for Australia.'

'I don't think he likes bad men and I expect he sees FIFA, and people around FIFA, as full of bad men.'

'Why didn't Hargitay like you?'

I laughed. 'I think that's a question for him really. But my guess would be because he doesn't like anyone who sees through him.'

'You don't think he can win us the bid?'

'All I saw Hargitay do was send copious emails criticising Lord Triesman, bully people and constantly tells us how important Jack Warner is. Then you've got Fedor Radmann who gets paid a lot of money. What is he doing with it? Andreas himself says the bid isn't won by the country with the best technical bid, the best Bid Book or the best presentation which is what he's getting paid for. If that's true, what wins it?'

I continued. 'Only you can be the judge of whether they can win it for us because you know what they do.'

'I always appreciate having your views Bonita, but I'm counting on you not to talk about them publicly.'

'I won't talk about them publicly until after the vote. Besides, if we win, my views will be irrelevant.'

His tired eyes crinkled into a smile and he gave a short laugh. 'That is true. And if we don't win?' He spread his hands and hunched up his shoulders in a question. 'If we don't win, you can write a book about it.'

Sydney: April 2010

THE TERM MAY not have been in use at the time, but fake news entered the bidding sphere with the appearance of a fake website.

Using the URL of qatar2022bidrevealed.com, it presented as an extended interview with FIFA's bête-noir investigative journalist, Andrew Jennings.

Both Jennings and another UK journalist, James Corbett, wrote that its creator was most likely to be the Hargitays.

There is no doubt that a fake website would fall within the Hargitays' skills base.

The extended pretend interviews with Jennings were focussed entirely on global geo-politics - Hargitay's interest, not Jennings' - and showed someone familiar with the operations of intelligence services in different countries. As well as Hargitay's background, including his ABI company that provided intelligence services for high net worth individuals, I recalled a conversation he and I had in Cairo about Australia's own intelligence services about which he was more knowledgeable than most.

The fake website was also prescient. 'Fake Jennings' predicted that Russia and Qatar would win.

According to 'fake Jennings', the two countries cut a deal via their respective embassies in Iraq. Qatar would provide the money to buy the votes for themselves for 2022 and for Russia in 2018. In return, Russia's Executive Committee member, Mutko, and his predecessor, Valeri Koloskov, would get the votes together.

Not that Russia was without their own mega-rich backers. The site mentioned prominent Russians Mikhail Prokhorov, Oleg Deripaska and Roman Abramovich. There was also the powerful chairman of the Russian bid, Igor Shuvalov, who was first deputy prime minister of the country and in charge of Russia's sovereign wealth fund.

One name not mentioned was former Gazprom boss, Alisher Usmanov, who through his Art, Science and Sport Charity Foundation, was a sponsor of the

Russian bid and today remains a sponsor of the 2018 World Cup.

The fake news site predicted that Russia would win 2018 with 15 or 16 votes in the first round, and Qatar would get eight votes in the first round for 2022. It was nearly right.

After the total number of voters was reduced by two, Russia won in the second round with 13 votes. Qatar managed 11 votes in the first round; it took another three rounds for them to win.

I wondered whether the fake site was an attempt to discredit Andrew Jennings further in the eyes of FIFA? Or was it using Jennings' name - loathed in FIFA circles - to deflect attention from any other deals that might be going on involving Russia or Qatar and possible partners? Who would have an interest in such a strategy?

Hargitay had other ideas. He promptly wrote a lengthy email to Blatter and others about the fake site, pointing the finger at Jennings and an unnamed German journalist. Hargitay suggested that it couldn't possibly be anything to do with him or the Australian bid as neither Russia nor Qatar were the Australian bid's enemies.

He wrote to Blatter: '*Who would profit from Russia being disgraced? Which other country? Who would profit from Qatar being disgraced? Which other country has an obsession with anti-Islamic slurs? Both answers are : NOT Australia.*'

Hargitay wrote that both he and Lowy were close to Bin Hammam and they would never '*resort to below the belt activities of this sort*'.

Did he protest too much?

Sydney: May 2010

ONE WEEK BEFORE the Bid Books were to be handed-over by all bidders to Sepp Blatter in Zurich, Ben Buckley invited me to lunch. I was surprised he wanted to meet, wondering what it could be about as I sat waiting for him.

He rushed in, phone in one hand, his black notebook in the other. He settled in, had the napkin shaken into his lap by the hovering waiter, poured himself some water and looked at me.

'I wanted to see how you were.'

He must have thought I was born yesterday. I didn't respond.

'What are you doing?' He tried again.

'Having a break. How are you?' I asked. He looked tired, stressed, unhealthy. His suit was grey, his hair showed more grey, his face looked grey.

'Terrible.' He looked down at the menu.

'How's the Bid Book going?'

'What Bid Book?' he asked, still staring at the menu. I assumed he was being sarcastic, but he looked up and said 'No really. What Bid Book? Right at the moment, we don't even know if we'll be going to Zurich to hand it in.'

Wow. Things must be bad. They were due to leave on the weekend.

'Oh well,' I said cheerily, 'at least I can't get blamed.'

The waiter took our order. Ben had a glass of red wine. I had not seen him drink alcohol at lunch time before.

'I don't think Andrew is talking to me anymore.' He was referring to Andrew Demetriou, his former boss at the Australian Rules Football League (AFL). The two were long time friends and former team mates from their playing careers as Aussie Rules players. They reportedly had a huge falling out over bid issues, especially after Lowy shouted at Demetriou at a meeting.

'But it's just business isn't it?' I asked. 'You'll both probably calm down eventually – and especially when we win and the AFL gets their share of $100 million. He'll want to be part of it then. And you can't help it if Frank loses his cool with him.'

He told me that the Bid Book was in Munich with Abold. They would pick it up on the way to Zurich, if they made it.

'How is Andreas?' I asked.

'He's fine. He's good.'

'And Pe ...' I was about to ask after the welfare of Hargitay and Radmann but he cut me off.

'Don't even ask. Peter is a nightmare. I've got so many stories to tell you when this is all over.'

DESPITE BEN'S PANIC, everyone came to the party in the end.

The other sports' compensation package was guaranteed. They knew they could go head-to-head with World Cup matches if they chose to do so.

The Australian government accommodated the government guarantees which government officials originally indicated were unconstitutional and even illegal.

Five years later, at the request of overseas colleagues, I tried to find out under freedom of information laws the extent to which the government guarantees were agreed by the Australian government. The requests needed to go to three different government agencies. All came back with almost every passage redacted. They still didn't want anyone to know!

It wasn't clear who would pay for the more than $5 billion worth of stadium and other infrastructure development that was required, but pragmatism prevailed. Tomorrow is another day.

Lowy handed over the 750 page kangaroo-leather bound Bid Book to Blatter and Jerome Valcke at a 15 minute stage-managed ceremony at FIFA headquarters in Zurich.

Never mind that according to its creator, Andreas Abold, no Executive Committee member would ever read it.

'We hope and pray that we might be the lucky country,' Lowy said as he handed it over. He told Blatter that 'Australia is a very competent country to do big shows.'

After ranking the Australian bid in the top two with England after the week of activities five months earlier in Cape Town, journalists Mark Bisson and James Corbett via their online publication, *World Football Insider*, now rated Australia at number six. Corbett was the only journalist in the world whose sole job for 18 months was to follow the progress of the bidding nations. He was uniquely placed to make the judgement.

WITH THE BID Books submitted, and after the obligatory photo opportunities with Blatter in Zurich, the bidding process stepped-up a notch. So did the dirty tricks.

The first one involved the head of the English bid, Lord David Triesman, a man Hargitay loved to hate.

Triesman was having dinner with someone he thought he could trust, a former woman employee whom he had mentored. Amongst other things, he made disparaging comments about the appointment of Spanish and Russian referees at the forthcoming World Cup in South Africa. The woman recorded the entire conversation and handed it over to an English newspaper which reportedly paid her £75,000 for the story.

As a result, Triesman resigned from his position as head of the English bid and the FA.

An overseas journalist alerted me to the story of Triesman's resignation with an email simply pointing to the story with four words: *'Hargitay at it again.'* There were no obvious links between the woman, the journalist who wrote the story and Hargitay. But it didn't stretch the imagination too far to know that it was the type of thing Hargitay would enjoy, even if he wasn't responsible.

He was obsessive in his hatred of Triesman - just as he was of Andrew Jennings and me.

Tokyo: June 2010

I LOOKED AT the time. It was 1.20am and my phone had just pinged a message. I thought to myself I must remember to put it on silent, but I looked at the message anyway. It was from an Australian journalist in Johannesburg to cover the World Cup.

'Australia has just been dumped in it big time. Bid is in disarray. No-one knows what's happening. Please call me when you can.'

Despite the hour and my now awake husband, I called. 'The most extraordinary thing has happened at the AFC Congress. Mohamed Bin Hammam just announced that Asia's backing Europe for 2018,' the journalist said.

This meant that Bin Hammam had finally made his move. I asked him what the Australian bid had said in response.

'Well that's the thing. Frank and Ben are all over the shop. They can't get their message straight. Frank said it doesn't matter and we're still going ahead with 2018. Ben admitted they didn't know anything about it beforehand. What do you think?' he asked me.

'I don't know why Ben would say it's a surprise. Blatter's been saying for well over two years that Europe would get 2018, so how can we continue to bid for 2018 when we know our own confederation doesn't support that position?

What is the USA doing?' I asked.

I could hear text messages or other calls coming through as we had the conversation. When I hung up I had another three calls and six text messages along the same lines.

More than a day later, and after 18 months of being publicly 'focussed' on 2018, Australia finally did what we knew we would need to do all along. We withdrew the bid for 2018 to focus on 2022.

Did Australia keep its public focus on 2018 as long as it did to deflect any attention from the fact that it might have been doing a deal with a European bidder, specifically Russia?

Lowy told the assembled media in Johannesburg that they had been in contact with FIFA 'for months' about withdrawing from 2018. It contradicted his earlier statement that Australia would continue to push ahead for 2018, but the journalists were either too tired to notice, or more focussed on, and interested in, the football to come.

CHAPTER 22
The first cracks appear

Sydney: June 2010

A TEXT MESSAGE at 5.52am. It was from a local football journalist.

'Have you seen the Herald?' referring to the *Sydney Morning Herald*.

It was a winter's morning, I was still in bed. I hadn't.

As soon as I did, it was clear what he was referring to. The Fairfax press, which includes the *Sydney Morning Herald* had a front page story about 'secret accounts' for Australia's bid written by two award-winning investigative journalists.

More reports unfolded over the next few days concerned with how much money the consultants were being paid, the existence of what they termed two separate bid budgets, one internal and one for government reporting, the backgrounds of the consultants, the favours shown to Reynald Temarii of Oceania and Jack Warner of CONCACAF, and the involvement of the diplomatic service and government Ministers. The latter was normal for an activity of this kind.

They made for fascinating reading especially when 'dumbed-down' to newspaper style. The paper also published a long response to the claims signed by Ben. Based on its style, I would guess it was written by Lowy's right-hand man at Westfield, Mark Ryan.

FFA's key point was that everything they did was within the rules set by FIFA.

What FFA of course failed to say – and what the newspaper didn't immediately pick up on – was that those rules were, at best, haphazard and, at worst, set up an environment conducive to inappropriate deals being done in the name of 'international football development'.

This was the environment FIFA had set. It was the environment in which FIFA conducted its business. At best, prone to dodgy practices; at worst, corrupt.

The arrangement with Oceania Football Confederation brokered by Temarii was a case in point. Using additional taxpayers money of $4 million, Australia was funding a project that was more than likely intrinsically worthwhile for development purposes – but there was no doubt that the money, as well as the other items sought by Temarii, were in exchange for his vote.

Amos Adamu from Nigeria was a focus of attention in the previous November.

The trip to Angola, which Ben ended up doing with Hargitay, Radmann and Abold within a day or so of sacking me in January, was arranged with the specific purpose of talking to two other African voters, Issa Hayatou and Jacques Anouma, to see what was needed to secure their votes.

Australia wasn't the only bidding nation targeting the same votes. All the bidders were.

Key people in FFA were actively briefing anyone who would listen that the newspaper reports from Fairfax were all my doing because I was a 'disgruntled former employee' who was 'bitter and twisted'.

The same tired old lines are generally trotted-out when the truth suddenly appears. It was noticeable that none of the FFA statements denied the accuracy of the reports. They didn't because they couldn't.

Anyone who knew me also knew I was neither bitter nor disgruntled. Nonetheless some people seem to think that if a critical opinion is expressed – even when it's a knowledgeable one – then that can be the only reason. It's the lazy way to deal with an issue when you don't have the capacity to deal with the argument. Football people who had known me for a long time or who knew me well and knew the depth of my commitment to football didn't have the same opinion. This included A-League coaches and staff, players, football journalists, administrators and fans.

Only weeks before, on his way to South Africa for the World Cup, Ben called me asking me to prepare background notes and speaking points for him for a debate on football development that he was to have with SBS-TV. Here was the man who sacked me asking a so-called 'bitter and disgruntled' former employee to prepare him briefing notes and speaking points.

Because the Fairfax newspaper reports emanated from Melbourne, many also saw the reports as an 'anti-football' agenda driven by Australian Rules Football which has its headquarters in the city.

It turns out they were right.

Seven years later in 2017, I learned that the tip-off came from Ben himself, although probably inadvertently. Ben was having a catch-up with his friend Andrew Demetriou, the head of the AFL. He was working hard to heal the personal rift since the argument between Demetriou and Lowy over stadiums. On one particular late night meeting with Demetriou, Ben apparently opened-up, saying that he was wracked with guilt by my sacking, declaring that he was 'forced to do a terrible thing to a truly good person'.

It was enough for someone within the AFL to let the journalists know that there may be something to investigate.

AROUND THE SAME time as Lowy and FFA issued a writ for defamation against Fairfax and the two reporters responsible for the reports, FIFA issued a statement officially clearing FFA of any wrongdoing.

This was not unexpected for two reasons. FIFA seldom admits to any wrongdoing. Plus the focus of their investigation had been around the pearl gifts which were given to the entire Executive Committee eight months before bidding guidelines were issued.

FIFA made some concessions, however, by changing the rules for bidders engaging with Executive Committee members not from their own country. In theory, it made the arrangement with Beckenbauer - whom I always assumed received a cut of Radmann's hefty consulting fee of $155,000 a month - even more challenging.

LOWY CALLED ME on a Saturday morning and asked me to meet him at his house that afternoon to talk about the media reports.

He opened the door and showed me directly into his study which was near the entrance. It was a beautifully furnished room; large enough for two oversized desks, two classic leather sofas, a large television screen, a Persian carpet beneath a coffee table, and a display stand and wall lined with mementos. There were photos of Lowy with world figures such as Ehud Olmert, James Wolfensohn and Henry Kissinger, thank you letters, awards, figurines and family portraits.

Lowy asked if I minded whether a trusted friend sat in on our meeting. I didn't.

Lowy and I sat opposite one another. He sat with his back to the wall, facing the room; I sat at one end of the sofa facing the wall, the third person at the opposite end of the same sofa. Lowy had a small notepad and a pencil in his hand. He looked at it.

He must have rehearsed his opening spiel because it was quite a long speech for him, unbroken and without hesitation.

'Bonita. We have always had a good relationship from the first time we met in 2001. You know I tried to get you into the game earlier than when I did. What happened this year is not something I wanted. But I need your help now. If you help me, I will get you back into football. I will help you get your job back.'

I told him I didn't want my job back.

He then said that people like him become targets for people wanting to make trouble. I wondered where this was going.

'Look at Nicolas Sarkozy and the cosmetics woman.'

'Lillian Bettencourt?' I prompted.

'Yes. And a few years ago there was the same thing for me with Ehud Olmert in relation to a sale. I spent $1 or 2 million defending that and I won. I will always win.'

The sale he was referring to was known as the Bank Leumi affair, in which Olmert was accused of selling the bank to Lowy and a business partner on favourable terms. No charges were laid due to insufficient evidence.

He paused while he looked down at his notebook, allowing me time to take in the significance of his last comment.

'You must realise that many, many people think you're the leak. People say it to me all the time,' he said.

'There are also many who don't think I'm the leak,' I said.

'Such as?'

'For example, journalists.'

'Well you cannot trust journalists,' he said. 'They say one thing to you and another thing to me and Ben.'

'I'm sure some of them do – but they probably feel they have to say that to you and

Ben, whereas none of them has any reason to be nice to me or to keep in touch with me. I am not important, and hold no position in the game, other than as a volunteer with a club. You are.'

'What I want to know is who would have access to that spreadsheet? Did you ever see the spreadsheet?' Lowy was picking up on the reference in the newspaper reports regarding the separate budgets for government reporting and for internal management reporting.

'Yes, I saw the spreadsheet. I don't know who had access to it. We were never allowed to take it out of the meeting room.'

'And what about the other bidders?' Lowy asked.

'How would they know any of this?' I said.

'Have any of them been in touch with you?'

'A few of them sent me an email saying how shocked they were after I left.'

'Have any of them offered you a job?'

'You know I wouldn't work for another bidder.'

'I know that Bonita, but some people think you could be working for another bidder.'

'Who would think that?'

'Hargitay, Radmann, Abold.'

I laughed. 'Who am I supposedly working for?'

'Qatar or the US,' he said.

Both the England and US bids made discreet approaches to me, both through third parties, but not Qatar.

Much later, I was told by a Qatar bid executive employee that they thought about approaching me also, but they were given a copy of my confidentiality agreement and realised I couldn't work for any other bidder. I have not been able to verify this, and I have no idea how Qatar could have a copy of my confidentiality agreement. If it was true, there was obviously a mysterious and potentially problematic information flow between Australia's bid and Qatar's bid.

'It's interesting that the consultants would think that way. I think you need to look at them and who else they might be working for,' I said.

We knew that Hargitay worked for Bin Hammam in 2009, primarily around Bin Hammam's campaign for the Asian Football Confederation Presidency against Sheikh Salman of Bahrain. In fact, this was seen as a positive for our bid.

We also assumed that Hargitay and Warner had a pecuniary relationship - although we weren't sure who paid whom. We also suspected that Hargitay might have been on a retainer from Blatter.

Radmann and Abold knew Bin Hammam well enough to have visited him in September 2008, at our request, to talk to him about Vision Asia and how Australia would secure votes in Asia and Africa.

There were also the close ties between the three consultants and the Russian bid. Radmann and Abold had been around FIFA and specifically the World Cup bidding environment for nearly 20 years. Radmann, in particular, knew everyone and had cultivated close relationships with Executive Committee members past and present.

And now, as well as being closely identified with the Australia bid, Beckenbauer was also named as an ambassador for Gazprom, the Russian energy giant, only the previous month. Gazprom was already a sponsor of UEFA and became a top tier partner of FIFA from 2015. It's unclear what a gas company ambassador actually does.

I told Lowy that some international journalists were of the opinion that it was Hargitay behind the fake Qatar Bid website and the Triesman sting.

'I also hear the Australian bid is pretty much disliked by most journalists,' I said.

'They don't vote,' said Lowy.

'No. You're right, they don't vote,' I said. 'But it's not good for Australia's reputation.' In fact, it was reputational risk due to the consultants which had long concerned me.

'How do you think we're going otherwise?' Lowy asked.

'I don't know. We haven't actually done anything locally to promote it, have we? We did have a whole program set out but none of it's been done. Ben told me when he spoke with me last month that there's no money left which is very curious. And you were in South Africa for a month with them all. How do you think it went?'

He shrugged his shoulders. 'I don't know. Some days I am hopeful, very hopeful.

Some days I am not.'

I told him I heard he got upset with journalists and some football officials in South Africa.

'Some journalists are so stupid. You know? They want to know answers. I don't want to give them the answers. It's as simple as that.'

I stayed silent.

'This week is important,' he said. The technical inspection was starting in two days time.

'That's not what Andreas used to say,' I said.

'That is why we had to stop Fairfax. We can't have any more reports coming out while the technical inspection is on or for the rest of the year. I'll do whatever is takes to keep them quiet,' he told me.

'I understand that. You have said it before. But it's only fair I should let you know that if the newspaper contacted me to help them in their defence, I would do so. I can't see anything in their reports that is fundamentally wrong and they have every right to raise the issues in the public domain.'

He sighed. 'Let us catch up again when this is all over.'

Lowy, his friend and I walked to the front door together. Lowy patted me on the shoulder and gave me a kiss.

THE FIFA INSPECTION tour, led by the Chilean FA President Harold Mayne-Nicholls, was organised with Abold's German precision. Even the winter weather was kind. The three day tour included inspections and stadium visits in Brisbane, Sydney and Melbourne, dinner with the new Prime Minister, Julia Gillard, and state Premiers at the Prime Minister's Sydney residence, green light corridors everywhere they travelled, and a few obligatory cultural highlights such as cuddling a koala.

After six months of little positive news domestically about the bid, it gave FFA an opportunity for picture opportunities to showcase the selling points of our bid above everyone else's – and to feed the perception to the public that a successful technical inspection was actually important for garnering the support of Executive Committee members.

A few days later, Lowy and Ben were in Kuala Lumpur presenting the 2015 Asian

Cup Bid Book to Mohamed Bin Hammam at AFC headquarters. It was a redundant hand-over ceremony. Australia was the only bidder.

With no trace of irony, Bin Hammam stated that he assured Australia that our bid for the Asian Cup would have his recommendation when it goes before the AFC Executive Committee.

Lowy said the Asian Cup in Australia would be 'bigger, better and more successful' than ever before. He was absolutely right about that.

Sydney: October 2010

'HAVE YOU SEEN this?'

It was a four word email from an international journalist who had noticed a report in a Jamaican newspaper about another 'donation' to a cause dear to Peter Hargitay's heart: Jamaica.

Hargitay's wife, and the mother of his second family, is Jamaican – coincidentally as was Andreas Abold's first wife. Hargitay has a home in Jamaica, as does Abold. And, along with CONCACAF chief Jack Warner, one of Hargitay's best buddies was the late Captain Burrell, President of the Jamaican FA. A former officer in the Jamaican Defence Forces, Burrell co-owned a chain of bakery stores in the Cayman Islands known as 'Captain's Bakery'. Burrell's business partner was the president of the Cayman Islands FA, Jeffery Webb.

According to the report, FFA signed a memorandum of understanding (MoU) with the Jamaican FA and the Jamaican Government for 'sports development' funding. It was part of a broader package of aid for the Caribbean from the Australian Government of $60 million over four years that the previous Prime Minister, Kevin Rudd, had announced in his visit the year before.

The precise amount for the Jamaican FA was not publicly known. A senior executive in government suggested to me that it was close to $2.5 million.

'The MoU officially says sport, but the two main sports in Jamaica are football and cricket, and you don't see cricket at the MoU signing ceremony, do you?' he asked.

If this was the case, the government's allocation to the bid now totalled $53 million.

I wondered how a donation to the Jamaican FA related to our bid strategy.

The senior executive laughed. 'What strategy? The only strategy appears to be *'Let's do what Hargitay and Radmann say'*.

The photo that accompanied the story had the Jamaican Sports Minister, Horace Burrell and John Boultbee, head of international relations from FFA, signing the MoU. Peter Hargitay was there too. He looked on like a cat that got the cream.

Meanwhile, the US Soccer President, Professor Sunil Galati, was bemused.

In London for a conference, Gulati said that 'We are very pleased that Australia is spending money in the Caribbean, that's fine, that's a good thing.'

Gulati also said what David Downs said to me in Zurich 16 months beforehand. If the CONCACAF vote went against the USA, all hell would break loose.

Gulati, along with his counterparts from every other bid except Australia, was in London for the 2010 edition of the Leaders in Football conference. FFA was hosting Paraguay, the home of Executive Committee member Nicolas Leoz, in an international friendly in Sydney. Leoz did not travel to Sydney for the match.

CHAPTER 23
Uh-oh

Sydney: October 2010

IT WAS EARLY on a Sunday morning. A few days beforehand the US bid finally withdrew from the 2018 vote and was focussed only on 2022, just as we had done in June.

An overseas journalist called. 'Have you seen the reports coming through from London? Adamu and Temarii are caught on tape asking for money.'

'That's no surprise,' I said. 'Who got them?'

'That's what I was ringing to ask you. Do you think it could be Hargitay?'

'It's not in Australia's interests. Temarii's vote was always ours. But Adamu, along with Anouma and Hayatou, were obvious targets for all bidders,' I said referring to three of the African voters.

'What do you think it means for the Australian bid?'

'A problem.'

The revelation occurred because Jonathan Calvert and Claire Newell from London's *The Sunday Times* posed as consultants for the US bid and met with Adamu, Temarii and others.

Adamu asked the fake consultant for $500,000 to be paid into a personal account to build practice pitches in Africa. When asked whether it would have an impact on his vote, he replied 'Of course it will.'

Temarii asked for $2.5 million for his long-desired project of a sports academy building for Oceania in Auckland – the one he had asked Australia to fund more than two years before.

Another person caught in the sting, Ahongalu Fusimalohi of Tonga, a previous FIFA Executive Committee member, was even more forthright. He told *The Sunday Times* team that Oceania was voting for Australia *'Because the Australian Football Federation persuaded its government to pay Oceania $4m (Australian dollars). He said the payment was unprecedented and was specifically done with the World Cup in mind.'*

The Australian bid team was worried. With Temarii caught on tape - still looking for a way to fund the academy building in Auckland - one-half of Australia's guaranteed support going into the first round was gone, leaving only Beckenbauer.

The initial report of the matter on the online site part-owned by interests close to Hargitay, *Inside World Football*, had an extensive section related to the Australian bid. Unless you knew the inside story, you might think it was irrelevant.

'In a letter seen by insideworldfootball, Temarii wrote last night to FIFA President Sepp Blatter to give his version of events and which has also been circulated to the nine bidders to host the 2018 and 2022 World Cups, including England and Russia.'

Temarii's letter to Calvert was also published on the website. Temarii noted that the commitment to vote for Australia was made in June 2008 and was confirmed by the Oceania confederation again in October 2010. That part was true.

Temarii wrote that Oceania was voting for Australia on the basis of historical football ties, Australia's experience with the Sydney 2000 Olympics and the Australian Government's historical investment in the region - all related to infrastructure, health and education, but not sport. He failed to mention that the decision was made on the back of a promise of $4 million specifically for the Oceania Confederation, together with another $1.5 million to $2 million in other benefits for Oceania via FFA.

He explained that, since Australia had withdrawn from 2018, Oceania's vote for 2018 was still undecided.

FFA was compelled to write to Calvert also. *Inside World Football* helpfully published extracts from that letter too. FFA rejected suggestions that it contravened the letter or spirit of FIFA guidelines. FFA also stated that its development activity was a *'matter of public record'* and done in conjunction with the government.

But within a few hours, the original version of the story was replaced. A much shorter version appeared. It expunged 22 paragraphs of the original article dealing with what Temarii had written to FIFA, and what the FFA wrote to *The Sunday Times*.

It was curious.

One of the reasons FFA would have been so keen to change the original article didn't become apparent for some time. Years later, contrary to their letter to *The Sunday Times*, we learned that FFA made a USD$462,200 payment that ended up with Jack Warner. The payment was not on the public record and was not made in conjunction with the government.

Sydney: October 2010

'HI BONITA, YOU must be looking at this FIFA stuff and shaking your head. Do you have any background on the deals between Russia and Australia vote swapping? I am at Olympic meetings in Mexico where it's the talk of the town!'

It was a text message from another international journalist. I ignored it for a while, wondering how to answer it.

I texted her back saying *'No surprise.'* The journalist called me almost immediately. She was in Acapulco for an executive board meeting of the International Olympic Commitee.

'You don't need to be all corporate and not talk to me,' she said. 'I absolutely know that there's a vote swap deal. It gives both of you five votes going into the first round. I just want to know how it came about. Isn't it against the rules? And who are the five? I can only get three – Beckenbauer, Temarii and Mutko.'

'It's probably worthwhile looking at those who are close to Mutko,' I said. I was referring to Marios Lefkaritis of Cyprus and Senes Erzik of Turkey.

'Do you think the deal will stick?' she asked.

'If one has been made, who knows? Especially given the Temarii situation. The only person I'd believe is the person who says they're not voting for you.'

'Someone told me that Zenit and Dick Advocaat were tied-up in this too. I didn't get that.'

I explained the background.

Advocaat, a famous Dutch coach, signed a contract to be Australia's national coach after a recommendation from Australia's 2006 World Cup boss, Guus Hiddink. Advocaat was enjoying great success at the Russian club, Zenit St Petersburg.

The club won the Russian league, the UEFA Cup and the UEFA Super Cup, and Zenit wanted to keep their man.

Flush with cash after being purchased by Russia's giant Gazprom from St Petersburg bankers, David Traktovenko and Vladimir Kogan, Zenit's new owners made Advocaat a counter-offer rumoured to be worth more than $5 million. It was an offer he couldn't refuse - and Australia couldn't match.

He pulled out two months before the 2010 World Cup qualifiers started in 2008. Lowy was livid. He hated losing anything. And losing a national team manager so close to the start of a vital qualification process was a big blow. He vowed to legally pursue Advocaat and Zenit through the Court of Arbitration for Sport.

When the discussions with the Russian bid began in 2009, Lowy's first task for me was to find out about Russian bid chief, Vitaly Mutko's ties to Zenit. Mutko used to be President of the club. It was the club of the Russian power elite including Medvedev and Putin. Ever since, everything on the Advocaat case had gone quiet. The case apparently never went to the Court of Arbitration for Sport and the only comment made by FFA was some years ago to the effect that a private settlement had been made.

To add to the intrigue, Gazprom was a major sponsor of Zenit and, only the previous month, UK journalist Charlie Sale reported that Franz Beckenbauer was to become an ambassador for Gazprom.

Doha: November 2010

MOHAMED BIN HAMMAM was slow to support the Qatar bid. His attitude started to change in October 2009.

He was home in Doha for the wedding of one of his sons, not long after Franz Beckenbauer's and Fedor Radmann's visit to the Emir in October 2009 on the Australian bid's behalf.

The Emir told Bin Hammam he needed to lift his game; that the country must host the World Cup; and Bin Hammam must do whatever it takes to make sure it happened.

Ever since the royal command, Bin Hammam was devoted to the cause. Most of all, he wanted to be the next FIFA President. He thought it was time for Sepp Blatter to go. But he wasn't certain that he could pull off a World Cup win and the FIFA presidency. He had no choice when his Emir called him to service.

Now, 12 months later, Qatar was in a strong position.

Bin Hammam knew Japan had no chance. He knew South Korea was mostly about Mong-Joon Chung advancing his political cause at home.

The US kept things close to their chest. Bin Hammam knew they had their supporters amongst the FIFA Executive. Everyone knew that the US could host the World Cup standing on their head, and bring in lots of money for FIFA coffers. But Bin Hammam was also confident that there were enough on the Executive Committee who didn't like the USA - the country. And if they didn't like the USA, they wouldn't like the US bid as a matter of principle.

Then there was Australia. The country he promised to support as long ago as 2006, well before he knew his own country was bidding. Even in 2008 when he met the former Prime Minister Kevin Rudd at the FIFA Congress in Sydney, and again promised support, Bin Hammam really didn't think the talk that Qatar might bid was serious.

So, at the time, he suggested to Frank Lowy that Australia engage Hargitay, Radmann and Abold. By hiring Hargitay, Radmann and Abold, Australia signalled to the FIFA Executive Committee that they were willing to do whatever it takes to win.

Everyone in the FIFA world knew what that meant. It was the old team back together: Bin Hammam, Beckenbauer with his fixer Radmann and assistant Abold. Hargitay too: Bin Hammam always figured he was better working for you than against you.

Bin Hammam and the Germans were especially close. They worked together to get Blatter elected - twice. They worked together to get Germany over the line for the 2006 World Cup. It was a system that Blatter and Radmann perfected years ago when they worked under Horst Dassler. He is widely recognised as establishing the system of financial patronage related to broadcasting, marketing and international development activity.

When FFA appointed Radmann and Abold in 2008, the two of them visited Bin Hammam in Doha. They talked about how much money was needed for Asia and Africa.

Eventually, FFA and the Asian Football Confederation signed an agreement for a $5 million gift to AFC over three years to Bin Hammam's pet Vision Asia project.

Other than a few specific activities, the money was not tied.

It was a win-win situation. FFA thought the grant to Vision Asia would guarantee support from the four Asian voters. Bin Hammam saw it as a means of continuing to give to the many people who came to him seeking help.

New York: November 2010

THE FACT THAT Qatar's campaign shifted up a gear and gained ground during the previous twelve months, thanks to Bin Hammam's support, was not lost on others.

David Downs, chief executive of the US bid told me as much when we caught up for coffee in New York. I asked him whether he thought the contest was between USA and Australia for 2022.

'Not at all,' he said. 'I'm sorry to tell you this but we're not at all worried about Australia anymore. Australia hasn't been in it since at least June.'

Downs said that no-one knew what the Australian bid stood for.

'There's no consistency of message. They've managed their relationships so poorly. It's hard to find someone who likes the Australian bid team. Frank, Ben, the consultants. We hear reports all the time about how they've put people off everywhere. None of us can understand how you can have that much public money and do so poorly.'

The US bid's concern was Qatar.

'They've spent a load of money. But they've also sold a coherent message. I have a lot of time for Hassan,' he said referring to his counterpart for the Qatar bid, Hassan Al-Thawadi.

We agreed Russia was the favourite for 2018.

'Russia hasn't had it; they have the capability; they've hosted the Olympics; they've got money; it would satisfy Blatter's wish for new lands. And, when it comes to Russia, who knows what else they're doing?' I said.

Zurich: November 2010

JEROME VALCKE WAS another who looked on from Zurich at Qatar's rise.

Valcke knew what a headache it would be if Qatar won. It wasn't just a question of dealing with Bin Hammam and his increasing power - which would be bad enough - but all the practical issues.

The FIFA administration had found it difficult enough dealing with South Africa and Brazil and the long distances they needed to travel to support the organising committees for the 2010 and 2014 World Cups.

Valcke feared it would be even more challenging with a Qatar win. For a start, everyone knew the World Cup couldn't be played in the desert in summer. It would mean they'd have to move the date. At least there was a clause in the bidding agreement that allowed FIFA to do so if they wanted. But Valcke knew that would be a major problem for the big European leagues, the American television networks, and so many leagues in other parts of the world too. They'd have to battle the European Clubs Association, the professional leagues association, Rupert Murdoch whose TV football interests spanned nearly every continent.

He also had a concern about revenue. As he had emphasised to bidders, the World Cup had to fund all of FIFA's activities for the next four years so there was no scope for revenue loss. Amongst the 2022 bidders, only the US could guarantee the type of revenue that was needed.

While Australia dealt with the issue by arguing the case for growth in television revenues coming from the Asian region in their time zone, Qatar took a more practical approach.

Valcke's concerns about revenue growth in relation to Qatar were assuaged when negotiations commenced in October 2010 for a bonus payment of USD$100 million to FIFA from Al Jazeera if Qatar won 2022.

But there was even more on offer. Not long after the vote in December 2010, Valcke told a highly-placed football official in Abu Dhabi that Qatar 'bought' the World Cup - using the same language as Peter Hargitay had 21 months beforehand. Valcke told the official that Qatar would double any sponsorship that needed replacement using a relevant Qatar commercial entity.

According to former FIFA staff, Valcke's share for negotiating commercial deals was generally 5%.

SEPP BLATTER FRETTED also. He thought about Mohamed Bin Hammam's end game: the 2022 World Cup or the FIFA presidency next year? Surely not both?

Like his CEO, Jerome Valcke, Blatter didn't want the World Cup in Qatar.

FIFA would be a laughing stock. Imagine the world's best footballers playing football in the desert heat! It just couldn't happen. Blatter wanted Russia and the USA to win. Two big countries that would make sure the World Cup was a financial success and would give the game more opportunities for growth.

Blatter also didn't plan to give up the presidency at next year's election. Not to Bin Hammam. Not to anyone. He needed a plan to deal with Mohamed's growing power and influence.

AUSTRALIA HAD LONG wanted Qatar out of the race.

Since 2009, Australia thought if they could get Qatar out of the way, they were a good chance against the US for the same reasons that Bin Hammam concluded: not everyone liked the US. They had tried, through Beckenbauer and Radmann, to convince the Emir to withdraw from the race. Qatar wouldn't budge.

With the vote only three weeks away, and with Australia's guaranteed voter, Reynald Temarii, now suspended Hargitay emailed Blatter with a *Spickzettel* - a cheat sheet - on why Qatar should be immediately disqualified from being a candidate for 2022.

It contained nothing that was news to Blatter. There was the heat. The lack of football pedigree. No infrastructure to speak of. Fans would hate it. The quality of football would suffer. They treated workers poorly. And 'rumours' of offering Africans money.

Hargitay also forwarded the email to Frank Lowy. He hoped it would give Blatter something to think about. Lowy replied to Hargitay saying he had done a 'great job'. Lowy was apparently convinced it would be enough to stop Qatar's candidacy from proceeding.

Lowy and the Australian bid team were even more hopeful when the FIFA Ethics Committee agreed to investigate the long talked-about allegations of collusion between the Qatar bid and the Spain/Portugal bid that had been referred to by another person who had spoken with the undercover journalists from *The Sunday Times*.

Reports also surfaced of a former employee of the Qatar bid team who claimed to be in the room in Luanda, Angola when a discussion took place between Qatar bid officials, including the bid CEO Hassan Al-Thawadi, and three African members of the Executive Committee. The former employee said that the three - confederation presidents Issa Hayatou of Cameroon, Jacques Anouma of Cote d'Ivoire and

Amos Adamu of Nigeria - were each offered money in return for their vote. The amount ranged from $500,000 to $1.5 million each, depending on who reported it.

The Qatar bid team denied the allegations, saying that they played within the rules set by FIFA. It was precisely the same thing FFA said in June when confronted with adverse reports.

Despite Hargitay's *spickzettel*, and a former Qatar employee helpfully speaking out only days later, Blatter was paralysed. There was nothing he could do to stop the vote. And even if he could, he knew it wouldn't help Australia.

Blatter reasoned he just had to let this play out. Perhaps his fellow Executive Committee members would also realise that the World Cup couldn't be held in the desert heat.

And if all else failed, the Al Jazeera $100 million bonus would help secure the financial success of the 2022 World Cup.

THE WORLD WATCHING, the FIFA Ethics Committee banned Nigeria's Amos Adamu for three years for breaching ethics rules on bribery. Reynald Temarii received a one-year ban for breaching rules on confidentiality and loyalty. The fact that Temarii specifically linked his vote for 2022 with the $4 million grant from Australia was not a concern to the Ethics Committee.

Four others received bans too. All were caught by the same *Sunday Times* fake consultants as Adamu and Temarii. All four were previous Executive Committee members. Ismael Bhamjee of Botswana, Ahongalu Fusimalohi of Tonga, Slim Aloulou of Tunisia and Amadou Diakite of Mali.

At the same time the FIFA Ethics Committee concluded that, despite the rumours which were circulating since at least mid-2009, there was insufficient evidence of collusion between the Spain/Portugal bid and the Qatar bid.

The rumours about Russia and Australia - which were a 'hot' topic amongst Olympic journalists, even if not football journalists - were never investigated. Why not? Perhaps no-one complained, as they had with Spain/Portugal and Qatar? Perhaps the FIFA hierarchy didn't mind if Russia and Australia won? Or perhaps they weren't taken seriously?

In announcing the sanctions against the six men, Blatter's hand-picked Ethics Committee chairman, Claudio Sulser, reserved most of his anger not for the men who were caught offering their vote, but for the journalists and the way they presented their story. He accused them of 'selectively' using excerpts of the fake interviews.

Blatter had his own perspective. 'It's a sad day for football because it's a sad day in life and you cannot always have sunny days.' He also said that he was surprised that people suggest FIFA is corrupt. 'FIFA is recognised in the world of sport as a good organisation.'

Jerome Valcke provided even more comedy. When asked by a journalist whether clarity was needed around the 2018 or 2022 vote, he replied it was a secret ballot and it was a 'clean and transparent process'. If Valcke recognised the implicit contradiction between a secret ballot and transparency, he wasn't letting on.

THE MEDIA TALK was that Temarii and Adamu would appeal their bans.

FFA's preference was to stop this happening in respect of Temarii. FFA's legal advice was that if Temarii accepted the one-year ban and didn't appeal, Oceania's senior vice-president could step into his shoes and vote. Nothing would be lost.

The view was that the least Temarii could do was the honourable thing, of not appealing, in light of the situation he put everyone in. Not to mention the $4 million grant that Oceania was given by Australia. Plus the further money in cash and kind, and all the other concessions Australia gave Oceania since joining Asia five years beforehand.

Oceania's chief executive, Tai Nicholas, joined FFA officials and legal counsel in Sydney to 'war game' the strategy and the possibilities. Unconfirmed rumours circulated that FFA's specialist external legal advisors were assisting Oceania, and FFA was covering Oceania's legal costs.

Even if not true, the rumours of FFA meeting Oceania's costs were not going down too well in Zurich.

By now, the FIFA Executive Committee were receiving daily media reports via the FIFA media department from around the world. They didn't read Bid Books; but they could manage media clippings.

Bin Hammam read the reports emanating from Australia with particular interest. He read that Lowy, in tones that varied from bullying to cajoling, publicly argued that Temarii should not appeal.

He also read what Reynald Temarii was saying. Temarii said that despite the pressures being brought to bear on him - Bin Hammam read that as being from Australia - and the issues at stake for Oceania, he wanted the chance to 'restore my honour, dignity and integrity'.

Knowing that Australia's first round vote would be reduced to one if Temarii appealed, and aware of the rumours circulating about the Australians being close to Russia who were bidding for 2018, Bin Hammam picked up the phone.

He asked his assistant to arrange for Temarii to visit him in Kuala Lumpur as his guest. Bin Hammam would give him the good news in person that he was happy to meet his legal costs, far away from the influence of Australia.

Bin Hammam also called Vitaly Mutko. He had visited Mutko in Moscow, along with his confidante Hany Abo Rida, only a few weeks before. He thought now was a good time to touch base again.

CHAPTER 24
Shunned!

Zurich: November 2010

BY THE TIME Andrew Jennings' much anticipated *Panorama* program was broadcast on BBC television a few days before the vote, the Australian bid team was ensconced in its headquarters at the Hotel Zurichberg.

The program detailed USD$100 million worth of bribes paid to FIFA Executive Committee members and officials over years by the Swiss-based marketing company co-founded by Horst Dassler, known as ISL. The company collapsed in 2001 because of the extent of its debts due to illegal payments throughout the 1990s. It showed documents that detailed the dates and the amounts.

The reaction from most who made a living from football – FIFA, other football associations, the nine bidding nations gathered in Zurich, journalists – was predictable. They either dismissed it as 'old news' or denigrated it as more work by a 'discredited maverick'.

Some went so far as to suggest it was part of a BBC plot to bring down the English bid. Bid chief, Andy Anson, described it as 'unpatriotic'. For months, if not years, afterwards, some members of the English bid team and some English journalists continued to think *Panorama* was the reason they lost.

Sepp Blatter and Jack Warner roundly condemned Jennings and the BBC. Both said they couldn't possibly vote for a country with 'such terrible media'. From their perspective - similar to Lowy, Hargitay and others - the media wasn't about fearlessness and truthfulness. It was to be manipulated, massaged, used and metaphorically at least, owned.

It was – and remains - an attitude common in football.

Lowy wasn't the type to rock the boat at any time, and certainly not a few days out from the vote. He told a media conference in Zurich that he questioned the veracity of the reporting about FIFA.

'I have never seen anything that worried me,' he added.

Yet even with that response designed to appeal to Blatter and the Executive Committee, FFA now had few friends in Zurich.

A Seoul-based English journalist John Duerden questioned: '...*How the Australian consultants with pockets deemed to be deep were, at a sensitive time, allowed to wander around Zurich and talk to committee members while Amos Adamu and Reynald Temarii were barred'.*

THE AUSTRALIAN BID team was buoyed by the fact that the technical inspection report from Chile's FA president, Harold Mayne-Nicholls, was positive. Mayne-Nicholls noted a few shortcomings compared with the powerhouse bids of England and the USA, but these were minor factors. Compared with the other bidders for 2022, Australia rated just as well as Japan, slightly better than South Korea and streets better than Qatar.

The only thing is Lowy and the rest of the Australians must have forgotten that it didn't matter. Andreas Abold told us almost two years beforehand and many times since - the FIFA Executive Committee does not read the technical inspection report. Just as they don't read the Bid Books. And even if they did, Abold also said the decision on who hosted the World Cup was decided on 'intangible things'.

A few days later, FIFA also released independent evaluations of the projected commercial revenues of each potential host nation. It was prepared by the blue-ribbon McKinsey consultants.

Australia's bid was ranked the last of the five bidders for 2022. Why? For the reason Jerome Valcke told us 18 months beforehand - the television revenue just couldn't compete with other bidding nations.

Amongst the 2022 bidders, the USA was given a perfect score by McKinsey as was England for 2018. Qatar only rated two percentage points better than Australia - presumably the Al Jazeera $100 million bonus wasn't included in McKinsey's calculations.

After a one-on-one meeting with Blatter at FIFA HQ in the days leading up to the vote, Lowy publicly railed against the McKinsey report. He questioned McKinsey's capacity to make such a judgement. He pitched his own business credibility as a billionaire against a team of consultants crunching numbers out of an office in smart Bahnhofstrasse in downtown Zurich.

'I don't want to give you a lesson in economics but I can tell you that if 2022 goes to Australia it will be very profitable, especially for FIFA.'

Lowy was also confident that there would be 23 voters. Oceania's senior vice-president, David Chung from Papua New Guinea, was on his way to Zurich as Temarii's replacement, so he could take part in the vote. Oceania's battle was now with FIFA.

Temarii had met with Bin Hammam; but Temarii also believed that David Chung should be able to vote, even if he did exercise his right to appeal. The Oceania confederation and FFA agreed.

But FIFA played hard-ball and said it would only allow Oceania to vote if Temarii admitted he was guilty.

'The banning of the OFC from voting is a decision made by FIFA, not by me,' Temarii said. 'It is my wish that FIFA authorises David Chung to vote.'

Even before the news, Lowy said he was hopeful Australia could still be successful without Oceania's vote. 'I sincerely hope it will not depend on one vote,' he said.

I WATCHED AUSTRALIA's final presentation in the early hours of the morning with nervous excitement and anticipation.

I knew it didn't count. Abold said so many times. But he also said that it needed to be 'perfect', and the world would be watching.

After about five minutes in, I knew we were watching something far from perfect. It was truly awful.

The entire 30 minutes demonstrated that Abold failed to understand Australia, what the bid message was, and the state of football in Australia. It also showed that those on the Australian bid in a position to intervene either didn't have the judgement to realise how bad it was, or the courage to admit their highly paid consultant got it so horribly wrong.

Five years later, when Lowy was departing his role as chairman of FFA, the Australian Academy Award winning director, Philip Noyce, revealed that he was brought in at the last minute to try to 'save' the final presentation. It was so bad that even someone of Noyce's talent and experience couldn't do it.

Who could blame him? What could you possibly do with a cartoon surfing, kleptomaniac kangaroo who stole the World Cup only to have it recovered by the fading Aussie actor, Paul Hogan? If it was possible to stuff every possible outdated cliche of Australia into one short film, this was it.

Or perhaps Abold was cleverly constructing a Pavlovian relationship between the kangaroo stealing the World Cup, and the impending disappearance of $50 million of taxpayers' money down the drain?

I felt unspeakably sad and sorry for the Australians on the bid team who worked so hard. If it wasn't sewn-up beforehand and if voters were wavering about us, the presentation was bad enough to lose us votes, especially compared with the USA's and Qatar's presentations, our main competitors for 2022.

The USA presentation wasn't spectacular, but it had star power with President Bill Clinton and Morgan Freeman fronting it.

Qatar, on the other hand, did have the 'wow' factor. The Emir's second wife, and mother of the bid Chairman, Sheikha Mozah bint Masser Al Missned, began and closed the presentation with a simple question: when will the world be ready for a World Cup in the Middle East.

Noyce's view was that the Qatari's were 'really slick. I had a bad feeling when I saw how professional they were.'

The reaction in Australia to our presentation was best summed up by a moment on radio the next morning.

The host of the blue-ribbon morning current affairs program on the Australian Broadcasting Corporation asked a colleague radio presenter from another program on the same network whether she had seen the final presentation. She said she had only seen the pictures, and put the question back to the host: what did he think about it.

There was an excruciating 15 seconds of silence. It seemed like an age on highly professional live radio from two of Australia's top radio presenters.

'Well, when I got out from under the desk I thought to myself maybe the 22 men making the decision might think it's good. $46 million it cost. $46 million of taxpayers' money to mount this bid,' said the first presenter.

Les Murray lauded it. He stated that the presentation wasn't for 'ordinary people' but for the Executive Committee. He was right about FIFA ExCo not being ordinary people.

An international journalist called me from Zurich to laugh.

'We're all doubled-over with laughter. It was amateurish, obscure, oblique, unfunny and embarrassing. It was so far removed from what we saw a year ago in Cape Town, it's just not the same bid,' he said.

Another journalist wrote to me.

'I watched some of the ExCo faces while it was on and you could see they just didn't get it. Qatar, on the other hand, was polished, professional and had meaning. USA dragged on a bit – but it was Bill Clinton - and at least there was a story to it and you knew what it was about. I asked the other bidders for their reaction and they said nothing on-the-record, but they're all killing themselves laughing. Whoever allowed this to happen should be shot at dawn.'

If you wanted to humiliate Australia and Australia's bid, this presentation orchestrated by Abold, would be hard to beat.

Zurich: December 2010

WHEN THE BID teams rolled-in to Zurich in late November, the intelligence services of each of the nine nations were there too - some in greater numbers than others.

Some were there undercover, as consultants working for Booz or IT fixers from CISCO. Others were there in diplomatic guise.

There were listening devices splitting the atmosphere in and around the Baur au Lac and the hotels where bidders were accommodated. That was until the Russians arrived when they jammed the lot. No ears left, only eyes.

That was when people such as former MI6 agent, Christopher Steele, who had been working for the England bid since 2009, came in to his own. Senior England bid team members knew before the vote was announced that Russia had won 2018. Seven years later, Steele was identified as the person who had compiled a dossier on allegations of collusion between Russia and the election campaign of President Donald Trump.

Vladimir Putin knew it also, which is why he didn't feel the need to be in Zurich until after Russia's win was announced.

It was also at this time that intelligence operatives also learned that, along with Executive Committee Franz Beckenbauer, whose role as a Gazprom ambassador was leaked to Charlie Sale in June, his aide Fedor Radmann was apparently also on the Russian payroll.

A SMALL GROUP was assembled in the elegant living room of Lowy's suite at Zurich's best hotel, the Baur au Lac. It was also the FIFA Executive Committee hotel. There was Frank Lowy, two of his sons David and Steven, his right-hand man Mark Ryan, biographer Jill Margo, and Ben Buckley. The group were apparently so confident of the outcome of the vote, that they were filming their meeting for posterity.

The Executive Committee were in their underground bunker six kilometres away at FIFA headquarters voting.

'Let's go through it again,' said Lowy.

Everyone around him swallowed a sigh. They had counted so many times. Not just in the 36 hours since the final presentation to FIFA's elite, but in the past two years and even prior to that. No-one objected.

Ben picked up his scrap of paper and pen and ticked off the countries as Lowy spoke.

'Germany. Cyprus. Switzerland. Belgium.' Lowy paused.

'There's the big country to the north,' said Ben. Everyone smiled as if taking comfort in a trusted partner.

Lowy continued. 'Russia. This is the five basics that we've had most of the time. All along. There's no doubt about this. Apparently we're going to get two basic Africans.'

'And the two Africans,' echoed Ben.

'That's seven. If we get seven, we can't lose,' said Lowy.

In other words, Australia was counting on the votes of Franz Beckenbauer, Marios Lefkaritis, Sepp Blatter, Michel D'Hooghe, Vitaly Mutko, Jacques Anouma and Issa Hayatou in the first round alone. No wonder Lowy thought Australia couldn't lose.

LATER THAT NIGHT, Lowy stood outside the Congress Hall in the Zurich snow in nervous anticipation of the big announcement.

With him was his closest advisor, Peter Hargitay. They waited to greet their counterparts from the Russian bid. Lowy had got to know a few of the Russians quite well in the past two years.

Photographers, journalists, camera crews and onlookers were milling around outside. All of them were watching who was coming and going. All were trying to assess the look on the faces of the voters and the bidders.

Lowy saw Igor Shuvalov and Vitaly Mutko arrive. He rubbed his gloved hands together and gave a little stomp. It was freezing cold, especially for someone who had come from early summer in Sydney. The sprightly octogenarian took a few steps forward towards the men, his hand extended. Hargitay followed him slowly, head slightly bowed squeezing his nostrils with his thumb and forefinger with a habitual soft snort.

The Russians walked by.

Neither Mutko the voter, or Shuvalov, the head of the bid and Vladimir Putin's finance tsar, looked in Lowy's direction. They didn't accept his outstretched hand. They walked on, staring resolutely ahead.

It was the moment Lowy knew that Australia hadn't won.

And I wondered whether he remembered the conversation with me in his office more than eighteen months beforehand and the story I recounted.

THE WINNERS WERE known at least 20 minutes before they were announced by Blatter. Al Jazeera announced it. Russia and Qatar.

Russia won 2018 at a gallop. It took just two rounds to get the necessary 12 votes to win.

Qatar won 2022 less easily. It took four rounds and came down to a showdown between them and the USA in the final round, with Qatar winning 14-8.

After the announcement, Lowy was in the middle of saying a few disappointed words to the media, his heart obviously heavy, responding to a question on how close Australia came to winning.

US Soccer President, Sunil Gulati, interrupted him discreetly to say that the vote count was released. Australia received one vote and was knocked out in the first round.

It was devastating news. It's one thing to have an acceptable loss. It's quite another to be humiliated.

Lowy finished the interviews as quickly as he could. He could see Mohamed Bin Hammam receiving congratulations from people.

Bin Hammam was so happy. Lowy walked over to him, tapped him on the back. Bin Hammam turned. A look passed over Bin Hammam's eyes. He was genuinely sorry for Lowy.

Bin Hammam embraced Lowy and shook his hand in one movement.

He also couldn't hide his delight that Qatar pulled it off. Not only was the Emir happy, but Qatar's win told Bin Hammam that FIFA was changing. Blatter was losing his grip.

The FIFA presidency was next.

HARGITAY WEIGHED-IN with an interview given to his good friend Les Murray, broadcast on SBS-TV.

Murray – still an Ethics Committee member while working for the government-funded broadcaster SBS – introduced the interview as being about 'at best (the) controversial, at worst scandalous, decision re 2022.'

The interview was Hargitay at his spinning best – flattering fans as the 'real losers' from the outcome – and suggesting that Australia's biggest problem was that they ran a clean bid. He also complained that 'several ExCo members lied to us' - an extraordinary admission from a so-called expert campaigner who apparently believed what he was told by people who were participating in a secret ballot.

'They shake hands, look you in the eye and tell you they're voting for you,' he wailed to the empathetic Murray. 'What motivates 14 men to vote for a country the size of Zurich or Fiji? The infrastructure still has to be created.'

'Are you saying the World Cup was bought?' asked Les Murray breathlessly.

'Ask those people,' said Hargitay.

There was no mention of both Hargitay and Radmann enjoying celebratory scotches and expensive cigars with the Russian bid team in the lobby of the Baur au Lac hotel well into the early hours of the next morning. The same Russian bid team who wouldn't look Frank Lowy in the eye earlier in the evening.

BEFORE CLIMBING INTO bed that night, Lowy was told separately by two Executive Committee members that they voted for Australia. He was a poker player. He was practiced at keeping a poker face. He gave nothing away.

It was a restless night. He tossed and turned, mulling everything over. The promises. The deals. The arrangement with the German FA. The people who told him they'd vote for him.

There had been one voice warning him about Hargitay, Radmann, the Russians and the way FIFA works - me. Not that he would ever admit that publicly.

He wanted to know who lied to him, who voted for him, how Qatar won, the relationship between the consultants and Bin Hammam, who was paid off. He wouldn't rest until he found out.

He spoke long into the night with his sons, who were deeply worried about him, as well as Mark Ryan and Jill Margo. He kept the circle of trust even tighter than usual.

Lowy didn't build the world's biggest retail property empire by giving in easily.

He reasoned it was a long time till 2022. Realistically, he had five years to get the decision overturned. If that happened, and it came to Australia, there would still be plenty of time for the country to get ready: build new stadiums, refurbish others, get other infrastructure up-to-scratch. It would cost the country more than $5 billion to be World Cup ready, but it was worth it.

Even if the tournament went elsewhere, like the USA, he could live with it.

The next morning there was only one thing on Lowy's mind. He intended to do whatever it takes to make sure Qatar didn't host the 2022 World Cup.

CHAPTER 25
Spooks

Doha: January 2011

OF ALL THE places on earth that Frank Lowy didn't want to be, it was Qatar.

But here he was for the 2011 Asian Cup, just a few weeks after the World Cup vote.

To make matters worse, the Australian team were performing well under new coach Holger Osieck which meant he had to stay longer. Putting aside his personal discomfort, Lowy knew it was really a good thing for Australia to make the final, especially as Australia was hosting the next Asian Cup in 2015.

The downside was it also meant that he had to spend time, and make small talk, with people he'd rather be a million miles from. Like Bin Hammam and Blatter, and other Executive Committee members who flew-in for the final between Japan and Australia.

It was times like this when his wealth came in handy. FIFA executives were used to the best, but Lowy could afford to go even better when it suited him. It did now.

Ensconced in the most spacious and luxurious suite in the Ritz-Carlton, assured total privacy and discretion, he was anxiously looking forward to the day ahead.

After deciding last month in Zurich that he would work to get the Qatar decision overturned, he summoned Andreas Abold - the only one of the three consultants he now trusted - to meet with him.

Abold suggested they engage someone with investigatory experience and who knew the underside of the football world. It was a good place to start, Lowy thought. Someone who had good contacts, good networks and could get people to talk when official channels couldn't. Lowy said he was happy with the approach - as long as it wasn't Andrew Jennings. Lowy had also decided to use his contacts in the US to find out more.

Today in his Doha suite, Lowy would meet with Abold and the recommended investigator. He would set them on a path, starting with Worawi Makudi of Thailand and Marios Lefkaritis of Cyprus.

Lowy knew Makudi asked for $5 million to vote for Australia, which he wasn't given. What else did he ask for and from whom? Lowy also suspected that Lefkaritis was doing something with the Russians and the Qataris - he wanted to know what.

London: January 2011

NOT THAT LOWY was the only one digging around.

Former MI6 intelligence officer, Christopher Steele, had been on the case since 2009. Steele was one of two intelligence agencies asked by the English FA to look into the competitor bids. The other agency was Hakluyt. The English FA was particularly interested in one country in which Steele was a recognised expert within the intelligence community: Russia, who England saw as their major competitor.

In September 2009, Steele had been in touch with Andrew Jennings. Steele visited Jennings in rural Cumbria in the north of England to talk with him about what he knew.

Jennings knew a lot. His book on FIFA corruption, FOUL! was published in 2006. Since then, he acquired more information from old as well as new sources, and through good, old-fashioned, hard slog, investigatory work.

Jennings characterised the bidding process as the 'greedy old men of FIFA wanting to get two sets of bungs at once before they dropped off the perch'.

The following year, in June 2010, Jennings was invited by Steele to a meeting in London.

Waiting for him in an anonymous office block off Berkeley Square, were three smartly-dressed Americans. Trim and fit, neatly dressed with crew cuts, good for a street rumble. Jennings said they looked like former Marines.

In that open, friendly, charming way that Americans have when they are at their best, they shook hands, smiles wide with pearly white teeth, while one of them handed Jennings his business card. It read:

Special Agent, Organized Crime Squad, Federal Plaza, New York

It was the FBI.

Another of the agents was the Chief of the Organised Crime and Racketeering Section of the Department of Justice in Washington.

These were the men who got Al Capone and John Gotti. And now they wanted Jennings' help to nail Blatter and his FIFA rogues.

It was a dream come true for the crusty investigative journalist.

Jennings was reviled by the Olympic movement and FIFA, and banned from attending their media conferences or events. Fighting sports corruption - to which Jennings moved after a long stint as a financial investigative journalist - was a lonely occupation that required nerves of steel and a focus on the long game. At last, here were serious people who shared his view about FIFA, asking serious questions.

The concern of the FBI the first time they met in June 2010? Qatar. They were convinced that something wasn't right.

It was the same as David Downs told me in November 2010; that, since June, the Americans were only worried about Qatar.

Now today, seven months after that first meeting and little more than one month after the vote, the FBI had returned to meet with Jennings again.

Jennings had knowledge, facts, dates, documents and archives. Each time he met them, there were more and more detailed questions. And as they talked, he also figured out where the biggest time bomb was ticking. It was sitting under a very large man four miles north of their Federal Plaza headquarters in Trump Tower - the US FIFA Executive Committee member and CEO of CONCACAF, Chuck Blazer.

Sydney: February 2011

FAR AWAY FROM spooks, Ben Buckley called me wanting to meet for coffee. I sat in the lobby lounge of the city hotel he nominated, watching the comings and goings. I noticed him as soon he walked through the door. He was on the phone.

He stopped and continued his conversation which, judging by the look on his face, was tiresome for him.

We headed for the adjacent coffee lounge where we found a quiet corner.

It was the perfect place for a private conversation in a public place.

After coffee and pleasantries were out of the way, Ben shifted and leaned forward in his chair.

'I'm really pleased that we're meeting. It's been a terrible twelve months,' he continued.

'It could have been better,' I said.

'And the worst part of it was what happened to you.'

He looked at me intently. I knew what he was about to say.

'I am so, so sorry.' He swallowed, looked down and then back at me. 'I had to do it.'

I said nothing.

'I didn't want to do it, but I had to.'

I was still silent.

'It has troubled me for ages. All year. I didn't want to hurt you. I thought the other job would be enough. But the consultants wanted you gone completely.'

He continued. 'But you know how much you and I enjoyed working together. You know I have immense respect for you. More than anyone I've ever worked with. You know what I said to you in Zurich. You know I think you are the best communications person I have ever worked with.' He swallowed. 'I want us to be friends again.'

For Ben, that was a long speech.

I paused. There was plenty I could say to argue the point, but it really didn't matter. Instead I said I was happy to be friends again too.

He told me the consultants became 'even worse' after I left.

'Peter became unbearable,' he told me.

Was that supposed to be a surprise?

'He got so bad even Frank had to talk to him a few times and tell him to cool it. I thought I was going to explode with it all at times. The year was a nightmare.'

It seemed now he had started talking, he wasn't going to stop.

'I knew the final presentation was weak. I mean, compare it with what you did in Cape Town. It was just so bad.'

'Yes it was,' I said. 'But Qatar's was superb,' I continued. 'They nailed it from beginning to end. Who can resist a World Cup in the Middle East?'

He went on, as if not hearing me. 'I almost walked out on the job a couple of times because of Peter and the others. It was unbearable.' That word again.

'There's nothing much I can say about that Ben. Except 'I told you so'. I indicated a quote with my hands.

He sighed. 'Yeah, I know, I know. You also knew you were going to be the loser against them. We couldn't let them go. They were part of the deal. You weren't.'

Sydney: March 2011

WHEN BEN SACKED me 13 months beforehand, I did what many others did in that situation: I signed a confidentiality agreement. An old friend, a well-known Australian economist, characterises them as 'We won't tell any lies about you if you don't tell the truth about us'.

This one was more onerous than most. It was specific about the World Cup bid and its consultants.

My meeting with Ben encouraged me to be less restricted by it. I focussed my criticism on FIFA and its decision-making processes. I went public via *The Australian* newspaper saying our bid was 'naive' for trusting in FIFA, and it was disappointing that FFA ran what I termed a 'reputational risk' with the hiring of its international consultants.

I was also critical of FIFA and its decades of corruption.

The decision to award the 2018 and 2022 World Cup tournaments to Russia and Qatar were merely a recent example of where the FIFA Executive Committee's decision-making was apparently made in their own best interests, rather than the best interests of the game.

Like others interested in these issues, I had read Professor Alan Tomlinson and journalists Andrew Jennings, Thomas Kistner and Jens Weinreich. I had also seen people like Blatter, others associated with Oceania football and the Asian Football Confederation at fairly close quarters, in addition to my bid experience. The deal-making was a way of life. Too many people had been in charge for too long and change was desperately needed.

Because of this, the decision made by the 22 men on 2 December 2010 was the best thing that ever happened at FIFA.

If, say, England and Australia had won, or Holland/Belgium and the USA, the same flawed bidding and decision-making processes and people would still have been in place. But those decisions would have been more acceptable, and the rest of the world may not have given the 'FIFA way' a second thought.

Qatar was such an outrageous choice for so many, on the basis of its size, its climate, its lack of football pedigree and an implicit cultural backlash, that it got the world watching and talking. Russia was less so because it was seen as a 'football country'.

TWO MEN WHO ran a social media group called Change FIFA were in touch with me in March 2011. They wanted my assistance in getting in touch with Lowy. It wasn't clear how, or why, but they found a candidate to stand for the FIFA presidency - 65 year old former Chilean great, Elias Figueroa. With nominations due by the end of the month, the two men who ran the social media account were searching for football associations to nominate Figueroa, and they figured Australia - having been so badly burnt by FIFA at the vote in December - might be a possibility.

Separately, US journalist Grant Wahl contacted me for the same purpose. Disgusted by the decision in December, he wanted to make sure there was an alternative also.

I contacted Lowy. I put to him what I saw as the advantages of him taking a leadership role in world football and nominating either Figueroa or Wahl, rather than supporting the alternatives of Blatter or Bin Hammam. I reasoned that if the Australian bid had nothing to hide - as he and so many proclaimed - there was no reason for someone in Lowy's position to have an allegiance to either of the declared candidates.

'I don't want to do this at this time, Bonita,' he told me. 'It doesn't suit what I want to achieve.'

It was some years later that I was able to piece together what else was going on that prompted Lowy to say it didn't suit him to take a stand against FIFA.

New York: April 2011

WORK HAD BEEN underway on Lowy's private investigation for three months. More people were recruited to the project. Lawyer, Roger Klein of Sheppard Mullin, was kept busy preparing contracts for project team members on the scope of work.

Now here they all were in a high rise midtown Manhattan office that belonged to Mark Bieler, a human resources expert. Besides Westfield, for whom he was a trusted consultant, Bieler's client list included Morgan Stanley, Ogilvy and Mather, Mercantile Trust and the CIA.

Abold and the investigator had flown-in from Europe.

There was William Green, founder and managing partner of TD International. Headquartered in Washington DC, TD International guides clients through the maze of political, regulatory and reputational risks.

There was also James Pavitt. White-haired, with a ruddy complexion, Pavitt had the air of someone used to authority and attention. He was a long-serving officer in the CIA's clandestine service and was its deputy director of operations for five years. He now worked as an intelligence consultant for the Scowcroft Group, another DC headquartered outfit providing business advisory services headed by former US National Security Advisor, Brent Scowcroft.

Even as the unlikely group were introduced to one another around the table, Pavitt had his Blackberry in his hand, constantly screening it.

On a video conference link from Australia were Lowy, his son Steven and Lowy's omnipresent right-hand man, Mark Ryan.

The investigation now had a name - *Project Platinum.*

With the group's access to information and intelligence - *'If we have a mobile phone number, we have everything'* Pavitt boasted at the meeting - this was a completely new stratosphere for Abold and the investigator.

But for all their extensive, high-level Washington insider knowledge and network, the others knew absolutely nothing about football, FIFA or the key actors.

IN THE THREE months since they met Lowy in Doha, Abold and the investigator managed to chase promising leads in Thailand and Cyprus.

A private detective was engaged in Thailand who managed to track down details of arrangements concerning the Thai FA's training and administrative headquarters at Chonburi. Similar to the arrangement Jack Warner had with the Joao Havelange Stadium in Trinidad and Tobago, the Chonburi development was paid for by FIFA; but the owner of the land was none other than Executive Committee member,

Worawi Makudi.

Coincidentally, part of Australia's $5 million gift to Vision Asia went to Chonburi to purchase new equipment after flooding in 2008. No-one seems to know if it ever arrived.

In Cyprus, they met a man who said he had documents that would prove who was paid-off by the Qataris via Executive Comittee member Marios Lefkaritis.

They talked of the two women who had gone public.

The first who worked for the Qatar bid, and whose claims revolving around a meeting in Angola in January 2010, were published in November that year. And me, who had been head of corporate and public affairs for the Australian bid.

'No, don't worry about her,' Bieler said, referring to me. 'Let's try to find the Qatari woman. She could be helpful.'

This was a priority.

The investigator also learned that Christopher Steele, who was originally engaged by the English FA, was still looking into the Russians. Steele was now so interested in the investigation that he was continuing it for his own purposes. The investigator and Abold also learned that Steele was willing to share the information with other bidders for a price. As *Project Platinum* was apparently not constrained by budget concerns, they raised this as a possibility.

'We're not interested in the Russians,' Pavitt said.

Not even when Steele said - much to Abold's apparent shock and horror - that Radmann, Australia's highest paid consultant, was also paid by the Russians? Or when Lowy was jilted by the Russians outside the Zurich Congress Hall on the night of the vote?

'Forget the Russians,' came the instruction from the Sydney video link.

London: May 2011

BEFORE A HOUSE of Commons Committee of Inquiry into the failed 2018 Bid, the former Chairman of the English FA and England Bid, Lord David Triesman, spoke under Parliamentary privilege about his experiences with some of the FIFA Executive Committee.

He told a packed Committee room that Jack Warner asked for £2.5 million for a school in Haiti which had been struck by a massive earthquake. The payment was to go via Warner's bank account.

Nicolas Leoz of Paraguay sought a knighthood.

Worawi Makudi of Thailand wanted a match against England and the broadcast rights for the game.

And Ricardo Teixeira simply asked him *'What do you have for me?'*

Lord Triesman didn't raise these issues with FIFA during the bidding process: not when he was still Chairman or even after he had been forced to leave in March 2010. The Committee criticised him on this point in their report a few weeks later. Triesman said that he did not do so as it would have undermined the English Bid for 2018:

> *"There was a huge amount of pressure to try and secure these games for England, a huge desire not to burn off any prospect of doing so, and although there have from time to time been some discussions with people at FIFA, the point was not pressed."*

Triesman was in the bid race reluctantly. The decision for England to bid again so soon after it was well-and-truly beaten in the race for the 2006 World Cup was made before he became President of the English FA. It was strongly supported by the then Prime Minister, Gordon Brown.

When Triesman started in the role in 2008, the nascent bid team had engaged ECN to be their strategic consultants. ECN was then co-owned by Peter Hargitay and former FIFA communications director, Markus Siegler. Triesman was aghast. Hargitay was not a man he wanted working for the England bid.

A person with a background in an intelligence service knew how to eavesdrop, he knew how to spy, he knew how to intercept signals, he knew how to set-up entrapments, he knew how to generate fake news, he knew how to identify people who might be whistleblowers, he knew how to intimidate and bully, he worked out who was vulnerable, and who might be helpful.

Triesman didn't want to win - or lose - that way. At the end of ECN's initial six-month contract, he insisted the bid team run a competitive process for their strategy consultants. ECN did not submit a proposal.

Ostensibly, Hargitay and Siegler parted ways after their contract was finished with the English FA. Within weeks, Hargitay turned-up with the Australian bid and Siegler with the Russian bid.

Triesman also talked with FIFA about withdrawing from the bid in 2009 after Blatter addressed bidders in Zurich and talked of his wish to see the two tournaments in 'new lands'.

When Jerome Valcke told Ben Buckley and me in July 2009 that we were not competitive due to television revenues - a point repeated by Hany Abo Rida in October that year and borne out by the McKinsey report 17 months later - Valcke also begged the English bid not to withdraw for the opposite reason. Like the USA for 2022, they were given a perfect score by McKinsey. A World Cup in England would be hugely profitable to FIFA.

DAVID TRIESMAN WASN'T the only person to appear before the House of Commons Inquiry.

The Sunday Times duo of Jonathan Calvert and his then investigative partner, Claire Newell, gave testimony about six football officials, in addition to Adamu and Temarii, that they spoke with in their undercover operation posing as consultants for the US bid from the fictitious Franklin Jones consultancy firm. They claimed that the interviews showed that 'vote buying was clearly engrained in the bidding process'.

They described the conversations they had with each of the men. In each case, they pointed to what Calvert and Newell presented as further evidence of Qatar's vote-buying.

They also testified that they also received information from the Qatar whistleblower. It was now widely known amongst journalists and others that the Qatar whistleblower was Phaedra Almajid, an American-born Iraqi who had worked as International Media Officer for the Qatar bid until March 2010.

According to Calvert and Newell, Almajid repeated the claim that Anouma, Hayatou and Adamu were promised payments of $1.5 million each 'no questions asked'.

Because Calvert's and Newell's testimony was made under Parliamentary privilege, every media outlet in the world was free to report what was presented to Parliament without fear of legal action. It drove much of the narrative around Qatar's World Cup win for years - and still does in the minds of many.

Washington DC: May 2011

THERE WAS A quiet air of excitement in the offices of William Green's TD International in Washington, where *Project Platinum* was having its second meeting.

The project team pored over the submissions and transcript of the House of Commons Inquiry. They wanted to find the 'Qatari woman' and discussed how they would deal with her testimony.

Already, they were having success in identifying influencers everywhere who were prepared to focus on the negatives of Qatar hosting the World Cup.

The International Trade Union Confederation would soon release a damning report that looked at the rights of the temporary foreign workers employed in Qatar. Researchers for Amnesty International were on to the issue also.

Their work was also bearing fruit within FIFA. Louis Freeh's company had just been engaged to assist in investigations.

Freeh was a former FBI agent, former deputy state attorney-general in the Southern District of New York (SDNY), former Judge of the SDNY court, and eight years as FBI director.

James Pavitt, of *Project Platinum*, knew Freeh. They were part of the Washington swamp together.

CHAPTER 26
An 'empty gesture'

May 2011

THE FIFA PRESIDENTIAL campaign between Sepp Blatter and Mohamed Bin Hammam was drawing to a close. Election day was 1 June 2011.

Bin Hammam announced his candidacy right on the deadline date at the end of March. If he was busy beforehand, he was even more so during the campaign, attending to people who sought money, criss-crossing the globe, responding to requests for media interviews.

After writing a flattering congratulatory letter to Bin Hammam at the end of 2010 following Qatar's win, Hargitay was back in his employ and busy in the thick of the action, coordinating media relations for Bin Hammam's election campaign.

He sent emails to Bin Hammam during the campaign bragging of his efforts in placing friendly media reports with Michael Wulzinger of *Der Spiegel*, Andrew Warshaw of *Inside World Football*, Osasu Obayiuwana of *New Africa*, and Philippe Auclair of *France Football*. He wrote that all the journalists were friends of his. He made note of his special influence with *Inside World Football*.

Bin Hammam's presidential manifesto outlined similar themes to the one Hargitay and occasional business partner/employee, Paul Nicholson, prepared for him two years before for his Asian Football Confederation election - but with a twist. Bin Hammam presented himself as the 'reform candidate'. Some actually believed it.

His campaign was also run closely with World Sports Group (WSG), the rights holder for Asian Football Confederation matches. Bin Hammam was godfather to the son of the head of WSG, Seamus O'Brien. Just as Bin Hammam was sent the invoice for work performed by Hargitay two years before, Pierre Kakhia of WSG was again sent bills for some of the consultants involved in Bin Hammam's campaign. Key amongst them were multiple accounts for a young South Korean web designer who over many months earned well over USD$1 million, some of it collected in cash.

SEPP BLATTER REALISED he was in trouble.

Bin Hammam had money. He knew what it takes to win in FIFA - after all, he helped Blatter win the presidency 13 years before. Bin Hammam's win with the World Cup was evidence of what he could do, and Blatter knew Bin Hammam had been preparing for his tilt at the top job for years.

FIFA staff - past and present - all agree that everything that happened at FIFA was about one thing and one thing only: keeping Sepp Blatter in the top job.

'Blatter will do whatever it takes to stay in power,' more than one former FIFA executive told me.

Blatter knew what he needed to do.

It was all about to come crashing down for Mohamed Bin Hammam, as well as Jack Warner.

One week before the presidential election, UK media reported that the pair were accused of attempting to bribe 25 Caribbean football officials with a payment of $40,000 each at a specially-organised meeting in Port of Spain. The travelling party accompanying Bin Hammam to Port of Spain included his good friends Hany Abo Rida of Egypt and Worawi Makudi of Thailand, both FIFA Executive Committee members at the time of 2018/2022 vote, Manilal Fernando of Sri Lanka who was at the time an Executive Committee member, and Bin Hammam's cashed-up South Korean web designer. Quite an excursion for a web designer.

On the same morning the media report about the meeting in the Caribbean appeared, Franz Beckenbauer was in touch with Bin Hammam. Beckenbauer retired from the Executive Committee two months before, his position taken by Theo Zwanziger, head of the German FA.

Beckenbauer learned that Lowy was spending big money investigating how Australia lost. He was on the warpath. Lowy thought all the promises were in place, and all the usual players lined-up to deliver it - Bin Hammam, Beckenbauer, Radmann, Abold. Lowy's view was he had a deal with the German FA, signed-off by Zwanziger and Schmidt. They should honour it.

Even before the business with Warner in the Caribbean became known, Beckenbauer wanted to tell Bin Hammam about Lowy's investigations. He also intended to tell Bin Hammam he is supporting Blatter, and that Bin Hammam should withdraw from the race.

When Bin Hammam returned to Zurich from London after meeting with Beckenbauer, he was invited to another private meeting. This time it was with his election rival, Sepp Blatter.

He arrived to find Sheikh Jassim of Qatar there also, son of the Emir and the former heir apparent.

The deal was already done between the Blatter and Sheikh Jassim before Bin Hammam got there. Bin Hammam was to withdraw his candidacy, and Blatter would continue to hold back the marauding lances wanting to take away the 2022 World Cup from Qatar - just as the Emir and Blatter had agreed the previous December.

A statement was handed to Bin Hammam announcing his withdrawal from the presidential race. Beckenbauer publicly welcomed the news, and called for football to unite behind Blatter.

Bin Hammam later told a trusted friend from Zurich that Blatter also promised at the same meeting that he would make sure the allegations against Bin Hammam and his trip to the Caribbean meeting to meet with football officials would disappear.

THE ETHICS COMMITTEE hearing was held the next day, Sunday. They met with Blatter, Warner and Bin Hammam.

Blatter was called before the committee because he knew that money would change hands in the Caribbean - Warner told him - but he did nothing to stop it.

Unsurprisingly, in a soft Ethics Committee hearing - comprised of members all appointed by him - Blatter was found not guilty. The basis for the decision was that it wasn't his job to stop people from doing the wrong thing - a metaphor for the administration of FIFA, if ever there was one.

Warner and Bin Hammam were suspended.

On the basis that Blatter promised him to help make the allegations disappear, Bin Hammam vowed to fight. Warner opted to resign from all football activity before the FIFA Ethics Committee could consider his case.

Blatter was happy because he had the FIFA presidential election all to himself again.

FFA did nothing.

Lowy went to ground. He was hospitalised and not able to travel to Zurich, although he was receiving regular updates on the progress of *Project Platinum.*

Meanwhile, in Zurich for the Congress meeting and Presidential election, a small group of member associations, led by the Scandinavian countries and England, abstained from voting as a point of principle.

I text messaged Ben saying *'Please tell me you voted the right way'* - meaning, that Australia would also abstain.

But no; FFA voted for Blatter.

MY LONG HELD view was that some form of intervention was necessary to see real reform at FIFA, and for it to be led by an eminent, independent person with no skin in the game.

There was a network of people around the world dedicated to raising this issue publicly. One of the most vocal was British MP, Damian Collins, who encouraged other MPs to join him in a call for reform of FIFA.

I wrote to several Australian politicians urging them to join him: the new Sports Minister, the opposition sports spokesperson, selected federal and state parliamentarians, and my two federal and state local members - who happened to be the federal Opposition Leader and state Treasurer at the time.

> *'The simple fact is that FIFA is not capable of reforming itself. Sepp Blatter has been in power as President or CEO since 1981. While FIFA has grown more commercially successful and has built the World Cup into being one of the most prestigious sporting events in the world in his time as President, it has also developed a culture where they are incapable of recognising good governance.'*

I told them that the World Cup bidding process was a symptom of FIFA's poor governance, and talked of the *'sticky fingers'* of football administrations worldwide.

> *'But the much bigger issue - and the reason why the bidding process was ambiguous and flawed in the first place - is that FIFA does not have in place the level of governance and accountability that we expect of our major institutions and organisations. Reform of governance arrangements to achieve democracy, transparency and accountability is the first order issue.'*

Only one Australian politician was interested. Senator Nick Xenophon contacted Damian Collins.

ON HIS RETURN to Australia from the Congress vote, Ben made a rare television appearance, in response to media pressure from me. He said that FFA would 'work with FIFA to review governance structures.'

'It was in the best interests of Australia to vote for Sepp Blatter,' Ben said. 'To do otherwise would be an empty gesture.'

Why?

CHAPTER 27
The search for a smoking gun

London: July 2011

THE *Project Platinum* team was spending money all over the world, talking to people. But they still did not have what was considered a 'smoking gun'.

What they did find was a receptive media, eager to expose how Qatar won. Influencing media and civil society organisations was a priority identified in their first meeting. Now their work was starting to bear fruit.

They were also tapping into freelance journalists and bloggers, people who might otherwise be seen as not being particularly close to, or friendly towards, those pulling the strings in *Project Platinum*; those with a reputation for independence.

What *Project Platinum* discovered - whether 'fake news' or not - was leaked strategically, mostly to unsuspecting writers who thought an 'exclusive' fell into their lap. For example, Jesse Fink in Australia - once close to Lowy as the editor of the first edition of Jill Margo's biography of him, but now estranged. Another, was an even more unlikely target: Jean-Francois Tanda in Switzerland. Tanda realised some time later that he was used.

The *Project Platinum* team held discussions with American *60 Minutes* about a documentary. They hoped the Qatar bid whistleblower, Phaedra Almajid, would feature in it. They agreed to arrange for a third party to approach her, rather than ask her directly.

Mark Bieler, the man coordinating *Project Platinum* wanted even more noise in the world's media; more stories and blogs about the issues to help spread the message and expand the global reach of their efforts.

There was one slight hiccup.

Not long before Bin Hammam was due to appear before the FIFA Ethics Committee, Almajid withdrew her claim against Qatar and the three African voters she implicated.

On a specially-created website, Almajid published an open letter saying she wanted *'to hurt the bid like they had hurt me.'* Almajid said she realised it had gone too far when Sepp Blatter said in Zurich that there would most likely be a re-vote because of her evidence.

'I want to make it clear that the Qatar 2022 bid committee never engaged in the behaviour I accused them of,' she wrote in the open letter.

It later emerged that at the time this happened, her ex-boss, Nasser Al-Khater, was in Washington DC near where she lived. He wanted to make sure she agreed to the affidavit that was prepared by London law firm, (formerly) Olswang, and to get it to media as soon as possible.

Somewhat incredibly, Al-Khater, who is now the deputy CEO of the Qatar 2022 Organising Committee, and his boss Hassan Al-Thawadi hoped Almajid's retraction would be the end of the constant speculation and innuendo that started even before they won. For those who were not inclined to believe Almajid, it was proof she was lying. For those who were inclined to believe her, the retraction made it worse for Qatar as it was widely viewed as coercion.

Almajid contacted journalist Andrew Jennings. She told him that Al-Khater had given her an ultimatum saying that they would invoke a $1 million confidentiality clause, and that she was frightened. Jennings let his friends in the FBI know.

The FBI sprung into action, ready to remove Almajid and her children to a safe location. They told her to shut down her communications and social media accounts. They took away her hard drive. They promised to protect her.

I WAS ASKED by journalists whether I knew Almajid, and what I thought about everything that was happening.

I met her once during the bidding phase, very briefly in Cape Town in December 2009. It was at the media expo at the international launch of the bids.

My view was that, regardless of whether she told the truth or not about what went on in that meeting room in Angola in January 2010, she must be feeling terrible. Either it was true and she was under pressure to retract, or it wasn't true and she was genuinely trying to right it.

I tracked down her contact details and got in touch to let her know I was thinking of her.

Sydney: July 2011

'BONITA, IT'S QUENTIN McDermott from *Four Corners*.'

Quentin McDermott was a veteran television journalist on the Australian Broadcasting Corporation's (ABC) blue ribbon public affairs program, *Four Corners*. I was aware that they had been interested in doing a program before the vote in 2010; I was approached by two third parties to find out if I would appear. I declined.

Even before the latest call from McDermott, I heard through player agent, Chris Tanner, that the program was back on the drawing board again.

Tanner was instrumental in getting *Four Corners* interested in focussing on the management decisions made by FFA – from the World Cup bid to botched expansion of the A-League and especially the bid with which he was involved for a team from western Sydney he dubbed the 'Wanderers'. The name, concept and colours of the team that would eventually be known as the Western Sydney Wanderers, and which won the Asian Champions League after its first season, originated with the work of Tanner and a business partner. They were credited with none of it by FFA.

McDermott wanted to know if I would reconsider being part of the program. He was taking a broader focus, was travelling to London, and would also speak with Andrew Jennings, Damian Collins MP and Peter Hargitay.

Quite a line-up. 'And FFA?' I asked.

'They're not cooperating, and they also say Frank Lowy is ill.'

It was no surprise that FFA was not cooperating, and it was known that Lowy had been hospitalised earlier in the year. He recovered well enough one month later in August to make a brief airport visit to Amman in Jordan, for a meeting with Prince Ali bin Al-Hussein.

Thanks to the patronage of Blatter, Prince Ali was now a member of the FIFA Executive Committee, as well as on the Asian Football Confederation Executive Committee. Prince Ali was also a good friend to Australia. Not long afterwards Prince Ali used his new position, together with longstanding FFA Board member and AFC executive member Moya Dodd, to push for an audit of AFC accounts by PwC.

McDermott contacted me again when he returned from London several weeks later. He said the first surprise for him was when Hargitay turned-up at the interview with two Schillings lawyers and his own camera man who was a stringer for Al Jazeera.

'I don't recall that ever happening before,' he told me over the phone. 'He said you were sacked because you were incompetent and he implied there was a confrontation with him.'

I laughed. 'Only one confrontation? There were more. And as for being incompetent, I know that's not what Ben or Frank thought.'

'I've met and interviewed many different people in all my years as a journalist. Some of them have not been nice people or good people. But he was so personally nasty and very vindictive towards you. I just couldn't believe it,' he said.

McDermott's crisp English accent was flattened only a little by many years living in Australia. As a seasoned investigative journalist, he also wasn't given to exaggeration.

McDermott also met with *The Sunday Times'* Jonathan Calvert and Claire Newell in London, and was shown the transcript of Ahongalu Fusimalohi from Tonga, who was also caught in their sting in November the year before. Fusimalohi, a FIFA Executive Committee member when the South Africa 2010 decision was made, had plenty to say about Australia.

The Tongan told the fake consultants on tape that Lowy 'wouldn't pay a penny' himself so he got the government to give the money to Oceania. He also told them that Australia had no chance of winning, as the head of the African confederation, Issa Hayatou, didn't like Australia and would do everything in his power to prevent their win. This was at a time when - we learned much later - Lowy was counting on two votes from Africa.

Calvert confirmed with McDermott that Oceania's vote was directed to Australia because of the $4 million FFA arranged to be given via the Australian government's aid agency.

'It seemed as if Australia had done a huge aid deal with Oceania to ensure that Oceania's vote was going to go for Australia. And he was quite clear on that, that the reason that they were voting for Australia was because they'd been given all this money.' Calvert said on the *Four Corners* program.

I did the interview with *Four Corners*.

FFA was informed beforehand of the issues the program raised and were given another opportunity to appear. Ben instead sent correspondence to football's stakeholders saying that the program contained nothing more than issues that had been raised previously and should be ignored.

The broadcast of the program was delayed further until September, because the government promised that the final report from FFA that acquitted the $46 million grant was on its way. It eventually arrived the day of the broadcast.

No-one had any time to examine it; McDermott could not do anything other than show it on camera.

Following the program, FFA senior executives and stakeholders disparaged and abused me on social media - helped by other people who had not even met me, and who had no familiarity with the bid.

THERE WAS NO time to examine the final report for the *Four Corners* program but when I did get a chance to take a look at it, it was clear it wasn't a forensic audit. It was a bureaucratic 'tick the box' action to satisfy the funding agreement.

The report wasn't an examination of what went right and what went wrong with the bid. And it certainly wasn't a full account of all the monies spent in the bid's name. For example, the $4 million that Reynald Temarii sought and received; while it was from a different 'bucket' of money to the principal grant, it was still government money and should have rated a mention in the report.

Despite the fact that FFA won a 'Dream Asia' award from the Asian Football Confederation in November 2010 for a $5 million gift, only one-quarter of that amount was accounted for in the final report. If the $5 million was paid, where did it come from? And where did it go?

At the time it would be almost three years before we knew about it, but there was no mention of the USD$462,200 given to Jack Warner.

The bid budget that was prepared after the government grant was announced, which the FFA bid management team were shown on four or five occasions when I was still there - and were never allowed to take out of the room - allocated $4 million to Africa. According to FFA's final report, we spent only $240,000 in Africa.

The final report showed that Hargitay's ECN received $1.45 million – around

$60,000 a month for 24 months. Hargitay says it was a modest fee that covered three consultants and a part-time assistant.

There was no account in FFA's final report of what Fedor Radmann did for the $3.63 million he received - more than $150,000 a month for 24 months, or how this money was used.

As such an amount was extraordinary, I always assumed that it included a cut for Franz Beckenbauer. This was confirmed to me many years later by more than one former high-level football official, as well as by Sepp Blatter who told me that Beckenbauer wouldn't publicly support Australia for nothing, and that Radmann always had 'some sort of scheme' going.

Apparently when Michel Platini found out Beckenbauer received money from Australia towards the end of 2010 and before the vote - thought to be more than USD$1.5 million - he was furious. With Australia, with Beckenbauer, and with Blatter.

Most perplexing of all, the bid budget also allocated $6.5 million in bonuses: $4 million to Radmann, $2.5 million to Hargitay. Yet Hargitay showed *Four Corners* a contract which showed no bonus.

And, if there were bonuses totalling $6.5 million, why wasn't this refunded in full to the government? FFA's final report showed that roughly only half that amount was returned. Where did the rest go?

The answer, according to the final report, is to the three things that didn't count: the Bid Book, the technical inspection and the final presentation. Despite being a world expert in these matters, the activities for which Andreas Abold was responsible cost $10.1 million against Abold's contract for $3.2 million. How did he underestimate the task by so much? Not only did Abold misjudge the final presentation utterly in terms of narrative, but he was way out of whack on his budget.

For me, it raised even more questions for which I did not yet have all the answers.

Doha: November 2011

'YOU DO REALISE that everyone thought Russia, Radmann and Hargitay, and therefore Australia, were colluding?' the man in the bar at the W Hotel in Doha asked me. He worked with the Qatar World Cup 'supreme committee'.

I was at a function for about 30 people, hosted by Qatar's 2022 Organising Committee, with journalists from England, Egypt, Ireland, Germany, Brazil and South Korea. The five hosts were Hassan Al-Thawadi, Nasser Al-Khater, Phaedra Almajid's replacement David Barrett, and two Australian women who worked for the Qatar Organising Commtitee.

I had travelled to Doha because I wanted to catch-up with one of the UK-based journalists who, along with the other journalists, was travelling to a sports exhibition and conference, combined with a friendly match between Egypt and Brazil. This journalist was in touch with me with information that could be helpful to my inquiries. The Middle East was a good mid-point to meet. Like the other journalists present, the journalists' trip was predominantly covered by the Qataris. I was there self-funded in a private capacity.

'It was fairly well known amongst the other bidders,' the Qatar employee said. 'And then we saw Hargitay and Radmann drinking with the Russians before the vote.'

'The night before? I heard it was after the vote.'

'Both. The night after the vote was a private party. We've got the evidence.'

'Really? I'd love to see it.'

'Lowy and Hargitay also went out in the snow to meet the Russians on the night of the vote.' He looked at me intently. 'Why would they do that? We thought it was very unlike Lowy.'

'Did you see this or did someone tell you?'

'I saw it. Others saw it too. But I personally saw it.' He looked at me intently again. 'You're not here as a Frank Lowy spy are you?'

I laughed. 'No, I promise I'm not. I haven't spoken with him since March. But I am writing a book and this conversation is likely to be in it.'

He smiled at me sideways. 'Well that's okay. You realise we had to send Lowy a 'cease and desist' letter? He was making inquiries everywhere, investigators all over the place. Last count, he had 20 or 30 private investigators, lawyers and journalists around the world working on the case. We also know he's been putting pressure on people.'

'What type of pressure on whom?'

'He's trying to find out how we won. He's trying to prove we did the wrong thing. He won't find anything,' the man said.

'No?'

'No.' His demeanour became more agitated. 'What people don't realise is that we worked very hard to win this. The other bidders made mistakes. We just stuck to our plan and kept going.' He looked away into the distance a little before turning back to me. 'We thought you – Australia – had it won in Cape Town. You had the best film. Without question. It was superb. The ambush marketing with the kids was brilliant. But then you – that is, Australia – just dropped off the radar.'

I shrugged my shoulders. He continued.

'We know that he will do whatever it takes - anything - to see this taken off us.'

'You may be right, but I really wouldn't know. Tell me, who voted for us?'

'Beckenbauer. Definitely. You would have had Temarii too.'

'And who voted for you?'

'Bin Hammam, Makudi, the three Africans, the three from South America. We're fairly sure of Erzik, Lefkaritis, D'Hooghe.'

'Plus Mutko,' I said.

'And Platini. More people said they voted for us than the number of votes we got. For example, Chung from South Korea and Ogura from Japan. They should have voted for us because it's Asia, but I think they probably voted for the US.' He paused. 'But really, Bonita, I don't want to upset you. Australia wasn't in it. In 2010, it was all down hill for Australia. By the time you guys finally decided in June only to go for 2022, you weren't even in the race.'

Exactly the same as the FBI told Andrew Jennings and Christopher Steele in June 2010, and what David Downs said to me in October 2010.

Sydney: November 2011

'IT'S JILL MARGO here,' said the voice on the end of the phone. Lowy's biographer. This was unexpected.

'I just wanted to say how fantastic you were on *Four Corners*. It would have been very difficult for you, but you came across as very measured, very professional.'

She told me she was working on an update of Lowy's biography and wanted to interview me for it.

'Frank knows I'm asking you,' she said. 'I particularly want your view on what went wrong with the World Cup bid, but I'd also like to go back to when you first met him.'

Lowy and I met more than a decade before. I convened a group of journalists, players, fans and administrators who wanted to see change in football from what was a moribund and largely unprofessional administration. The group involved journalists Matthew Hall, the late Michael Cockerill, Neal Jameson and Kyle Patterson, retired players Andy Harper and Robbie Slater, and an acquaintance who was a passionate fan and had a title, that we knew would be useful for public engagement, Dr Mark Bowman, of all things, an IVF specialist.

At that time, all of us saw Frank Lowy as a 'white knight'; someone who could bring instant credibility to our game because of his business success and contacts. Once we settled on Lowy as the man who could help save the game, journalist Jesse Fink joined the group also at Hall's recommendation. Fink's access to Lowy meant that we were granted an opportunity to pitch our case to him in June 2001. Lowy told us he'd consider coming back to the game if we sorted out the politics.

We did. It took another two years, another interim administration, a government inquiry and a personal invitation from the Prime Minister, but Frank Lowy was parachuted into the role as President of FFA in July 2003.

Soon after we first met, Lowy offered me a job at Westfield. I turned it down.

I visited Jill Margo in her upmarket, trendy cottage-style home in exclusive Vaucluse on two occasions. Both times the tape was running for more than two hours. When she published her updated volume to coincide with Lowy's departure as President of FFA four years later, she related many of the things I told her as if it came from someone else. There was no mention of me, and no mention of our group who lobbied him as well as politicians from 2001 onwards.

It was if the group or I never existed. We were inconvenient to Lowy's version of history.

Margo's new tome was not so much a biography as a hagiography.

LOWY WAS RE-ELECTED unopposed towards the end of November 2011 to another four-year term as Chairman of FFA. He was buoyant.

It was now his third term and would be his last according to the FFA Constitution. Also re-elected were his two closest confidants who had been with him from the beginning and throughout the bid process – Brian Schwartz, who was also deputy chairman of Westfield, and Phil Wolanski, a childhood friend of Lowy's sons.

Lowy was thrilled with the progress of *Project Platinum*.

When he read the testimony of *The Sunday Times* pair in the House of Commons, he realised there was an easy way to locate the woman from the Qatar bid who *Project Platinum* had never been able to track down. *The Sunday Times* was owned by his good friend, Rupert Murdoch. Lowy had a close, personal, longstanding relationship with Murdoch. Either man could pick-up the phone to the other at any time and his call would be taken.

Through Lowy's lawyer, Roger Klein of Sheppard Mullin, an offer was made to Phaedra Almajid. They promised her consulting work. They said they would meet the education and care costs of her two teenage sons.

A draft contract promised to indemnify her if Qatar took legal action against her. It agreed to meet the costs of Almajid's British lawyer that was arranged for her by *The Sunday Times*, Steven Barker of Barker Gillette in London.

Lowy used his time speaking to the media in Australia to tease people with the prospect of Qatar losing 2022.

'I don't know whether you recall when I came back from that fateful day and I said '*This is not the last word about awarding the World Cup*'. Well it wasn't the last word and the last word hasn't been heard yet. Don't ask me to elaborate because I don't have a crystal ball. But the media all over the world is talking about that, the awarding particularly of 2022, the state of the FIFA Executive Committee. It's not over. I don't exactly know where it will bounce. The only thing I know is it's not over yet.'

Washington: December 2011

IN WASHINGTON, ANOTHER stranger made contact with Almajid. He told her he had 'contacts' with America's *60 Minutes* program. They wanted to build an entire program around her testimony.

The stranger was David Larkin, one-half of Change FIFA, whom I had brought to the attention of Lowy eight months before. Change FIFA, which to this day is a Twitter account that has never published a manifesto, started-up in July 2010.

Larkin introduced himself to Almajid as a bioscientist with a law degree from Texas who now lived and worked around Washington. Almajid told me she couldn't understand why someone with no background or experience in football or Qatar was so vehemently against Qatar hosting the World Cup, or how he came to have contacts with 60 Minutes. She didn't pursue the offer.

Former FBI boss, Louis Freeh, who had been engaged by FIFA, was also in touch with Almajid. This approach was more acceptable to her than the one via Roger Klein. Freeh arranged for the British lawyer hired by *The Sunday Times* to be replaced by an American lawyer, Stuart Pierson.

The first thing Pierson did, acting for Almajid, was to write a 'cease and desist' letter to Lowy's lawyer, Roger Klein of Sheppard Mullin. That was two 'cease and desist' letters for Lowy in the space of two months.

CHAPTER 28
Promises, promises

Zurich: January 2012

BLATTER HAD TWO visitors from Australia in snowy winty weather in the third week of January.

The first was Frank Lowy. The second was his good friend, Rupert Murdoch, the billionaire media mogul with substantial investment in football broadcasting on six continents.

Lowy's presence was not widely noticed. He kept out of the way of photographers.

The images of Blatter and Murdoch, smiling broadly and shaking hands, were placed proudly on FIFA's website. Murdoch tweeted how much he enjoyed his visit to FIFA HQ.

Blatter told me that when Murdoch arrived the automatic sliding doors at the entrance to FIFA headquarters wouldn't open.

'Rupert Murdoch. He is a great man,' Blatter said. 'The doors wouldn't open. You know the doors at FIFA House? The automatic doors. They were stuck. There is Rupert Murdoch outside and he couldn't get in. The alarm was ringing. It was very funny. Rupert Murdoch locked out of FIFA. He was on the outside. We were on the inside.'

Someone else working closely with Lowy was in Zurich too. Jim Pavitt. The key member of Lowy's *Project Platinum* group. He didn't attend the FIFA meeting, but he did catch-up with a few other people, inside and outside FIFA.

After the meeting at FIFA, Lowy invited other people with close links to Blatter to his suite at the luxury Baur au Lac hotel. There was much to talk about.

After a miserable year in which he was ill, then wore some flack for supporting Blatter for re-election as President of FIFA, and despite questions being raised publicly about the Australian bid by me on national television, Lowy was as excited as he had been for some time.

Lowy told those in his hotel suite that Blatter promised Qatar would not host the 2022 World Cup.

Of course, Lowy had no idea that Blatter had also promised consecutive Emirs of Qatar that he would ensure the World Cup was not taken away from them.

Zurich: July 2012

PROFESSOR MARK PIETH was perplexed.

Pieth, a Professor of Criminal Law from the University of Basel was appointed as head of FIFA's new-look Governance Committee at the end of 2011. He had made some progress in updating FIFA's approach to governance and ethics that had, so far, been accepted. Key amongst these was a recommendation for a new-look Ethics Committee. He suggested two parts to it: an investigatory chamber headed by a prosecutor and an adjudicatory chamber headed by a judge.

For Pieth, getting the right people on the Ethics Committee was a vital first step in getting FIFA on the path to redemption. He made recommendations for people to appoint to the two roles. But Blatter ignored the top two nominations from Pieth for the investigatory chamber. Pieth didn't know why.

Instead, Blatter named a former prosecutor from the USA to head the investigatory chamber. Michael J Garcia, once US Attorney for the Southern District of New York (SDNY), now a Partner with Lexington Avenue law firm, Kirkland Ellis.

The Director of Interpol, American Ron Noble, recommended Garcia after Interpol had struck a sponsorship relationship with FIFA in May 2011 for USD$20 million over ten years.

Noble was the long time head of Interpol, a position he was nominated for by Bill Clinton's former Attorney-General Janet Reno, and Louis Freeh, whose firm was taking on more and more work for FIFA - also on Noble's recommendation.

Before becoming director of the FBI, Louis Freeh was a Judge in the SDNY. It coincided with Michael Garcia's time as a prosecutor in the same district.

Noble and Garcia also knew one another well, Garcia having served as a vice-president of Interpol for three years before joining Kirkland Ellis.

James Comey, the FBI director from 2013 to 2017, who was involved with the investigations that would lead to the 2015 arrests, was another alumni of the SDNY. He was a prosecutor in the same period.

In an amazing coincidence for a country of more than 300 million people, the Americans involved with FIFA - Ron Noble, Louis Freeh, Michael Garcia and James Comey - knew one another and had worked together in New York from more than 20 years before.

Garcia's first task was to look at the implications of the ISL case from a FIFA ethics perspective. The actual legal proceedings of the ISL case had been locked-up in a Zug court for years as FIFA spent large amounts of football's money fighting in the Court to prevent their release.

The case involved a series of kickbacks from FIFA's former marketing partner, International Sport and Leisure, known as ISL. The marketing firm was established by Horst Dassler of Adidas which had partnered with FIFA in the mid 1970s. Fedor Radmann and Sepp Blatter worked closely together on Dassler's unique funding model for football development. Radmann later moved from Adidas to ISL also, although he has never been implicated in the ISL case.

The ISL scandal went to the very top of FIFA. Joao Havelange, his son-in-law Ricardo Teixeira, and Paraguay's Nicolas Leoz all took millions. It directly implicated Blatter who, at the very least, turned a blind eye to it. Blatter's stated reasoning was that it was not a crime to pay or accept a bribe in Switzerland at the time the offences took place - and who was he to upset the apple cart that kept FIFA turning?

Andrew Jennings wrote about it extensively in 'FOUL!' and showed the list of bribes in his December 2010 *Panorama* program that was broadcast just before the World Cup vote.

ONE MONTH AFTER his appointment, Garcia announced that he would also hold an investigation into the conduct of the 2018 and 2022 World Cup bids. He did so in the knowledge that he had access to the PwC report into the finances of the Asian Football Confederation, a cache of other material from the AFC, as well as material from the private investigations conducted for Frank Lowy.

It was a move that was widely viewed as a mechanism to take the World Cup away from Qatar. Hardly anyone mentioned Russia.

It was just as Lowy wanted it.

Tokyo: December 2012

MICHEL PLATINI WAS furious.

He saw Stevie Hargitay, Peter's son, coming towards him in the VIP area of the International Stadium in Yokohama. They were at the Club World Cup. Platini strode over to Hargitay junior.

Platini cornered him. Stevie Hargitay was taller and 20 years younger, but Platini still fancied he was smarter, quicker and stronger.

Michael Platini had read the excerpts from this book published for free on Andrew Jennings' website the month before. The excerpts were so popular that Jennings reported his website crashed from all the traffic.

Platini read that Hargitay referred to him as a 'dangerous little faggot'.

Platini vowed that if he ever became President of FIFA, courtiers such as Peter Hargitay would be gone.

Stevie Hargitay protested when Platini confronted him. 'It's not my father you should be upset with,' he said. 'It's that woman. From Australia. She's lying.'

He meant me.

Stevie continued his protest. 'And Jennings. He hates my father. He's a maniac. Together, they will do anything to destroy him.'

When Hargitay senior found out about the incident, he wrote to Platini. He took umbrage that Platini dared to 'attack' his son so publicly. He wrote that if Platini had a problem with him, Platini should take it up directly, not with his son.

Then his language shifted from faux anger to conciliatory, verbose, flowery. It was the verbal equivalent of stroking a cat.

Hargitay threw-in that I was incompetent, bitter and twisted - yawn - for good measure. Yes, so incompetent that my boss gave me the maximum performance bonus for how well I did my job just four weeks before he sacked me.

He added, not for the first time, that Andrew Jennings was a discredited moron who had a vendetta against him. Another yawn.

And he, Peter Hargitay, would never say any such thing about someone as esteemed as Monsieur Platini. Hilarious.

The person who showed me the letter said that Michel Platini referred to it as a 'polemic' against Jennings and me. Platini was also in no doubt that I recounted Hargitay's words precisely.

'Not least because Hargitay knew that Platini had no time for him and, therefore, the Australian bid,' the source said.

HARGITAY WROTE TO journalists saying he would take legal action against Jennings and me because of the book excerpts.

I heard nothing more about this supposed legal action until more than a year later when Jennings contacted me to say there was a letter addressed to me at his Cumbrian home. It was from the Swiss prosecutor's office. He received one also.

The letters informed us that the prosecutor wouldn't be taking action in the complaint against us. That's alright then, because we didn't know there had been one.

It turned out Hargitay lodged an action against both of us in the Swiss courts over the book excerpts. Rather than saying I lived in Australia, Hargitay directed the Swiss authorities to me via Jennings' Cumbrian address. Presumably he hoped I would never find out about the court action, wouldn't turn-up, and a judgement would be issued against me in my absence.

His plan didn't work. Not only did he try to pull the wool over Swiss prosecutor eyes about where I lived - but also where he did.

The Swiss authorities were thorough. They visited his ex-wife, who lived in Zurich, to check on his whereabouts. She gave them full chapter and verse about where, and how long, he had lived in London. His action failed at the first hurdle because he had no right to lodge it in Switzerland.

Sydney: March 2013

THE MAN WHO eventually assumed part of my former role at FFA was on the phone.

We hadn't talked in just under two years. He happily called me on his first day in the job, saying he'd be in touch.

But when he realised that the World Cup bid issue just wasn't going away, that I was seen as the source of all of FFA's problems, and the official policy was to denigrate me, he turned. He briefed journalists against me, tried to get me taken off volunteer football committees, and peddled the usual lazy line that I was bitter and twisted and there was nothing to see.

As I did with many people in football in Australia, we went way back, getting on for 20 years.

He had been part of the group I convened that led to Lowy returning to the game. On the day Lowy was elected as president of FFA in July 2003 he text messaged me to say I should feel proud about all I had done to make it happen.

But none of that meant anything to him now.

'How's the book going?' he asked.

He was referring to the same published excerpts that exercised Michel Platini.

Eventually, Jennings' website was hacked and the entire site was taken down. At the same time, a website I co-owned with a business partner and friend, dealing with parenting issues, suffered the same fate; a massive distributed denial of service attack that took out the entire network for five days emanating from Russia.

'It's going well, thanks,' I said to the FFA executive.

'Do you have a publisher?'

'Yes.'

'I just wanted to offer to look at it first.' He went on. 'It's important that Frank and others who were involved with the bid are comfortable with what's in it.'

I remained silent and wrote it all down. I knew this conversation would be included in the book when I eventually published it. I heard more papers being shuffled. Was he reading from a script?

'You might have a different understanding of what is on the public record and what is confidential,' he said. 'I think it would be a very useful tool for us to see the manuscript before it's published to ensure there is no disappointment from either party.'

A useful tool? What does that even mean? And why did he think I would be concerned about what 'Frank and others' thought was important?

'The bid vote is long over. Frank knew I would write something.'

'It doesn't matter. If you give people some visibility and let us approve what you say, it could save you a big disappointment. You wouldn't want you and your family to lose everything,' he said.

Wow. Quite a threat. They must be really worried.

'I'll think about it. For the record, I don't owe FFA anything. And I will always do what I think is best for football.'

'FRANK LOWY IS still very cut up about the World Cup bid. Al-Thawadi was in Sydney last week and met with him.' A former FIFA executive, who remained a confidant of Blatter, was on the phone.

He was referring to Hassan Al-Thawadi, the CEO of the successful Qatar bid and now of the organising committee for the 2022 World Cup.

'That would have been interesting,' I said.

'It was the second meeting that was the most interesting. The first one was just standard. You know, meeting Lowy, the new CEO, and some others to talk about his candidacy for the ExCo position for the Asian Football Confederation. The second was just Lowy and Al-Thawadi.'

'What happened?'

'I'm getting it second-hand, of course, but before Al-Thawadi could even sit down, Lowy said *'How did you do it?'* Al-Thawadi told him *'We worked hard. We went to places and you weren't there. Australia just didn't turn up.'* Lowy was incensed, and went on and on about how he was humiliated. As if the Australian bid was all about him. Lowy told him that Qatar wouldn't get away with it, that they would lose it.'

'Is that the view in Zurich too?' I asked.

'Put it this way. Blatter promised Lowy he'd take the World Cup off Qatar. Zwanziger told Blatter that FIFA needs to have a re-vote on 2022. He's the most vocal on the Executive Committee, and now all of a sudden he cares about migrant workers too. Where did that come from? Now we've got the Garcia inquiry happening. The rumour is that Garcia has recommended a re-vote.'

'Garcia hasn't handed down his decision on ISL, let alone the World Cup bids,' I said.

'No. There's one other thing I thought you'd want to know. Hargitay is touting for business in Doha.'

A proposal was received from *Inside World Football* to the Qatar 2022 organising committee to "invest" £12,500 per month in return for favourable coverage. When Andrew Jennings also published this information - not via me - he received yet another threatening letter from Hargitay's favourite law firm, Schillings.

The other business for Hargitay was from Qatar's Aspire Academy by way of sponsorship of conferences his company organised.

The Aspire Academy was a regular presence in the Qatar 2022 bid team. The director of international affairs, German Andreas Bleicher, would accompany the Qatar bid team on international visits. Amongst other things, he arranged the multi-million Qatar Foundation sponsorship of Barcelona football club.

While Australia dipped into taxpayer monies, Qatar had the Aspire Academy, the Qatar Foundation, the Qatar Investment Authority and large corporate sponsors to call on, such as Al Jazeera, Qatar Airways, Qatar Gas and its sovereign wealth fund of which the Qatar bid CEO was a Board member. Russia also had its many oligarchs, its sovereign wealth fund headed by the chairman of the Russian bid, and corporate sponsors, most notably Gazprom.

Sydney: April 2013

THE EMAIL I found when I awoke on a Saturday morning contained nothing but a subject line which read: *'Look at page 96'* with an attachment. I almost didn't open it, thinking that perhaps it was malware.

It was a report of the Committee of Integrity appointed by CONCACAF, the confederation for North America, Central America and the Caribbean, to look into the finances of the confederation after the departure of both Jack Warner and his number two, Chuck Blazer. Both had served on the FIFA Executive Committee.

For the past two years, Blazer had been referred to as a whistleblower ever since he informed Blatter and Valcke about gifts of $40,000 in cash distributed to each of the 25 Caribbean member associations of CONCACAF at the time of Bin Hammam's visit in April 2011.

When Blazer found out about it, he instigated the investigation and took the findings to Blatter that led ultimately to Bin Hammam's ban. Bin Hammam referred to it as a 'kangaroo court'.

Blazer didn't have quite the same reputation as Warner but he was well known within football circles for having a vast appetite for the good life that football offered. First class travel, generous expense accounts, gifts, hospitality, even women. And more.

Andrew Jennings revealed in August 2011 just how good that life was for Blazer. There were lucrative marketing 'commissions', a Fifth Avenue apartment in Trump Tower - actually two Fifth Avenue apartments, as one was for his cats - and a Rolls Royce housed in the underground garage at FIFA HQ. All of it was paid for by CONCACAF.

I SCROLLED TO page 96 as the email suggested.

> 'The evidence reviewed by the Committee also shows that Warner obtained through fraud and then misappropriated USD$462,200 provided to CONCACAF by FFA in 2010.'

Earlier in the report, the Committee noted that:

> 'These funds were provided through Australia's international football development program in connection with its 2022 FIFA World Cup bid.'

This is what I had been wary of all along: targeting pet projects of FIFA Executive Committee members under the guise of football development with no accountability for what happened to the money. The fact that Jack Warner was involved was no surprise at all. Here was proof that money from Australia never reached what purported to be its intended target.

The grant was ostensibly to upgrade the Joao Havelange Stadium, and was made two months before the bid vote.

The name of the stadium should have been a clue. It was built with FIFA money, on land owned by Warner and bought with FIFA money, for a football club owned by Warner.

Why did anyone in Australia think it necessary to spend USD$462,200 on upgrading a stadium in distant Trinidad and Tobago - which just happened to be the home of one of the most wantonly greedy FIFA Executive Committee members?

Lowy had obviously been worried about the payment for some time. Before the Committee of Integrity discovered Warner's pocketing of the money, Jim Pavitt was on the case for *Project Platinum* sniffing around in Trinidad and Tobago.

A memo addressed to Pavitt from one of his investigators which surfaced in 2011 talks of the *'complicated situation surrounding the $500,000 Australian grant to Trinidad'*.

The Trinidad Prime Minister of the time expected Warner's resignation from FIFA in 2011 to stop any investigation into the 'final use of the money' by both FIFA and the Australian authorities. Pavitt's investigator wrote that *'This is also an indicator that there are problems with the $500,000 payment.'*

The Trinidad government was concerned that any exposure of Warner's activities would *'only serve to confirm the view in the region that Trinidad is one of the most corrupt countries in the Western Hemisphere …'*. Pavitt was briefed that the Trinidad Prime Minister understood *'that the bulk of Warner's funds come via corruption'* but Warner's corruption was seen as 'minor' compared with the alleged systemic corruption of the previous Trinidad and Tobago Prime Minister.

After reading the Committee of Integrity's report, I wrote an article that was published online revealing what happened in relation to the Australian money.

FFA was not happy; they thought the report would go unnoticed in Australia and it would slip under the radar. It largely did as mainstream media wasn't that interested - other than *The Age* - and no Australian politician wanted to rock the boat of a generous donor.

Eventually, in 2015, the Australian Federal Police investigated the payment. Australia is recognised internationally by academic experts as not having strong laws relating to potential bribery and corruption.

More than two years later, in 2017, the police found that public monies were not used for the alleged gift to Warner. The only public money used was for the expenses incurred by staff and consultants who travelled to the Caribbean to give the gift, so that is all they examined. They concluded that because the travel was in the course of their work, and no employees individually benefited, no offence was committed.

The Australian Federal Police missed the point. What was the true purpose of the payment? And, if it wasn't paid from taxpayers' money, whose money?

FOR JACK WARNER, who gave up all his world and regional football positions two years beforehand, the net was closing-in.

Two years previously in 2011, Andrew Jennings revealed that Warner's sons, Daryan and Daryll, were apprehended in Miami and put under house arrest. Not wanting to spend the rest of his life in a US gaol, Daryll eventually pleaded guilty to charges brought against him by the US authorities in July 2013; Daryan joined him in October 2013; after assisting the FBI with their inquiries, Chuck Blazer pleaded guilty in November 2013.

According to Pavitt's investigator, Warner continued 'to profit from graft' as a Minister and senior figure in his political party at least until he lost his seat in Parliament in 2015.

Daryll and Daryan Warner are due to be sentenced in 2018.

Chuck Blazer died in July 2017.

At the end of 2017, Jack Warner was still fighting extradition to the USA from his home in Trinidad and Tobago. Both aged in their 70s, Warner and his wife Maureen face the prospect of never seeing their sons again.

CHAPTER 29
'Call me Mike'

Sydney: May 2013

ANOTHER SURPRISE IN my inbox. An email from FIFA's chief ethics investigator Michael Garcia.

He wrote that *'I understand you have been trying to get in touch with me.'* He invited me to share my concerns with him.

I was curious. Why did he suggest I had been trying to contact him, when I hadn't? How did he get my email?

The fact is, I had barely given the Garcia inquiry a thought. I saw it as an exercise where the only outcome would be the one FIFA wanted.

The Garcia inquiry was established to find a rationale for taking the World Cup from Qatar and giving it to the 'second place' getter, the USA. If Garcia could find a smoking gun against Qatar, then FIFA would be well placed to move the 2022 World Cup which is what Blatter preferred. Australia's bid - and anything I had to say about it or FIFA - would be incidental. So why would he want to talk to me?

Garcia also had no ability to compel people to talk with him, no capacity to trace financial transactions, no penalty to hand-out for those who didn't cooperate with him or who didn't tell the truth, and he was banned from visiting Russia. In other words, there was no reason to have much confidence in the work he was doing.

But having been contacted by him, thinking about it, and talking it over at home and with close colleagues, I decided to respond. My reasoning was that the only way Garcia, a former US Attorney-General with the Southern District of New York, had a hope of doing his job properly was by people who had some knowledge or experience about the World Cup bids cooperating with him. And the only way world football would ever change is by getting the issues out into the open.

Not long afterwards, we had our first telephone hook-up. Me in Sydney; Garcia, at least one of his law firm associates, and one of Louis Freeh's right hand men, Tim Flynn, in New York. Flynn was a former 23-year veteran of the FBI now working as one of the managing directors of Freeh's consulting firm registered in Delaware. The Freeh Group was working for FIFA more or less full time on security and investigatory issues.

The first discussion was mostly concerned with process. I let them know I was bound by a confidentiality agreement.

'We'll fix that,' said Garcia. 'FFA has to let you talk with us. FIFA has made that clear to all bidders.'

It was a flawed concept from the outset. By the very fact that they needed a release from my confidentiality agreement, FFA would know I was talking to them when those who met with Garcia were supposed to remain confidential.

Many weeks afterwards, when Garcia obtained a release from the FFA, he told me they had been the 'most difficult' of all of the bidders. 'It got quite tense. I really had to put my foot down and call in FIFA over it,' he said.

Great, I thought. So FIFA knew also.

'It only made me think they've got something to hide,' he continued. 'Why would they go to such great lengths to try to stop you talking with us?'

He may have received a slowly-extracted and grudging signature from FFA for me to speak with Garcia, but I knew there would be some form of retaliation. It would either be from FFA, the bid consultants, FIFA or all of the above. I expressed my concern about it.

'You don't need to worry about that. What you say to us is protected. It's confidential. It's anonymous. We'll do all that we can to protect you,' Garcia said.

Aarhus, Denmark: October 2013

I WAS IN Aarhus, Denmark, to attend a conference of journalists, sports academics and sports associations who were interested in corruption in sport.

Even though it was almost three years after the vote for the 2018 and 2022 World Cups, the principal topic remained FIFA, those World Cup votes and the Garcia investigation.

Professor Mark Pieth, head of FIFA's Governance Committee, was a keynote speaker, as was FIFA's head of communications Walter de Gregorio. I spoke briefly with both of them.

The first thing De Gregorio asked was when my book would be published.

'Is it all about Peter Hargitay?' he asked.

'No, he's a bit player in the end,' I said. 'But don't worry, Walter, it's mostly a comedy.'

While I was at the conference, another email arrived from Garcia's assistant.

After Garcia eventually received the release from FFA, I had other, lengthy phone discussions with him, Flynn and their team.

From the outset, I said I didn't have so-called 'smoking gun' evidence, other than the report of the CONCACAF Committee of Integrity about the USD$462,200 pocketed by Warner. What I could help them with is observations, what we were doing, how the consultants worked, and how I saw that fitting in with how FIFA operated. They asked for any documentation. I explained that, because of the way I departed the role, I didn't have much.

The email informed me that they were making arrangements for me to travel to New York to see Garcia in two weeks time.

The first question I was asked by many journalists as they greeted me at the conference, unsurprisingly, was whether Garcia was in touch with me. I informed them I was travelling to New York to see him soon.

New York: November 2013

AFTER SNOW ON the ground on the day I arrived in New York, the next morning was fine, sunny and cold. Even colder than Aarhus.

I walked the five blocks north on Lexington Avenue to Garcia's midtown Manhattan law firm, colder than I had felt for some years.

Garcia's 500-person New York office was located on the top floors of a 59-storey tower with friendly security staff on the ground floor. The express lift whisked me to the top which opened into a spacious reception area that took up almost one half of the building. Before me was a spectacular view of Manhattan looking north past Central Park and east to Roosevelt Island. Groups of leather sofas were placed around the floor with a large reception desk strategically placed to observe all comings and goings.

I felt like I had walked on to the set of an American legal drama TV show.

One of the associates who sat in on our telephone conversations and organised my travel, greeted me and led me down a corridor to a meeting room.

It was easy to recognise Tim Flynn, the former FBI man. He rose immediately as I entered the room. He held out his hand. I judged him to be early-to-mid-50s, trim, fit-looking, average height, with a short haircut, in a stance as if he was ready to pounce at any sign of trouble.

There were ten chairs around a comfortably-sized meeting room table. Recording equipment was already set up. There were several folders of material and some loose pieces of paper on the table in front of the two associates, and one folder in front of Flynn and an unoccupied seat at the end of the table. A cupboard under the window that faced west across the Manhattan skyline, offered coffee, tea, water and cookies.

I helped myself to a coffee, and made small talk about the weather and my flight.

Garcia arrived a few minutes later. He was short, much shorter than he looked in the photos. Perhaps my height. He held out his hand. The other one was holding a Blackberry.

'Call me Mike,' he said.

THE FIRST THING Garcia said - before the recording started - was to inform me that the proceedings were confidential, as he also told me over the phone previously. My identity would be protected, he told me - notwithstanding both FIFA and FFA knew I was talking with him - and what we talked about would remain confidential.

'I know you know a lot of media. You are not to tell them you're here, that we're talking or what we're talking about. And especially Andrew Jennings. He's not to know anything about any of this. Andrew Jennings must not know.' He emphasised the last sentence.

A specific mention of Andrew Jennings? Twice? Now who at FIFA could possibly have briefed him about Jennings? And why wouldn't Jennings be someone Garcia would want to talk to? After all, he unveiled the ISL scandal years before - and was one hundred per cent correct. Wouldn't Jennings be a useful person to speak with for this inquiry?

I said to Garcia that it may be a bit late for that. I explained that I had already informed some journalists, including Andrew Jennings, that I would be meeting with him a few weeks beforehand in Denmark.

I also thought, but didn't say, that I was under no obligation to him or to FIFA not to say anything to anyone if I wanted to.

He shrugged his shoulders. 'Well don't tell them anymore,' he said. I thought no more of that exchange.

The recording equipment was turned on. I asked him what would happen to his report, noting that his Ethics Committee investigation into the ISL matter - separate from the legal findings of the Zug Court - was not published.

He gave the predictable answer, the comfortable one for him. It was all up to his colleague head of the adjudicatory chamber, Judge Eckert.

'What will happen from there, it will really be up to Judge Eckert. Where it goes from there, I really couldn't tell you.'

That may be so, but I couldn't help but think that it was a cop out for a man who once told the *New York Times* that his credo was to do *'the right things for the right reasons'*.

By this stage, he had already been working on his World Cup bid investigation for 15 months. It would be another ten months before he submitted his report. And yet he couldn't say, and didn't seem that fussed about, what would happen. Was he merely a hired gun?

He homed-in very quickly on the cost of the Australian bid. He wanted to know how much I knew about the 'level of expense detail'.

I explained that what I could talk about was how the budget shifted, and could point out the inconsistencies between the various budgets and the report by FFA on final expenditure.

'The first budget that PwC put together was around $90 million.' His jaw dropped when he heard that amount. 'Exactly, I had that reaction when I heard it too.'

I explained that we eventually asked the government for two amounts of money: $54.3 million for the main grant - the government gave us $45.6 million - and $28.5 million for the second grant for unspecified development projects.

I told him I used to manage budgets in previous government roles of up to $8 billion, including preparing budget papers and funding submissions for Cabinet. I understood budgeting and financial management. I knew how government budgeting worked. But I said that I did not understand some strange differences between the internal budget for the bid, and other documents I had seen, specifically FFA's final report to government that was tabled in the Australian Parliament.

A copy of the spreadsheet setting out the internal bid budget was distributed around the table - the one we were never to take out of Ben Buckley's office.

Garcia focussed on the amounts for 'international football development', $4 million for Africa, $2.5 million for Asia; the almost equivalent amount of bonuses for the consultants, $4 million for Radmann, $2.5 million for Hargitay; and the amount budgeted for the Bid Book. I said again that he needed to look at the spreadsheet in conjunction with the final report on expenditure to government, as well as some other documents.

There were lots of questions about our consultants. Who were they close to on the Executive Committee? What favours did they seek? What were their roles exactly? Why didn't we announce the appointments of Hargitay and Radmann?

Garcia was totally aghast when I pointed out that Radmann was paid more than $150,000 a month, via Abold. I said that Hargitay told me *'never to put Radmann's name on an email because to do so would jeopardise everything'.*

I told him that I read this particular email as I walked through the front door at home one evening quite late, and the brief conversation my husband and I had about it.

Hargitay had copied the email to Mohamed Bin Hammam's personal assistant, Jenny Be. I thought perhaps he made a mistake. But there was no mistaking what he wrote.

!!!!!!!! Dear Bonita

Many thanks for this

Will revert with input

Please do not list Fedor in the recipient lines!!!!! You simply MUST NOT do that.

Why? Because you are thus jeopardizing everything.

I had asked my husband how he interpreted it.

'One of two options: Fedor is up to no good; or Hargitay's a drama queen. Ask Ben what he thinks. If he doesn't have an answer then you've got your answer,' he told me.

I told Garcia that I did ask Ben about it.

'He just basically said to forget anything Hargitay says and ignore it … it was further evidence that Radmann was up to something in my view … I raised the question so many times. Not once did these people with whom I worked closely, Ben being one, Lowy being another, say *'There's nothing going on here'*. They never did.'

He said that he was particularly interested in the German connection with our bid, and who came first. Beckenbauer, Radmann or Abold? Who else from the German FA was involved? I told him about the 2007 cooperation agreement with Germany. 'The same people were involved in 2006 and 2010,' he said.

He then stopped the recording. 'I'm actually looking at your bid in the context of those two other tournaments, going back to 1998 or 1999 when the Germany World Cup was awarded.'

We talked further before the recording was turned on again.

Once it was, he was surprised to learn that the $4 million for the Oceania Confederation was an additional amount from government via the aid agency.

'This is a separate pot of money that you're tapping into, other than your 46 million,' he asked. I confirmed it.

'Was there ever any discussion about Lowy financing any of this?' he asked. I told him I raised it.

He wanted to know when Temarii told us he would vote for us. His eyebrows raised when I said at least as early as March 2008, officially June 2008.

We talked of the $5 million Australia promised for Vision Asia and how we got to it starting with the meeting between Bin Hammam and Prime Minister Rudd on the sidelines of the May 2008 FIFA Congress in Sydney. Garcia wondered where the money was paid from. I told him it was a mystery as only one-quarter of it was accounted for in FFA's final report to government, yet we won an award from the Asian Football Confederation in November 2010 for the $5 million gift.

I also pointed out that the $4 million budgeted for Africa was referred to by Amadou Diakite, a football official from Mali, in his discussion with the fake consultants from the 2010 *Sunday Times* sting. Diakite was a member of the FIFA Executive Committee that awarded the 2006 World Cup to Germany. Radmann knew him well.

The transcript of part of Diakite's discussion with the fake consultants was on the website of the Court of Arbitration for Sport. I said I did not know if the money was paid, but Diakite clearly refers to it - just as he did to offers from other bidding nations also. Curiously, *The Sunday Times* and other media outlets at the time only reported him talking about an offer from Qatar.

Garcia asked me to send through the link to the transcript. Later, after I did so, an email came back asking whether I could also supply an English translation of it. I was taken aback by that request from a well-resourced committee.

We talked about how Australia distributed money to confederations and Jack Warner, compared with how Qatar might have done so.

I told him the vehicles Qatar might have used - based on nothing more than observation - included the Qatar Foundation, the Qatar Investment Authority of which CEO Hassan Al-Thawadi was a Board member, or the Aspire Academy. Andreas Bleicher, director of the Aspire Academy, travelled regularly with the Qatar bid team. Aspire also later became a sponsor of various activities associated with Hargitay.

Like almost everyone else when talking about the Australian bid, the talk returned to the pearl pendants, the ones that were given to the partners of Executive Committee members at Lowy's mansion in May 2008, before the bidding process formally commenced.

He asked me about the pearl gift for Maureen Warner, clarifying that this was the only one given during the bidding process. I told him I felt uncomfortable with having to purchase it while we were bidding, as the gift was inconsistent with bid guidelines that dictated gifts should be 'incidental' in value. I recalled that I wrote an email to Lowy and Ben about it at the time.

We all laughed at the thought that what was 'incidental' to a billionaire such as Lowy, and certain members of the Executive Committee, would be different from what we might consider incidental. He wanted to know whether the $2,000 pendant was paid for by bid monies, and I told him I didn't know this level of detail.

I said that there was much more done to curry favour with Warner at Hargitay's constant urging.

I mentioned that we had also funded the under-20 Trinidad and Tobago team to take part in a training camp in Cyprus. One of our junior women's teams played a game against Trinidad's junior women's team. I said I wasn't certain but the travel for these trips may have been organised via Jack Warner's travel company. We signed a cooperation agreement with the Jamaican FA, headed by Warner's good friend, the late Horace Burrell. Prime Minister Rudd had a one-on-one meeting with Warner in Port of Spain. And, of course, there was the USD$462,200 donation to help upgrade Warner's stadium.

I mentioned Russia and the many overtures we made towards them through political circles as well as via the consultants and their links. I said that Lowy invited Mutko to join him on his super yacht in the Mediterranean in the northern hemisphere summer of 2009, but I did not know if the meeting happened.

We talked of the friendly matches organised by all bidders. He wanted to know how an international friendly would be helpful to Executive Committee members.

I explained that it would be one or all of the match fee, who picked-up the expenses, what was included in the expenses, and the broadcast rights. Even at a younger age group, such as the matches against Trinidad and Tobago, match fees and paying expenses could be helpful. We discussed how these were paid. I suggested he look at friendly matches beyond the date of the bid vote, as some were still happening in 2011 and perhaps even into 2012.

Unrelated to bidding, I shared a story with them from 12 years previously when Australia played Colombia in a friendly match when I was the operations manager of the men's national team, the Socceroos. The comparatively modest match fee of USD$40,000 was paid in cash.

'It turned-up literally in a brown paper bag in cash from a man with a ponytail wearing a white lace shirt,' I told them.

They laughed.

Garcia asked me what changes did I think should be made to the bidding process.

I identified six - besides fundamental changes to FIFA itself.

Opening up the World Cup vote to the entire Congress. Having a non-refundable fee to be a bidder that can help form part of a football development budget once the bid is decided. Limiting bid budgets to the extent that was possible - in other words a type of 'financial fair play' for bidders. No legacy requirement as part of the conduct of the bid, but only as a result of staging a World Cup, once awarded. Making sure every one in a bid team, including consultants, were aware of, and subject to, the bidding rules and regulations. And never have more than one tournament open at a time.

I also reiterated what I said to him in an earlier telephone conversation that I thought none of this was possible because FIFA wasn't interested in, or it did not suit them to, reform.

'They are incapable of reforming themselves,' I said. 'Their culture, their way of doing business runs deep.'

'As a country, using taxpayers' money, we ran a reputational risk with our conduct because we employed Peter Hargitay and Fedor Radmann,' I told him.

The great shame for Australia was that our bid had a strong argument on merit, but FIFA simply isn't interested in merit-based arguments. It was about what went on behind closed doors.

Garcia thanked me for taking the trip to see him.

'It's been incredibly helpful for us,' he said, as I rose and shook the hands of Flynn and Garcia's two associates. 'We're an open door. If you do think of anything, please contact us, and we'll do the same if we see something we didn't ask or you might have some insight on.'

He said they would be in Australia soon and we would meet again then.

Garcia walked me out into the corridor and to the large reception room, where we chatted for a few minutes. He told me that he had three children, and he lived in the outer suburban reaches of New York City to the north of the scene laid out before us. He confided that his wife preferred living in Washington DC, as the housing was better and everything was closer. I took some photos of the splendid view from midtown to Central Park and beyond.

I put on my coat to venture out into the cold. I realised I was exhausted. A combination of jet lag and concentrating for more than six hours on events and conversations that were now up to six years old.

We shook hands. He gripped my forearm with his left hand, politician style.

'Thanks, Bonita. Thank you again.'

CHAPTER 30
Follow the money

Sydney: April 2014

I DID NOT give the Garcia inquiry much thought after my trip, though I followed the regular media articles about his investigation. Some seemed well-informed; others were speculative.

His team were now visiting Sydney as part of their world tour. They asked to see me again. I took the ferry into the city and walked the few hundred metres up the hill to the five-star hotel where they were spending the week. This time it was Garcia, Flynn and yet another associate from Garcia's law firm.

Tim Flynn greeted me and took me to the meeting room. It was small, closed-in with no windows and no fresh air. It smelt slightly stale. Even though there was just three of them, the room looked crowded with multiple folders open before them.

'Let's get one thing out of the way first, Bonita,' said Garcia, before I had a chance to settle myself. 'I told you not to talk with media.'

He was referring to a report run by journalist Nick Harris in the UK's *Mail on Sunday* newspaper which focussed on the payment to Jack Warner and the money for Oceania and Africa, as well as the fact that Garcia himself was 'ruffling feathers' of the FIFA Executive Committee in Zurich. Garcia had been in Zurich a few weeks before, prior to an Executive Committee meeting, to interview each member of the committee who had voted in 2010. The Executive Committee members concerned were so incensed that they attempted to stop his investigation.

Harris' story certainly referred to information he heard from me, but I was not his only source.

'And as I told you in November, Mike, Nick Harris has known that I met with you since last October. He sat on that information for almost six months, as did others,' I said.

'Who told him we were coming here?' Mike asked.

'He already knew, but I confirmed it when he asked me.'

I also said that, to be fair to Harris, I thought he and some other journalists believe their reporting is doing the investigation a favour.

The view around media circles after Garcia's recent Zurich visit was that, despite the on-the-record comments from Blatter supporting the Garcia investigation, it was actually Blatter, his people and those close to him on the Executive Committee who wanted to stop the investigation.

'The general view is that, to the extent there are any 'good guys' on the Executive Committee, they will be more emboldened if they realise that you're making progress. This may not be a correct assessment, but it's not an illogical one,' I said.

He didn't say anything.

'Besides, I've been getting calls from German journalists for months. Guys I haven't even heard of before. They seem to be very well briefed and asking very relevant questions.'

One of the German journalists specifically told me that he was briefed by Garcia more than once.

I held Garcia's gaze.

'Well, you shouldn't have talked to Nick Harris,' he said haughtily, ignoring the comments about the German journalists.

He shifted in his seat, shuffled some papers.

THE ADMONISHMENT MAY have been over, but Garcia's demeanour was different. He seemed tired. Lacking in energy. Uninterested. He was going through the motions. It was as if he put up barricades in his own mind about any further inquiries.

As well as his recent experience in Zurich, where the attempt was made to cut short his inquiry, I wondered whether the change in Garcia had anything to do with a noticeable shift in Blatter's rhetoric too.

Initially, Blatter was hopeful that the Garcia inquiry would come up with a 'smoking gun' on Qatar so the World Cup could be hosted by the USA. The material from the Asian Football Confederation, Frank Lowy's private investigations and Phaedra Almajid were paramount to that happening.

From 2012 when the Garcia inquiry was announced, and throughout most of 2013, Blatter was relatively critical of Qatar. Blatter clearly sent a message during this period that Qatar 2022 was not a guaranteed event. He made pronouncements that holding the World Cup in Qatar 'may have been a mistake' and it was 'not rational' to hold it there.

Qatar could read the tea leaves as much as anyone. Blatter was invited to visit the new, young Emir in November 2013, where the Emir reminded him of the arrangement with the retired Emir struck after the vote in 2010: that, in return for Bin Hammam being out of the Presidential race and maintaining his silence, Qatar would keep the World Cup. Come what may.

It was also a view Blatter was hearing from his CEO Jerome Valcke who was satisfied that Qatar 2022 was viable commercially with the help of the Al Jazeera bonus. Valcke also knew that, from a legal perspective, FIFA could be ruined if they tried to change the decision made in December 2010.

After the visit to the new Emir, Blatter started to shift his position to say it was 'much too soon' to say what would happen.

A few weeks later, after years of resisting a change to the timing of the World Cup, he said for the first time that the tournament would need to be held at a different time of year because of the 'mistake' of ignoring the technical assessment regarding the oppressive and excessive heat in Qatar in June. Others such as Platini, and the German FA chief Theo Zwanziger, had been saying the same thing for years - although each for different reasons. A few weeks later, Blatter claimed that those who criticised Qatar's win were 'racist'. It was also something I first said in 2011 - although the rest of my sentence was '… without other bidders first examining their own behaviour'.

Garcia was an expert, but he was also a paid consultant with limited scope to do the proper job of an investigator. Was he given another set of instructions in Zurich? Had he been told what the outcome should be?

FLYNN SHOWED ME my email to Lowy and Ben written in July 2009 after I purchased Maureen Warner's pearl pendant in Dubai. The one I told them I wrote.

'Why did you send that?' Flynn asked.

'For precisely the reasons I say so. We were in bidding mode and a gift that expensive was, in my view, outside bidding guidelines. I felt uncomfortable about it.'

'What happened when you sent that email?' A pretty stupid question considering the response was in front of them.

'Ben said *'Never to write an email like that again'.*'

'Why did he say that?' they asked.

'Because he didn't want in writing a suggestion that I was concerned about us breaching the bidding guidelines.'

'Could it be that he didn't want you writing to Frank Lowy?'

I sat back in my seat and looked at them. Obviously this was how FFA and/or Ben rebutted it to them. I laughed out loud. It clearly didn't say that. *'Not writing to Lowy'*, and *'not writing an email like that'* were two different things.

'No. I had free rein to write directly to Lowy on anything as long as I copied Ben, which I always did. In fact, that was his general rule and part of the problem in the organisation; he wanted to be copied on everything.'

Flynn asked if there were any other documents I could give them.

Why did they keep asking that? I explained once again that I had very few documents because of the nature of my departure, but they were welcome to have what I did have. I added: 'If I still had the same computer, you could have it,' I said. 'But I gave that back. They probably still have it if you want to check it.'

They asked to see my personal notebooks. 'No problem,' I said. 'Just as long as you're not expecting diary entries. I'm not a spy who makes detailed records. I take notes as an aide-memoire for myself.'

I looked down at my note pad. 'Just like I have here,' I added, showing them my contemporaneous notes of our meeting.

'That would be really helpful,' Garcia said.

The three of them each had a copy of FFA's internal bid budget spreadsheet in front of them. 'Have you thought any more about that spreadsheet?' Garcia asked.

I shook my head.

Garcia leaned forward in his chair. The sleeves of his white shirt were rolled-up about three-quarters of the way. His elbows were on the meeting table. Other than his little tantrum over Nick Harris' article, it was the first time he seemed engaged in the meeting.

'We just met with your former colleague,' he said. 'He said these two different budgets might be unusual but not improper.'

He was referring to the former chief financial officer, and the fact that the budget provided to the Government for reporting six-monthly progress was so different from the one that was being used for internal management reporting purposes.

It was a mystery why Garcia was so keen to meet with him. What I actually said in New York was that the former chief financial officer had no oversight of the bid budget; that another, more junior member of Stuart Taggart's operations team was responsible for bid finances. Garcia had asked me who that was, and I spelled out the staff member's name. The fact that the chief financial officer had no insight into the bid budget was a matter of tension and contention between him and Ben: that was the point I had made.

Yet, in November when we were in New York, Garcia had persisted for some reason.

'He leaves at some point, too?' the transcript shows Mike asked me the previous November.

'Yes, he leaves in September 2009.'

'And why does he leave?'

'I think Ben got rid of him because he ... they just didn't get on. They were chalk and cheese. He was a typical accountant, very careful, very cautious. I think it became uncomfortable for Ben when the CFO ... was concerned that he didn't have any insight into the bid budget.'

'Do you speak with him at all?'

'Maybe once or twice a year, to wish him a Merry Christmas or something, yes.'

'Do you think he would speak with us?'

'I can ask him if you like.'

'Give us his contact (sic) and I'll reach out for him and see if he would be willing to speak with us.'

One of Garcia's associates chased me twice for the former chief financial officer's details after I returned to Sydney.

I thought now about what Garcia just said. Almost anyone could have told them that two budgets were not necessarily improper, but he was asking the wrong question of the wrong person. I said nothing.

Garcia continued. 'We've looked at it. We've thought about it. We looked at the other documents. And we think the answer to your bid is in that spreadsheet,' he said.

There was more silence in the room.

'I just wondered whether you had any more thoughts about it at all,' he added.

I shook my head. 'No, I haven't given it a thought.'

More silence.

'Do you think Beckenbauer, Radmann and Abold were part of a package deal?' He asked a similar question in November.

'I have thought about that more since the last time you asked me,' I said. 'It could be cut and spliced any way, but the more I think about it, I believe it was Beckenbauer as early as 2007, followed by Radmann and Abold together. I have no doubt they were part of a package deal.'

Garcia looked at Flynn. They both made a note.

32,000 feet: May 2014

DESPITE GARCIA SAYING he thought the answer to our bid was in the spreadsheet, I still did not intend giving it another thought. I was both perplexed and annoyed that he persisted on meeting with the former chief financial officer who was not a member of the bid team, and had zero insight into our World Cup bid.

Having spoken with Garcia four times, met him twice, shared my personal notes with him, I thought I fulfilled my duty to his inquiry and, more broadly, to football.

That was until I received a phone call the following day. I was about to leave home for the airport and a trip to north Queensland.

'You'll never guess who I ran into last night,' a Melbourne journalist said to me.

He hardly paused. 'Ben Buckley.'

'Oh. How was he?'

The journalist lowered his voice and spoke staccato-like.

'Happily drunk. It was about 2am. At the casino. He'd been to some function and so had I. Everyone sort of convened in the bar. I was introduced to him. We got talking. I asked him about his time at FFA. He said something really interesting.'

'Oh?'

'He said that all those articles back in 2010 about the World Cup bid missed the really big story.' He paused. 'He said – and I quote – *The real scandal was right under their noses all the time*'. What could that mean do you think?'

I knew straight away it was the spreadsheet. Lowy was anxious about it; it was the first thing he asked me about when he called me to his mansion in July 2010. Garcia said the other day he thought it contained the secret to our bid.

The early-morning conversation with the journalist, together with Garcia's comment and Lowy's anxiety, piqued my interest. As I was leaving home, I grabbed the spreadsheet and some other documents, and packed them in my bag to have a look at on the flight.

And here we are. At 32,000 feet. It's an amazing feeling when something that was opaque suddenly becomes clear. With clarity comes a sense of lightness.

I felt like laughing. I looked around at my fellow passengers. I was sitting in the middle of a three-seat aisle in fairly empty flight with the computer open and several documents spread around me. They might have thought I was bonkers if I laughed out loud, so I grinned to myself instead.

The answer wasn't entirely in the spreadsheet by itself. It was when the spreadsheet was read in conjunction with other documents and publicly available information. It was just as I suggested to Garcia.

The spreadsheet for the World Cup bid reconciles two separate budgets: an internal working budget for management reporting, and another budget for reporting to government.

Included in the government reporting budget was $14.8 million for consultants and community programs. A comparison with the management reporting budget shows that these items were reduced by $9.3 million. A further reduction between the government reporting budget and management reporting budget of $3 million was also made to the allocations for the Bid Book, public relations and administration.

In other words, the budget for these items for government reporting purposes was overstated by $12.3 million, compared with the budget for internal management reporting purposes.

What the spreadsheet also tells us is where the $12.3 million was reallocated to under the internal management reporting budget.

Under 'international football development' there was $2.5 million for the Asian Football Confederation and $4 million for the African Football Confederation. A further $6.5 million was allocated as bonuses to Hargitay and Radmann, in the amounts of $2.5 million and $4 million respectively, with an annotation that the bonuses were payable if Australia won the 2018 tournament.

Yet FFA's final report to government which, of course, mirrored the format for the government reporting budget, indicated that only $1.5 million was paid to Asian football and only $240,000 was spent in Africa, although not via CAF, and no bonuses were paid.

It didn't make sense.

We knew that Australia had won an award for a $5 million gift to AFC, but there was no mention of the gift in the report, and only $1.5 million of the allocation for Asia was accounted for.

The final report to government showed that the final amount paid for Radmann's and Abold's work was $13.7 million, roughly in line with what the internal management reporting budget showed as far back as April 2009. Yet the total in the internal management reporting budget included the bonuses which were, of course, not payable. And that assumes, of course, that Abold's share was genuinely the $7 million budgeted, rather than the $3.2 million that was the value of his contract.

It was curious.

Why did Radmann and Abold get the entire amount of money that was budgeted for when at least $4 million of it was allocated for a bonus that wasn't payable? Did some of it end up in 'Asia' or 'Africa' or elsewhere? If so, who received the money and for what purposes? Did the money stay with Radmann and Abold via their

'Beyond Limits Marketing' company?

In the years since the end of the bidding process, the company has had changes of name and ownership. It is now known as the Lammershoek Winery in South Africa. The marquee wine of the Lammershoek Winery? The Franz Beckenauer Libero No. 5, of course.

My thoughts were that only a forensic financial audit which 'followed the money' could get to the bottom of the apparent contradictions between what was planned to be spent and what was reported to government. Such a divergence would surely draw the attention of even the most novice auditor.

CHAPTER 31
The Americans are coming!

East Midlands: April 2014

BLATTER'S SHIFT IN rhetoric was noticed around the world.

People who met with Mike Garcia, or had some familiarity with his inquiries, were telling similar stories to what I had observed at our Sydney meeting. 'Something has changed. He's no longer interested,' they would say.

Journalists who said they had 'very off-the-record, never-happened conversations' with Garcia recounted that he was becoming increasingly despondent as he realised that he couldn't get anywhere with reforming FIFA.

The briefing against Garcia stepped-up also. Charlie Sale of the *Daily Mail* reported that the Garcia inquiry had so far cost £6 million (USD$9.4 million) with apparently no end in sight. What wasn't reported was that the bill included Garcia, his multiple associates working on the case, Flynn and his offsiders, as well as a lawyer for Phaedra Almajid.

Lowy and the remnants of his *Project Platinum* team were becoming increasingly concerned too.

They managed to put a lid on the reporting of the donation to Jack Warner within Australia. They successfully convinced Australian authorities that it was all just a terrible mistake. But Garcia was asking far too many uncomfortable questions of Lowy and the Australian bid. That wasn't what was supposed to happen.

Lowy and his team saw me as the source of all these problems and continued to cast me in the role of Australian football's pariah. They apparently did not realise that other bidders, journalists and football officials also had information relevant to the

Australian bid and were willing to talk to Garcia and others about it.

The remnants of the *Project Platinum* team learned that the nine terabytes of data from the audit of the finances of the Asian Football Confederation conducted at the instigation of Prince Ali were in the possession of an investigative team in the East Midlands of England. They wanted to get hold of it before anyone else did. The data from the audit report was Garcia's initial reference point; staff from AFC had transferred to FIFA to assist him with his lines of inquiry for his investigation.

For one, the *Project Platinum* team thought it might help their case against Qatar just as Blatter seemed to be faltering. And if Blatter really was reneging on his promise, the AFC material would at least be useful for some anti-Qatar, anti-Bin Hammam headlines.

Lowy also saw it as insurance. Just in case there was something in there that might be uncomfortable for him that was causing Garcia to ask him uncomfortable questions.

Lowy despatched his trusted consultant, the coordinator of *Project Platinum*, Mark Bieler, to track down the investigative team in England who held the AFC treasure.

The gatekeeper to the AFC treasure was a man who was sickened by the people in football who put themselves and their positions above those who played the game, loved the game, volunteered for the game. He experienced FIFA and AFC at close quarters and didn't like what he saw.

Like everyone else with exposure to the Garcia inquiry, he also thought it would go nowhere. He decided to find someone who could make use of the material. He was in contact with media outlets and journalists in England, and offered them access to the material. The BBC were in talks and pushing it through their bureaucracy. The Guardian believed they were close to a deal.

And then Mark Bieler came knocking, introduced by a mutual contact. Bieler wanted to know how his client, Frank Lowy, could have exclusive use of the material, and how soon could he have it.

Sydney: June 2014

THE HEADLINES WERE big and bold from *The Sunday Times*:

'Plot to Buy the World Cup - huge email cache reveals secrets of Qatar's shock victory.'

Weeks before the 2014 World Cup in Brazil was to start, Jonathan Calvert and Heidi Blake told the world they had access to a secret cache of documents from a FIFA whistleblower that lifted the lid on how Qatar won the 2022 World Cup.

Except it wasn't. If you read beyond the headlines of the multiple stories they wrote each week over the next four weeks, it didn't show files that revealed *'How the former head of football in Qatar bought crucial votes to secure the 2022 World Cup.'*

What it detailed was a comprehensive list of payments made by Mohamed Bin Hammam to almost any world football official who asked for it.

With a few exotic non-Anglo Saxon names to add to the headlines, such as Seedy Kinteh of Gambia who asked for and received money from Bin Hammam, very few bothered to look at what was really going on. By Calvert's and Blake's account, Bin Hammam gave money to at least 30 officials in African football. They said this was to buy the World Cup for Qatar.

Yet not one of those officials had a vote for 2018 or 2022.

Only one person had a vote amongst the many other people to whom Bin Hammam provided hospitality or gave money - Jack Warner. But the series of payments made to him were six months after the vote and associated with the trip Bin Hammam made to the Caribbean as part of his Presidential campaign.

Bin Hammam also made payments to former Executive Committee member Reynald Temarii, who didn't vote because he was suspended. Bin Hammam met the expenses for the appeal against Temarii's ban - the action which meant Oceania confederation did not have a voter.

While this took away a certain vote for Australia for 2022, and probably for England in 2018, the payment wasn't part of a pre-meditated, planned campaign by Bin Hammam but a reaction to - for him - fortuitous circumstances.

In the second week of their serialised reports, Calvert and Blake recounted the visit of Franz Beckenbauer and Fedor Radmann to Doha in October 2009 as an initiative of Bin Hammam. It wasn't. Worse, they sought no comment from the Australian bid, which employed Radmann.

That was when I contacted Jonathan Calvert.

The Australian bid asked Beckenbauer and Radmann to visit Doha in October

2009. Calvert didn't want to know.

His lack of interest is what made it clear to me that, regardless of who held the material, the benefactor behind Calvert's and Blake's access to it had to be Frank Lowy. There was no other reason for the story of Beckenbauer's and Radmann's visit to Doha to be so wrong, and for a journalist of Calvert's experience and high standing not to care.

And this was when I realised there was a compelling backstory to be investigated and told.

Sydney: November 2014

"HOW CHUCK BLAZER became a confidential informant for the FBI!" screamed the headline.

It was the front page lead story in the New York Daily News outlining how Blazer was detained on his motorised scooter by the FBI and the IRS on Fifth Avenue, New York, three years before in November 2011 - just as Andrew Jennings' report in August of the same year pointed to.

Blazer, an American, was the long time CEO of the CONCACAF confederation and FIFA Executive Committee member, who worked closely with Jack Warner for decades. Along with Warner, he was implicated in the report of the Committee of Integrity into CONCACAF finances in 2013.

Since his arrest, Blazer had been assisting the FBI by recording conversations with other world football officials and spilling the beans on decades of dishonesty.

The persons of interest whom the FBI asked him to secretly record included Russian Executive Committee member Vitaly Mutko, Russia 2018 CEO Alexey Sorokin, Frank Lowy and Peter Hargitay.

The report revealed that the FBI was involved in other investigations from *'the Caribbean to Zurich, from Australia to Moscow to Qatar'.*

Blazer was the first person arrested with intimate knowledge of FIFA, and the third person arrested with deep knowledge of CONCACAF. The other two were Jack Warner's sons, Daryan and Daryll, who had also been under house detention in Miami since 2011.

Just like Al Capone, the authorities pinged Blazer initially on unpaid taxes.

With the help of people such as Andrew Jennings, and former MI6 officer Christopher Steele who had been on the trail since 2009, they had enough information on Blazer from his life in world football to throw the book at him.

CHAPTER 32
Popcorn time

Perth: November 2014

I WAS IN PERTH, Western Australia, on a work assignment when a friend in the UK sent me a text message.

'You need to look at the Eckert Report. Urgent.'

Judge Hans-Joachim Eckert, chairman of the adjudicatory chamber of the FIFA Ethics Committee published his summary of the Garcia report that was submitted in September 2014. It wasn't the 'full Garcia' but a 42-page summary of a report that was thought to be ten times longer than that, excluding the attachments.

I turned on the computer, and read this about me:

'The relevant individual undermined its own credibility by talking to the media.'

After reading the entire summary, including critical remarks about Phaedra Almajid also, talking it over with a handful of people, thinking about it, and getting through the shock, the anger and the hurt - I was delighted.

Here was a supposedly reputable German Judge putting his name to a summary report of Garcia's 25-month investigation which was clearly deficient.

The investigation didn't speak to Spain or Portugal.

The Russians told Garcia's deputy, the Swiss prosecutor Cornel Borbely, and Garcia's offsider Tim Flynn, that they leased their computers, which had since been thrown out. Because of this, the Russians said they couldn't really help as they didn't know how to access the data. Borbely and Flynn accepted this. Here was a country that could launch a dog in space as far back as 1957, but apparently couldn't back-up the data on their computers.

Garcia himself did not get involved in the inquiry into Russia because he was banned by Vladimir Putin from entering the Russian Federation in April 2013. Garcia was one of 18 Americans banned by Russia related to the United States' Magnitsky Act.

Eckert's summary report indicated that Garcia identified 'problematic' conduct from Australia as well as other bidders.

The two winning bidders of Russia and Qatar had absolutely nothing to answer.

What stood out like a sore thumb was that the summary singled-out two women - Phaedra Almajid and me - from more than 70 witnesses, and all but identified and discredited us. In fact, while everyone else was a 'witness' we were referred to as 'whistleblowers' and 'it'.

It was disgraceful treatment, but also typical of how large organisations and institutions treat people who do dare to raise questions. I also realised that if the summary report was this brutal, the 'full Garcia' - if ever it came out - would be worse.

Despite all the assurances - by telephone, in writing, in person and, in Almajid's case via her Louis Freeh-arranged, FIFA-paid lawyer - of confidentiality, Garcia did this. Or was it Eckert? Or, was it FIFA?

I reasoned that it was FIFA.

Garcia's law firm and Eckert were in a fiduciary relationship with FIFA. As much as they might use the adjective 'independent' to describe the Ethics Committee, it simply wasn't. If FIFA was paying them a bucket load of money, Garcia and Eckert really only had two options: to walk away, or do as the client asked.

Under the leadership of its former president, Joao Havelange, and under Sepp Blatter, FIFA and its courtesans long lurked in the shadows away from the boundaries of normal, day-to-day conduct.

Whose narrative did Phaedra Almajid and I upset?

FIFA's and Blatter's. And the two parties to whom conflicting promises were made: Qatar's Emir and Frank Lowy.

FIFA would have reasoned that Almajid needed to be discredited because Qatar would host the World Cup in 2022. Her story, and her continuing presence in the media, were getting in the way.

And while Blatter could no longer fulfil his promise to Lowy regarding the 2022 tournament, the least he could do as a favour was to discredit the inconvenient woman - me - who caused him so much trouble.

All Garcia needed to say was that he could find no corroborating evidence to support what Almajid or I told him. While it wouldn't have been true in my case - and that is all I can comment on - it nonetheless would have done the job if that is what he truly thought to be the case.

Instead, FIFA reasoned we needed to be intimidated, discredited and silenced. Garcia obliged. It was textbook treatment of whistleblowers.

It allowed FIFA to brief journalists to ignore us, and it worked with many journalists; those who value their connection to FIFA.

For others, the Eckert summary report showed just how broken FIFA and their deeply rotten culture is, and how FIFA would do whatever it takes to maintain their position.

BACK IN MY hotel room, the phone was ringing hot.

My family, 4,000 kilometres away in Sydney, were worried about me. Almajid was talking with me on Skype and alternating between white hot anger and deep distress. Friends and journalists from around the world were calling.

I only spoke with a few people that night. One was journalist Nick Harris, who was close to Almajid. He wanted to do a back page feature on both of us for the UK's *Mail on Sunday* in two days time. Almajid was keen; I was reluctant because I didn't want the tabloid treatment of being viewed as a victim of big, bad FIFA. I didn't want to accept that label from them.

But because Almajid was keen, and I was happy to stand with her, I agreed to talk with Harris.

'I'll do it on one condition,' I told him. 'I want change out of this. I want football to be better. I want this to start to make a difference.'

A few hours later, Harris fulfilled his side of the bargain - and I did too.

He connected both Almajid and me with British MP, Damian Collins, who had been championing FIFA reform.

Collins said he would invite both of us to speak at a forum in Brussels to be convened by three members of the European Parliament. Almajid wasn't interested, but I was.

I spoke further with Collins and suggested that we also talk with Swiss-based Australian businessman, Jaimie Fuller, whom I met in Aarhus 12 months before and had come to know well.

Since our first meeting, Fuller and I had a few discussions about a campaign to rock FIFA's boat, as he had done through his company SKINS with world cycling. We were waiting for the right opportunity - and now here it was. The Eckert summary report, the apparently toothless Garcia report, its treatment of whistleblowers, and a forum at the European Parliament, were giving us the exact platform we were seeking.

Collins, Fuller and I talked, and we agreed it was time to do something about FIFA. The campaign group #NewFIFANow was born.

AS IT TURNED out, Almajid and I were not the only ones who objected to aspects of the Eckert summary report.

Mike Garcia said he did too. By the next morning, he issued a statement from New York saying it was 'materially incomplete and erroneous' with 'erroneous representations of the facts and conclusions.'

His biggest concern appeared to be the conclusion from Judge Eckert that there would be no further investigation into the issues surrounding the conduct of the 2018/2022 bids.

Blatter emphasised this aspect of Eckert's report also. Not surprisingly, Blatter's assessment was there was nothing to see here.

Garcia appealed against the summary report, as did Almajid and I, although for different reasons than Garcia.

The basis for Almajid's and my appeal was that our confidentiality was broken when we were both promised we would be protected - in direct contravention of a FIFA statute.

My appeal was denied because FIFA deemed it was not admissible. FIFA claimed I was no longer involved in football so the FIFA statutes were not relevant to me. Wrong. I was an active volunteer with two grassroots football clubs in Australia, a member of an A-League club, and a volunteer Executive Committee member of Australian's then football media association. I also, by this time, had started-up an independent football news website. What more did I need to do to be 'involved' in football?!

Almajid was given similar reasons.

Garcia's appeal was also dismissed. FIFA declared his complaint was 'not admissible' because the report was 'neither legally binding or appealable'.

Hilarious.

Writing an oped in The Guardian with a call to action to fans to unite behind the need for change that Collins, Fuller and I were pursuing via #NewFIFANow, I said:

> *'Let the Fifa pantomime play out: Garcia reports; Eckert summarises; Garcia appeals against the summary; Eckert admonishes Garcia for talking to the media. In other words pull up a chair, take out the popcorn and see what happens next.'*

What happened next was three things.

FIFA engaged American legal counsel. In addition to their ongoing arrangement with Swiss firm Niederer Kraft Frey, they engaged Quinn Emmanuel at the end of 2014. They were a perfect fit: one of Quinn Emanuel's co-founders boasts as one his career highlights that he won a case for a big corporate against a whistleblower.

Quinn Emanuel's engagement by FIFA came about after they wrote to FIFA in December 2014 offering their services to defend FIFA in action to be brought by the US Department of Justice (DoJ).

Blatter told me that he did not know about this until 2017 when he read it in a German newspaper. Blatter said neither of the two signatories to the Quinn Emanuel contract - his CEO, Jerome Valcke and Head of Legal, Marco Villiger - thought to inform him either of the Quinn Emanuel contract or the reference to DoJ action.

FIFA also engaged external PR help through another American firm, Teneo, that was co-founded by two people close to both the former President of the United States, Bill Clinton, and the former Secretary of State, Hillary Clinton. It now employs the former CEO of the English Bid, Andy Anson.

Quinn Emanuel and Teneo joined the Freeh Group as three powerful US firms in FIFA's employ.

The third thing that happened?

Michael Garcia resigned. After 30 months in the job, Garcia concluded what others, including me, had long known. That FIFA was incapable of reforming itself. That its culture was deeply flawed. And that it needed a change in leadership.

CHAPTER 33
Smelling a rat

Brussels: January 2015

THE MEETING ROOM at the European Parliament was packed with several hundred people.

Members of the Parliament, including hosts Ivo Belet of Belgium and Emma McClarkin of England. MPs from both sides of the House of Commons from the UK. Journalists from all over Europe, England, Ireland and the USA. Lord David Triesman. Plus Damian Collins, Jaimie Fuller and me who were the co-founders of the #NewFIFANow campaign group.

Mike Garcia told Collins he would try to attend also, if he could change a court appearance. He didn't make it.

Two men who declared they may stand for the FIFA presidency in May were also invited to share their views. They were former FIFA senior executive Jerome Champagne, and the head of the technical inspection of all the bids for 2018/2022, Harold Mayne-Nicholls of Chile.

The Brussels forum launched #NewFIFANow, a loose coalition of people who agreed it was time to reform world football governance.

What we called for was an independent, time-limited administration, led by an eminent person, to completely overhaul world football and its way of doing business. We said there was a need for systemic and cultural change throughout football's six confederations and the 200 plus member associations, as well as a change of leadership at FIFA itself.

'The failure of governance with the bidding process is not a one-off. There is a litany of scandals that have plagued the organisation for decades,' I said to the audience.

'Without transparency and external scrutiny, flawed governance practices inevitably emerge and pervade the culture of an organisation.

'Such organisations are also inured to change from within, as FIFA has demonstrated time-after-time.'

I told the audience that my view was - and remains - that 'evolution' is not enough.

'A pretend Damascene conversion to transparency should not be tolerated. It is a revolution we need. It is the equivalent of the tearing down of the Berlin Wall.'

'It is time to reclaim football. It is time to build a new FIFA,' I said.

Mainz: March 2015

THOSE FIGHTING WORDS didn't go down too well in Zurich.

If I thought that Blatter and his close advisors had me in their sights with the Eckert summary report, they now saw a need to step it up a gear.

The interest of German journalists in my experience with the 'German connection' of Franz Beckenbauer, Fedor Radmann and Andreas Abold, continued unabated. I was asked to speak to multiple German print journalists, and radio and television programs about Radmann's and Abold's role in the Australian bid.

I was also invited to talk about #NewFIFANow and the need for reform, live on German television. The television station flew me to Germany for their premier sports talk show. It happened to coincide with an international friendly between Germany and Australia - ironically, one of the obligations arising from the 2007 cooperation agreement.

When FIFA learned that I was to appear on the show, they demanded of the station - one of their host broadcasters, ZDF - that they appear also.

What I was confronted with was the then communications director of FIFA, Walter De Gregorio, stating that I should be ignored when talking of anti-corruption measures and FIFA reform, because of a matter from my past that he referred to and exaggerated.

As I sat on live television listening to a translation of what De Gregorio was saying through an earpiece, I thought to myself *'Is this the best you can do, FIFA? Is this your only answer to all the corruption you've overseen for decades?'*

The matter to which De Gregorio referred is a minor matter that is unrelated to football and is more than a quarter-of-a-century old. The Judge directed I be found not guilty, but the jury disagreed. That's life. However, the law of Australia, and many other western countries including Germany, considers this matter so minor and so old that it is officially a non-matter. It is a breach of law to refer to it or discuss it unless I agree to it.

Of course, from an organisation whose President thought it was perfectly acceptable to turn a blind eye to more than $100 million worth of bribes over several decades, respect for law was a foreign concept.

The day before the live television show, De Gregorio - whose principal concern two years before when asking about my book was Peter Hargitay - was in Moscow enjoying the company of the man himself. The pair were giving a seminar on crisis communication. I later learned Hargitay was beyond excited about the planned 'gotcha' moment for me and flagged it to a few people ahead of time.

De Gregorio mumbled and bumbled through the rest of the interview. He was yet another football bully who was incapable of dealing with the substance of issues.

Tipped-off by Andrew Jennings that the FBI and US Department of Justice investigation that began in 2009 was homing-in on some high-profile targets, I asked De Gregorio twice whether he could guarantee there would be no more scandal, or that there would be no arrests.

Of course, he couldn't.

On the day following the television show, Hargitay's occasional business partner, Paul Nicholson - the one who was so keen to work for the Australian bid in London - weighed-in with an article in his new role as editor of Hargitay's favourite online publication, *Inside World Football*. Blatter's hand-picked, supposedly independent head of audit and compliance, Domenico Scala, circulated material to journalists imploring them to *'Look at this!'*.

On my return home I was in the air for less than an hour when I logged-on to the onboard WiFi. The first message to appear was from journalist Matthew Hall in the USA.

He smelt a rat.

Hall noticed a new website in my name which, amongst other things, was seeking funds via a Bitcoin account to publish a book - presumably this one. Hall not only recognised a fake website when he saw one; he also knew me well enough to know that it was fake.

The creators of the site copied some of my genuine blogs from my football website and from a parenting website I co-owned, which my business partner and I had literally just sold with the sale to settle in two months time. They made up other parts of it. As for Bitcoin, I had no idea of how it worked, let alone had an account with them.

At 41,000 feet, on a 24-hour trip home to Sydney, and heading into the four-day Easter shutdown, with slow and intermittent WiFi, I was trying to find a lawyer to help start action on shutting down the fake website, fake email address and fake Bitcoin account. It took almost one month and thousands of dollars to do so.

This cyber crime came on top of two previous massive distributed denial of service attacks on websites I owned and on my computer and my mobile phone.

I reported this latest one to the appropriate authority in Australia, the Australian Cybercrime Online Reporting Network. They were polite, but essentially told me they were much too busy chasing terrorists to worry about a fake website using my identity.

The Australian authorities may not have been interested; the Swiss were. Months later the Swiss Office of the Attorney-General said if it was to ever happen again, I should report it to them immediately.

Who could possibly want to do this? Who would have the skills to do it? Who would be motivated? Who would go to this much trouble to continue to try to intimidate me? Who would authorise it? Why? And why now?

FIFA WITH THE help of their friends played the woman and not the ball.

What it told me is that something I was saying was deeply concerning to them.

The campaign for #NewFIFANow enjoyed good publicity and worldwide attention. But that wasn't such a big concern to FIFA. Without the support of governments, sponsors and major international institutions, and with only voluntary labour, we are simply a modest, but well-organised and well-presented grassroots campaign with three effective spokespersons in Collins, Fuller and me.

I realised that what concerned Blatter and the FIFA hierarchy, were the same as those that concerned Frank Lowy and FFA hierarchy: that is, the issues I brought to the table of Mike Garcia.

This included identification of the the modus operandi of FIFA that dated back at least as far as Blatter's election as president in 1998. What I was saying and what I observed implicated individuals and how FIFA had operated its business for decades - the 'FIFA way'. It was also about the inconvenience of raising issues about the Australian bid and its 'problematic conduct', when the original intention of the Garcia inquiry was designed to be about Qatar.

Far from intimidating me, it emboldened me to keep fighting.

Later in the year, the same German television station that invited me to Germany, ZDF, sent a three-person crew to Australia for a week to interview me for an hour-long television program on the role of the German FA in past bids. The journalist, Markus Harm, won an award for his work.

I appeared in another 90-minute documentary film on corruption in sport, made by German filmmaker Benjamin Best, released in 2016. It has been shown in film festivals around the world - as well as a shortened version on the in-flight program on Australia's national airline, Qantas. It has won international film festival awards in London, New York, Hollywood and Germany.

AUSTRALIA IS SUCH a big country that when you cross the north-west coast on return from Europe, there's still another five hours to go before landing in Sydney.

It was still daylight as my flight made the Australian continent on return from this trip. I looked out the window at the wonderful, wide, brown land below me - and never, ever felt so glad to be home. Far from the sewer rats of world football.

CHAPTER 34
The Enterprise

Zurich: May 2015

NO WONDER WALTER De Gregorio tried to deflect my questions about more scandal at FIFA. And no wonder FIFA had the need to engage more legal support.

On 27 May 2015 at the luxury FIFA Executive Committee hotel, the Baur au Lac, the Swiss authorities, on behalf of the FBI, swooped in the early morning to make arrests. It was five years after the June 2010 meeting between Christopher Steele, Andrew Jennings and US authorities.

The 164-page first indictment included some of Blatter's closest allies; two FIFA vice-presidents, Eugenio Figueredo of Uruguay and Jeffrey Webb of the Cayman Islands. Webb, the man who was tipped to be most likely to succeed Blatter as President once he retired, had succeeded Jack Warner as the president of CONCACAF.

Those who were caught napping at the Baur au Lac, literally considering the hour of the morning, and who were arrested in Zurich were Webb, Figueredo, Eduardo Li of Costa Rica, Julio Rocha of Nicaragua, Costas Takkas who was an assistant to Webb, Rafael Esquivel of Venezuela and José Maria Marin of Brazil. Others were arrested overseas.

The US authorities had already secured guilty pleas. The football officials amongst these were Chuck Blazer and Jack Warner's sons, Daryan and Daryll. The fourth individual to plead guilty, in December 2014, was Jose Hawilla, the owner and founder of Brazilian sports marketing company, Traffic Group; his company joined the guilty parties a few weeks before the arrests.

Eventually, two more would be found guilty, and one acquitted, at the first trial conducted by the US Department of Justice at the end of 2017.

A 47-count indictment showed that the defendants were part of a racketeering, wire fraud and money laundering conspiracy dating back at least 24 years. While not everyone was named, it wasn't hard to guess some of the co-conspirators.

The charges were announced by the US Attorney-General Loretta Lynch, Mike Garcia's former colleague James Comey, now the director of the FBI, and other officials from the Attorney-General's office for the eastern district of New York, the FBI and the IRS.

'The indictment alleges corruption that is rampant, systemic, and deep-rooted both abroad and here in the United States,' said Loretta Lynch.

'It spans at least two generations of soccer officials who, as alleged, have abused their positions of trust to acquire millions of dollars in bribes and kickbacks. And it has profoundly harmed a multitude of victims, from the youth leagues and developing countries that should benefit from the revenue generated by the commercial rights these organizations hold, to the fans at home and throughout the world whose support for the game makes those rights valuable,' she continued.

'Today's announcement should send a message that enough is enough,' said the acting Attorney from the Eastern District of New York. 'After decades of what the indictment alleges to be brazen corruption, organized international soccer needs a new start – a new chance for its governing institutions to provide honest oversight and support of a sport that is beloved across the world, increasingly so here in the United States. Let me be clear: this indictment is not the final chapter in our investigation.'

'Whether you call it soccer or football, the fans, players and sponsors around the world who love this game should not have to worry about officials corrupting their sport. This case isn't about soccer, it is about fairness and following the law,' said the IRS chief.

It was a tremendous day.

It was music to the ears of so many people. Perhaps not in Zurich or football association headquarters around the world.

But to Andrew Jennings, Jens Weinreich, Thomas Kistner, Jean Francois Tanda, Jamil Chade, Robert Kempe, Jochen Leufgens, Grit Hartmann, Lasana Liburd, Camini Marajh, Nick Harris, and others. Journalists who had gone out on a limb, and risked their livelihoods in pursuit of the truth about FIFA and world football.

To people like me, a former insider who was prepared to put their head above the parapet and say *'There is something deeply rotten in the state of FIFA'*. Knowing that the more you talked, the more desperate they became, the more you'd cop retribution.

Of even greater consequence is how the US authorities described FIFA and its confederations. They saw it as an 'Enterprise'.

The Enterprise was involved in RICO conspiracy, wire fraud conspiracy, wire fraud, money laundering conspiracy, money laundering and obstruction of justice charges. RICO - a racketeering influenced corrupt organisation - is a term created for the mafia.

'The government's investigation is ongoing,' the US statement read.

With Asia, Africa, Oceania and Europe not even looked at yet, it was only the beginning.

Time for more popcorn.

NOT THAT A few arrests would stop Sepp Blatter.

The FIFA presidential election was due at the end of the week. Many around the world used the arrests to call for Blatter to step down. Some senior figures in world football called for the election to be postponed. Even some of FIFA's sponsors - some of whom #NewFIFANow had been quietly talking with for weeks prior to the arrests - were beginning to agitate.

The words 'FIFA reform' were on everyone's lips.

In Blatter's mind, the only person who could possibly right this sinking ship was him. He defiantly proceeded as if it was business as usual.

Blatter did have a challenger. It was Blatter's former prodigy, Prince Ali bin al Hussein of Jordan, backed by the brains of his sister, the money of his brother-in-law, the Sheikh of Dubai, the UK security firm Quest, and Shimon Cohen from the PR Office. Not having been known for saying much publicly previously, Prince Ali stood on a platform of reform.

Even with the arrests - or perhaps because of them - Blatter knew his position was safe with Prince Ali as an opponent. The Prince would get some votes but not enough to topple him. Blatter reckoned that with Mohamed out of the way for good, there was no-one to organise against him where it counted - in Africa, parts of the Prince's own Asian confederation, South America and the Caribbean.

In a speech to the FIFA Congress ahead of the vote, Blatter argued that the arrests were because of rogue individuals, not because of systemic corruption within world football and certainly not within FIFA. He did not accept the characterisation from the US authorities that world football via FIFA was an Enterprise that was a racketeering influenced corrupt organisation.

'It's not the entire organisation!' he said. He called on delegates to 'repair the damage. Immediately!' He argued that he was the only person who could do this.

His appeal worked. Blatter missed out by seven votes in gaining the two-thirds of votes required to win on the first ballot. Prince Ali withdrew his candidacy before the second ballot took place.

MANY PEOPLE THEN, and still today, including Blatter and Michel Platini, suggested that the arrests occurred because the US was upset they didn't win the 2022 vote.

They believe that an angry former President Bill Clinton returned to New York in December 2010, picked-up the phone to his friend Loretta Lynch and to his former FBI Director, Louis Freeh, and said 'get FIFA'. Blatter's circle cites as further evidence the approach by law firm Quinn Emanuel referring to future action by the DoJ, and the subsequent engagement - on Quinn Emanuel's recommendation - of PR consulting firm, Teneo, both of which have close links to the Clintons.

A former senior FIFA executive, who is still close with Blatter told me in 2017 that 'all of the investigations are about appeasing Bill and Hillary Clinton.' The speculation was that investigations might all disappear into nothing as the FBI, the IRS and the US Attorney's office in eastern New York find other priorities once Hillary Clinton was not elected President of the United States.

Blatter and his friends had no idea that the investigations started with a match-fixing investigation by the FBI and the IRS in Europe. The FBI and IRS work led to Christopher Steele's work for the England bid, who turned to Andrew Jennings as early as mid-2009.

The indictments and arrests made so far pre-date the 2018/2022 World Cup bidding process. That remains the subject of ongoing investigations by multiple authorities.

CHAPTER 35
Legacy

Zurich: May 2015

FOR THE REMAINDER of 2015, it was about being 'on the right side of history'.

At #NewFIFANow, we put that thought to fans, sponsors, broadcasters, the FIFA Congress and the Executive Committee in May - weeks before the arrests. We challenged them to think about what was best for football, rather than what was best for their role in football.

It had little traction prior to the May arrests.

But by the end of the year, so many people were scrambling to prove themselves to be in that place - the right side of history. They were not prepared to say anything beforehand, but now they were concerned for their legacy, and wanted to win the narrative.

Less than a week after his re-election as President, Sepp Blatter announced his impending resignation. He said it would happen in February the following year, after he presided over necessary reforms to be led by audit and compliance chief, Domenico Scala. Blatter told me two years later that this was his decision and his decision alone.

In his two-year tenure with FIFA so far, Scala was not notable for having achieved anything.

However, with a Swiss corporate pedigree to uphold - and, as his self-written bio details remind us - a now 50-something World Economic Forum 'former young global leader', Scala became the new power behind Blatter.

After Professor Mark Pieth's resignation from the Governance Committee in 2014, Scala was presented as a FIFA's latest expert on governance reform. His background was finance in the dental implants area of the pharmaceutical industry.

Sydney: July 2015

A RESEARCHER WROTE to me around the middle of 2015 saying that her television production house was *'producing a documentary about Frank Lowy's tenure as FFA chairman and his endeavour to take Australian football to the world stage. We are looking at key moments in Australia's football's history since 2003, which include the FFA's move to the AFC and the World Cup bid.'*

What she didn't tell me was that the production house had a history with the Lowy Institute, Lowy's Westfield property empire and the Lowy family in a private capacity.

The researcher and I had only one phone call.

'Do you agree that Frank was naive and misled by the consultants?' she asked.

'No. To the contrary,' I said. 'He may well have been misled by the consultants but Frank absolutely knew what he was getting into,' I said.

I never heard from her again.

Zurich: August 2015

IN AUGUST, Blatter announced a reform committee to be headed by his friend from the International Olympic Committee, another Swiss, Francois Carrard. Blatter felt comfortable with one of his own in charge.

Joining Carrard were two people from each confederation. There was nothing independent or necessarily expert about the Carrard committee. It comprised three people involved with the Olympic movement; two who were in fiduciary relationships with football organisations; and ten with a direct role in football.

Two of the committee members have since resigned from their football positions. One, Sheikh Ahmad Al Fahad Al Sabah, because of his alleged involvement as a co-conspirator in a football-related indictment by the US authorities in 2017. Another, Gorkar Villar, was arrested along with his father, longstanding football heavyweight and former FIFA Executive Committee member Angel Maria Villar Llona, for alleged corrupt dealings in Spanish football.

A third member of the Carrard Committee, Hany Abo Rida, was a voter in the 2018/2022 decisions. A close colleague of Mohamed Bin Hammam, Abo Rida was one of the passengers on the private jet that visited Trinidad and Tobago in 2011 - a visit that ultimately saw Bin Hammam and Jack Warner leave football for life. He is still on the FIFA Executive Committee.

Sydney: August 2015

IN AUSTRALIA, FFA Board member Moya Dodd prepared some basic policies around women's participation in the management of football. A former vice-captain of the women's national team, the Matildas, by 2015 Dodd had already spent eight years on the FFA board, was seven years an executive member of the Asian Football Confederation and almost three years as a FIFA Executive Committee member.

It was good to see Dodd take positive action in 2015 after the FIFA arrests.

This work occurred in conjunction with a high-profile and expensive public relations campaign for re-election to the FIFA Council. Dodd's efforts were supported by tennis legend Billie-Jean King who, seemingly out of nowhere, also became an advocate for gender issues at FIFA.

FIFA's American PR firm, Teneo, is a partner of King's business and philanthropic endeavours.

Dodd has so far been granted more than $500,000 from her fellow otherwise voluntary Board members at FFA to assist with her 'representative duties'. The FFA contribution was on top of her USD$300,000 annual stipend from FIFA while she was on the Executive Committee.

I had called on the three women members of FIFA's Executive Committee to do something to help improve the position of women in football in a speech two years beforehand, in 2013. I asked: what would it take for a woman to be president of FIFA?

However, to this day, none of the high-level women at FIFA, the AFC or Australian football have ever bothered to contact or offer support to Phaedra Almajid or me when it was obvious two women in senior roles in football were singled-out and discredited by the male-dominated FIFA machine.

Zurich: September 2015

BY SEPTEMBER, SEPP Blatter and Michel Platini were suspended by the FIFA Ethics Committee now overseen by Garcia's former deputy, Cornel Borbely, and Judge Eckert.

Borbely was the man who went to Russia and accepted the excuse about thrown-out computers, apparently not aware that they would be backed-up and the data not lost.

Eckert was the man who, according to Garcia, erroneously concluded that no further action should be taken in relation to the 2018 and 2022 World Cup bids.

Roundly ridiculed after the US arrests that happened in May, Borbely and Eckert realised they needed to salvage their own reputations and take some action. This was made more urgent when, one month after the arrests, Swiss Attorney-General, Michael Lauber, announced he was investigating Blatter and Platini.

Of all the many pieces of puzzle that many assumed could possibly implicate Blatter, a so-called 'dishonest payment' was at the centre of the Swiss inquiries and the Ethics Committee suspensions.

The payment allegedly dated back to work undertaken by Platini for FIFA in 1998, for which he was only paid a portion. In 2011, 13 years later, Platini supposedly asked for the remainder of the payment, approximately $2.5 million. Many saw this as a reward authorised by Blatter for Platini not standing for President in 2011.

When I asked Blatter about it in 2017, he told me that it was exactly as he and Platini described it. He added that he was 'shattered' that the Swiss authorities, his own country, and for whom he had served in the military, would take action against him.

Aarhus: October 2015

TWO YEARS AFTER my first visit to Aarhus in Denmark for a conference in 2013, I was there again for another. I arrived in Aarhus from London where Andrew Jennings interviewed me for his forthcoming BBC *Panorama* documentary on his long and successful history tracking FIFA and its big personalities.

I was one of the keynote speakers at the opening session of the conference. I followed an interesting group.

The FBI sent a supervisory special agent, Nicholas Cheviron, to take us through a comparison of how FIFA is organised and how the mafia is organised. They were the same.

Journalist Jonathan Calvert was another speaker. He was warmly received as he took people through a powerpoint presentation on his award-winning newspaper reports *The FIFA Files* that were expanded into the book, *The Ugly Game*, co-written with Heidi Blake. At this stage, I did not know for certain about the backstory behind the book, but I did know it wasn't all that he said it was.

At a happy hour after the presentation, I tackled Calvert again about how and why he ignored parts of the story. He couldn't think of anything to push back on my claims. He simply turned his back and talked with someone else.

The eminent sports lawyer Professor Richard McLaren, who later chaired the World Anti-Doping Agency investigation into state-sponsored doping in Russian sport, talked of his work to date in looking at doping in world athletics. The previous year he kindly gave me some time, along with a Melbourne Queen's Counsel barrister, about dealing with some of the issues and threats I had received to that point.

Two of the whistleblowers who alerted the world to the doping regime within Russia, Yulia and Vitaly Stepanov, were interviewed via Skype. They talked of their experience and courage in exposing the systemic doping within Russia. It was also an inestimably sad one because they were forced to leave the country of their birth, probably never to return - simply because they told the truth.

Because I was specifically asked to by the conference organisers, I talked about my experience as a 'whistleblower' - not that I ever set out to be one. In essence, a short sketch version of this story.

'Just as the media is the fourth pillar of democracy, I see whistleblowers as the fifth pillar – auditors of accountability and guarantors for good governance. People who are willing to ask questions for no personal gain and invariably at great personal cost.

'I am committed to reform in world football not because I'm bitter and twisted, but because I'm a football fan, parent and global citizen who values democracy, accountability, transparency and probity in our international institutions.'

New York: November 2015

THE DONATION FROM Australia's FA that ended-up with Jack Warner in 2010 came under a little more scrutiny following the FIFA arrests. It was mostly friendly fire.

'I have never spoken to Warner about this subject,' Lowy declared with outrage to a journalist from Rupert Murdoch's SKY News who travelled from Sydney to New York especially for an exclusive interview. 'He made no promises to me,' he said.

Lowy's words were no doubt true. Unfortunately, the reporter didn't know enough about the FIFA world to follow-up.

In the FIFA way of doing business, it is the consultants that have such conversations. It gives football officials plausible deniability. Football officials are theoretically subject to FIFA ethics rules; consultants are not.

Lowy admitted in the interview that the payment was to create 'goodwill'. Part of his defence of the payment was that Warner actually asked for $4 or $5 million but he only agreed to the half-a-million, as if that made it acceptable.

What was known is that the Australian aid agency refused to give FFA more money for this particular payment. When asked why FFA went ahead with it anyway, Lowy said that 'Time was running out. The vote was approaching. There were other things to do. I don't think there was anything strange about it.'

Although FFA wrote to *The Sunday Times* in October 2010 saying that '*All donations were a matter of public record*', Lowy admitted to SKY News that 'There was no media release about many of the things that happened. It wasn't a major event,' he said.

Perhaps when you're in the world's top 250 rich list, USD$462,200 isn't a major event.

For Jack Warner, it was. It was also major enough for Warner to want to keep it all for himself - to add to the rest of his alleged loot.

Someone in FFA also thought it was a major event. Rather than an electronic transfer, a travel agency cheque was drawn that circumnavigated the globe from Sydney to London to New York to Port of Spain. And, according to the Australian Federal Police, the payment didn't come from government-provided bid monies.

Yet it initially did. When the payment was first made by FFA to the travel agency, it was made from bid monies. It was later recalled and paid from FFA's own funds.

Lowy's admission that not everything was made public begged the question what else they didn't announce in addition to the Warner donation.

The advice from the Australian Federal Police that the payment to Warner came from FFA's own revenues - around 7% of which is provided by the hundreds of thousands of children who play and who pay an annual fee to FFA - has never been disclosed in any of its statutory annual financial reports. It also begged the question of what else has not been disclosed.

But no-one has ever asked either question.

Sydney: November 2015

FRANK LOWY'S BESPOKE documentary - the one about which I was contacted by the researcher earlier in the year - was exquisitely titled. *Played*.

In it, the cast of real-life characters presented a tale that global property billionaire Frank Lowy, with business and personal interests across the world, was naively 'played' by everyone's favourite football whipping boy, Mohamed Bin Hammam, the machinery of FIFA and the consultants Fedor Radmann and Peter Hargitay.

The producers employed Australia's most prominent and high-profile political affairs journalist as the presenter, giving added credibility when shown by the Australian Broadcasting Corporation as a genuine documentary.

What it showed is that the people 'played' were the journalist and those who actually believed most of what they were hearing.

Those appearing included Lowy, his sons David and Steven, Ben Buckley, Brian Schwartz, Jill Margo, Mark Ryan, Andreas Abold, Sunil Gulati, former Prime Minister John Howard, former FFA CEO John O'Neill and Jonathan Calvert.

Lowy and his closest advisors said they did not know how the big bad world of FIFA operated. They didn't know anyone. They didn't understand what was going to happen. They said they were advised by Blatter and Bin Hammam to employ the consultants, and that they were lied-to by Bin Hammam and others.

'We didn't know that world. We didn't know the people in that world. That's why we needed help,' said the deputy chairman of FFA and of Lowy's Westfield, Brian Schwartz.

It was curious. Lowy met regularly with 'people in that world' from 2004 onwards when he sailed into Piraeus Harbour during the Athens Olympics. He employed Peter Hargitay on Les Murray's recommendation as far back as 2004 to help Australia join the Asian Football Confederation. How could he not know what they were like?

Lowy said he didn't know anything about corruption within FIFA ranks. 'At the time, we didn't know what FIFA was like,' he bemoaned.

Yet his friend, former Prime Minister John Howard, thought differently. 'There's a helluva lot of corruption in world sport,' he said.

Lowy's Westfield right-hand man, Mark Ryan, who had no formal role with FFA or the bid, tried to set the story straight. 'There is a very clear line between helping football associations developing their infrastructure or sending footballs to poorer nations for kids to play with. That, in fact, is what FIFA requires you to do when bidding for a World Cup,' he said.

Actually, the bidding guidelines didn't require it. It was a commonly-held belief that it was required, and FIFA did nothing to dispel this, but it was not specifically in the bidding guidelines.

Ryan continued. 'But there's a world of difference between doing that and using secret bank accounts to funnel money into what might be personal bank accounts of people who are voting for the World Cup.'

Quite.

Such as the USD$462,200 payment that ended up with Jack Warner two months before the vote, that journeyed from Sydney to London to New York to Port of Spain via an unmarked cheque? The payment that was originally paid out of the bid budget using government monies, but was subsequently withdrawn and paid from FFA funds?

Jonathan Calvert from *The Sunday Times* popped-up in the guise of an independent, expert voice.

'Mohamed Bin Hammam was actively campaigning for Qatar even when he was talking to Lowy in the early stages of the Australia bid,' Calvert said.

He referenced 'junkets for African officials' in May 2008, but failed to mention none of those officials had a vote, or that those votes were an essential part of Bin Hammam's strategy to win the FIFA Presidency. He also didn't mention that Bin Hammam invited Lowy to meet with him in Kuala Lumpur after Bin Hammam's meeting with the African officials.

Calvert also talked of the gas deal with Thailand, and the land deal in Cyprus - the same ones discovered long ago by *Project Platinum.*

Sunil Gulati, head of the US Bid and US Soccer, inadvertently revealed that he and the CEO of the US Bid didn't talk much.

Gulati said that he realised Qatar's bid was strong but the US bid team 'thought it was between Australia and the US.' Yet his own CEO told me in November 2010 that they knew Australia was out of it in June of that year, just as Qatar thought, and just as the England bid's former MI6 officer, Christopher Steele, knew.

The presenter told us that Australia didn't realise Qatar was bidding until February 2009.

What? Was I the only one listening when Blatter told us that in May 2008 at a media briefing? What about when Blatter actually announced that Qatar was a likely bidder at the FIFA Congress, also in May 2008? Was I the only person in the Sydney Opera House who heard him?

Mark Ryan said 'We had a quiet chuckle about Qatar bidding'.

Putting aside the arrogance implicit in that remark, those of us who were in Zurich in July 2009 and heard Blatter talk about the World Cup going to 'new lands' didn't have a quiet chuckle.

Ryan also said that we didn't know at the time that the Bid Book wouldn't be read.

Of course, he couldn't be expected to know as he wasn't in any of the meetings. But the $10 million man, Andreas Abold, told us the Bid Book wouldn't be read by the FIFA Executive Committee as early as January 2009.

Abold made a cameo appearance also. 'Money makes the vote go around, and the world is round like football,' he said cutely. It was a neat paraphrase of another thing he told us in January 2009 - that the bid would be won because of 'intangible things'.

In other words, it was absolutely nothing to do with the $13.8 million paid in total for his and Fedor Radmann's work - described by Lowy, when he was questioned ever so gently by the presenter about the cost, as 'expenses'.

Inexplicably, there was no follow-up.

Abold's company specialises in bid books and marketing related to bids around the world. That's what he does. Yet, for Australia, he apparently under-estimated big time.

The expenditure on the three elements by the Australian bid for which Abold was responsible - and let's remember, they didn't count - is thought to be more than twice the amount spent by any other bidders on the same items.

It was more than the entire US bid budget.

The same items for the England bid cost less than half that of Australia.

And, by way of contrast, Australia's Bid Book for the 2015 Asian Cup - for which we were the only bidder - cost $290,000.

In 2014, Jonathan Calvert and his new investigative partner, Heidi Blake, from *The Sunday Times* quoted an unnamed source from the England bid team in their submission to a House of Commons inquiry on the bidding process for the World Cup.

> *'Where Radmann is working is where Beckenbauer is. And you know about Andreas Abold? The bid book will cost a fraction of what the hiring fee is. That's how the vote is procured.'*

Calvert and Blake had no doubt at the time they wrote this submission that Australia engaged Radmann and Abold. Once again, they felt it was not necessary to obtain a comment from Australia's FA. Just as the host of *Played* didn't think to probe further.

But they weren't alone. It didn't matter to the Australian government either.

Many years later, one of the most senior people in the Prime Minister's department told me that because Lowy was Lowy, there was never going to be a detailed examination of what went on.

Steven Lowy, the successor to his father as president of the FFA, said 'It felt like dad had been shockingly misled by a whole group of people.'

And that's what *Played* was all about. It should have been called *Legacy*. Frank Lowy wanted to exit his 12 years as FFA chairman with his legacy told his way, his reputation intact as being on the right side of history. For much of the 12 years, it was.

As always, the last word should go to Sepp Blatter.

'It's not my problem where the money has gone,' he said. 'This is the problem of those who have given the money.'

Except in Australia. When it comes to wondering what happened with $50 million of taxpayers' funds, the Australian Parliament apparently has 'no worries'.

Brussels: January 2016

WITH Blatter and Platini facing legal action and banned from FIFA, the February presidential election was a contest between five candidates.

Prince Ali of Jordan was trying again. The Asian Football Confederation president, Sheikh Salman of Bahrain. The CEO of UEFA, Gianni Infantino, who was an accidental candidate as it was widely assumed his boss Michel Platini would run - and win - until he was suspended by the FIFA Ethics Committee. 'Tokyo' Sexwale of South Africa; in some ways a celebrity candidate having been incarcerated in Robben Island with Nelson Mandela, and also involved with South Africa 2010. And, finally, former senior FIFA executive, Jerome Champagne. A former French diplomat, Champagne was sacked from FIFA in January 2010.

After weeks of negotiation #NewFIFANow organised to host a live televised forum with the candidates in the European Parliament building, via ESPN.

It was well-intentioned, but the plan fell apart.

Sheikh Salman of Bahrain, was never going to attend. He said he had a prior AFC engagement.

Gianni Infantino was in South America and said he could not make it to Brussels in time. He sent a friendly video message for the broadcast.

Jerome Champagne and 'Tokyo' Sexwale were committed to attending, and Prince Ali said he would travel through the night to reach Brussels from where he was also campaigning in South America.

And then something FIFA-esque happened.

Prince Ali wrote to the co-host, Damian Collins MP, to inform him he could not attend the forum as it would *'constitute a breach of FIFA election rules.'* He told Collins that one of the candidates not attending made a complaint about the forum.

It didn't make a lot of sense. Salman was never going. Why would Infantino go to all the trouble and expense of making a video, merely to complain about it?

Even more curiously, Prince Ali's letter incorrectly stated that the date and venue for the debate had changed several times. Collins wrote to all candidates on 3 November 2015 proposing the date of 27 January 2016 at the European Parliament in Brussels. That hadn't changed. What was Prince Ali talking about?

Collins contacted the man in charge of the FIFA election, Blatter's hand-picked Domenico Scala.

As the self-promoting big 'reformer' in FIFA, this was Scala's big chance to walk-the-walk as well as talk-the-talk.

Scala could easily have nipped Prince Ali's misunderstanding in the bud. If you're committed to genuine reform of FIFA, and introducing transparency and accountability, a debate between Presidential candidates is a good thing, right?

What followed was a series of incredible email exchanges between Scala and Collins.

Scala was unable to answer a very simple question from Collins: did the debate breach FIFA election rules? The answer to that question was either a 'yes' or a 'no'.

Both Infantino and Salman stated publicly that they did not make a complaint. And when asked, Scala would neither confirm nor deny whether he received one.

It exposed Scala as working not in the interests of transparency and accountability to the true stakeholders of the game, but to vested interests within the football world. In other words, it was business as usual.

In the end, Jerome Champagne turned-up in Brussels and was able to have the media who attended all to himself. Strangely, even though it was against the election rules, according to Prince Ali's letter, Champagne has never been sanctioned for supposedly breaking them.

We didn't need more proof, but it was ready-made evidence that, as we always maintained, FIFA would not change merely with a change of personnel at the top. Blatter, Platini, Beckenbauer, Warner, Webb, Bin Hammam and many more may have been gone for different reasons; the culture lives on.

ONE MONTH LATER, the modest reforms proposed by the Carrard Committee were adopted by the FIFA Congress.

Quinn Emmanuel held briefing sessions with journalists before the Congress to get the message out that the reforms would have to be adopted by FIFA in order to avoid losing its victim status under US and Swiss law. Although not formally part of the Quinn Emanuel briefing, there was a view put about in the briefings that a Sheikh Salman win would present a risk to FIFA's victim status.

Gianni Infantino was elected President after he won the second ballot against Sheikh Salman. This was also a relief to many.

Salman's chief campaign backer was his friend Sheikh Ahmad from Kuwait, who has since resigned from his football positions. Salman's behind-the-scenes strategist was considered by almost everyone on the FIFA circuit to be Peter Hargitay - apparently also known as James Dostoyevsky - although he denied this. The regularity of letters from Hargitay's preferred law firm, Schillings, to anyone who dared question Salman over alleged involvement in locking-up athletes in Bahrain, tended to fuel this rumour. Certainly, Stevie Hargitay was spotted happily accompanying Salman on his campaign travels.

A LITTLE MORE than one year after Gianni Infantino's election, he announced that an internal investigation conducted by Quinn Emanuel into multiple allegations of corruption and fraud was complete.

The investigation was key to FIFA maintaining its victim status with both the US and Swiss authorities. It was conducted in conjunction with the authorities.

A visit to a Swiss prosecutor would mean FIFA's representative would also be in the room, either from Quinn Emanuel or FIFA's long-time retained Swiss firm Niederer Kraft Frey, or perhaps even both.

Quinn Emanuel is said to have compiled yet another enormous report: 1,300 pages with 20,000 pieces of evidence on matters of 'primary concern to the Swiss and US authorities'. They interviewed some of the same people Garcia spoke with, as well as many others who had not previously come forward but who were now more willing to share information.

The report is with the Swiss authorities. FIFA's legal bill for the investigations was at least USD$50 million.

CHAPTER 36
The backstory confirmed

East Midlands: June 2016

'BONITA, I'VE GOT something to tell you,' said the man in front of me as he handed me a mug of instant coffee.

We were sitting in the kitchen of his home in rural England. It was a large, comfortable and spotlessly tidy kitchen. Modern, with every convenience, but containing a tilt to English tradition with an Aga as the centrepiece, framed by a picture postcard outlook beyond the back garden to patchwork fields leading to gentle rolling hills.

I was on my way home after travelling to Switzerland. The Swiss prosecutor's office asked me to meet with them at the beginning of the year, and I was required to sign-off on my testimony.

He sat down opposite me with his own mug of coffee. 'You were right about that book.'

The book he referred to was *The Ugly Game* by Calvert and Blake, the book based on *The FIFA Files* which had been serialised in *The Sunday Times* in June 2014. The man I was sitting with in the kitchen of his home, sharing a cup of coffee, is the person Calvert and Blake refer to in the book as their 'source'.

We were in touch more than a year beforehand. Not on this matter specifically, a related one. We got to know one another well when I visited nearby in Nottingham. We talked about all things football over numerous cups of coffee.

The 'source' had football in his blood like I did. And he knew, from our first meeting, that I thought Frank Lowy had a hand in both *The FIFA Files* and *The Ugly Game*.

He didn't mention Lowy's middle-man, Mark Bieler, by name. I learned that from sources in Zurich. The introduction between him and Bieler was made through a third person known to both of them. Bieler wanted to know how his client could have exclusive use of the material lifted from the Asian Football Confederation servers at the time of the PwC audit.

He spoke about how quickly Calvert and Blake appeared at the hastily-arranged office in Beeston, outside Nottingham, once the contract was signed.

He said Calvert and Blake barely touched the surface of the information available to them. They were given access to nine terabytes of material, approximately equivalent to 765 million pages.

'They looked at 100,000 – maybe 120,000 – pages. That's all. They only seemed to want stuff about Qatar. What they really found was stuff about Bin Hammam.'

He shook his head. 'There's so much more.'

The kitchen was quiet. There were no usual Saturday morning sounds of children playing outside, or lawns being mowed. No household cleaning or radio blaring. Just the modest tick of a clock on the far wall.

He shifted on the stool. 'You were right all along,' he said again. 'It was paid for by Frank Lowy. I felt you were owed the truth. You of all people deserve to know this.'

I said nothing.

'What I can't figure out is what Lowy was trying to achieve from it,' the source said to me.

'Was it to 'get' Qatar and/or Bin Hammam? Did he think it would overturn the decision and Australia would get it? Or was it to cover his own backside by making sure anything in there about him or Australia was not uncovered by someone else?"

'Probably all of the above,' I said.

It was a quick visit. The 'source' had work to do as well as weekend chores. I had a commitment in London.

'It's a big story. It's another piece of the puzzle. I've been right about everything so far,' I mused as we headed to the train station.

'It is big,' he said.

'What can I do with it?' I asked.

'It's your story to tell. You do whatever you like with it.'

CHAPTER 37
Collateral damage

Sydney: June 2017

A SIXTH SENSE woke me in the early hours of the morning. An overseas friend alerted me via text message to the release of the 'full Garcia'.

FIFA was forced into publishing it because, somehow, a German tabloid newspaper with no track record in investigations got hold of it. Rather than simply publishing it, the newspaper alerted the world to the fact they had it and wrote that they would eke out stories from it over a period. Even if FIFA was their source - and many believe they were - it was a clumsy way of dealing with one of the most highly sought-after reports in world football.

FIFA then did the logical thing and published it themselves.

There was no skin off the nose of FIFA President, Gianni Infantino, in doing so. For a start, he wasn't implicated. And he also knew there was no smoking gun in respect of the hosts of the next two World Cup tournaments, Russia and Qatar.

I crept downstairs in the cold, turned on the computer and had a read.

It was exactly as I predicted it would be back in December 2014. Even more brutal on Phaedra Almajid and me.

Contrary to Mike Garcia's assertion on his resignation - that there were '*erroneous representations of the facts and conclusions*' in Judge Eckert's summary report two-and-a-half years beforehand - Eckert appeared to have summarised the 'full Garcia' reasonably fairly.

The key difference was in relation to Sepp Blatter: Garcia criticised his leadership, Eckert chose not to highlight this in his summary.

Line-by-line, I could dismiss the misleading and inaccurate commentary from Garcia on me - and it definitely was me because he named my role, the time of the termination of my employment and my gender. No other woman has held the role. So much for the 'protection' he promised in May 2014.

A current member of FIFA management, as well as a former member of the FIFA Ethics Committee, both said to me that 'Everyone knows it's you'.

THIS IS WHAT Garcia got wrong in relation to my testimony, either intentionally or unintentionally.

He made a point about me offering him access to my computer. It was in the context of me explaining - yet again - that I did not have access to much material, for which he had asked repeatedly, by the nature of my immediate dismissal from the job. What I did say was that if I still had my computer, he could have it.

He suggested that the evidence did not support my recollections and allegations. But I made no allegations, and told them from the outset, that I had no evidence. I told them what I knew, what happened at meetings I attended, what I observed, what I had written, what I had read. I raised questions. I gave them lines of inquiry.

Coincidentally, about a week before the 'full Garcia' came out, I caught up for coffee with my former boss, Ben Buckley.

I contacted him as two international journalists asked me to check something with him for an investigation they were pursuing. After an hour or more of friendly chatter about our lives, our families, travel and work, I raised their specific issue with him - related to Russia.

'I don't remember anything about the bid. I've put all that behind me, at the back of my mind. I don't remember anything. I don't want to talk about it,' Ben said.

I said jokingly 'That's a shame. You won't be able to write a book.'

'My father always said I should take notes and write a book about all of it. But I took no notice of him,' he replied. 'But what about you?'

'Yes, I've written one. It's more or less finished. Just waiting on a few things.'

'Should I be worried?' he asked.

Ben continued: 'I have a good memory, but you have the best memory of anyone I've ever met, and you write better than anyone I know, so I figure

I should be worried.'

However, contrary to the view of Ben, my former boss who knew me well, Garcia alleged I had a 'mistaken recollection' of an email about a the purchase of a pearl pendant for Jack Warner's wife.

Garcia contrasted what I said about how I felt about the incident when we first met in New York, with an email I wrote more than four years beforehand. He cited as evidence that my recollection was wrong by quoting one paragraph of a seven paragraph email. Not only did he selectively quote from the email, but he also dismissed my response to the actual question he asked.

Garcia also pointed to the spreadsheet setting out the internal budget for the bid, stating my concern it *'concealed certain bid expenditures documented on internal budgets.'*

What I said was, as the transcript confirms, that it was unclear why we couldn't share the internal budget with the government. 'The fact is, if we had gone to government and said '*Well, this suits us to report this way,*' they wouldn't have cared less,' I said to him. The fact that we didn't potentially pointed to the possibility that there was something to hide.

Clearly Garcia missed the point.

To this day, it begs the question why FFA didn't want to inform, or make progress reports to, the government of the significant sum set aside for international football development in Asia and Africa, and consultants' bonuses.

I also said that he needed to look at the spreadsheet in conjunction with other documentation, including FFA's final report to government published in September 2011. I told him FFA's 'final report actually raises more questions than it answers, if you know the detail.'

Garcia then stated that I suggested he contact the former chief financial officer to verify this. Wrong.

The point I made clearly in the transcript was that the former chief financial officer had no insight into the bid budget, that he was not a member of the bid team and that, in itself, was a point of contention between him and the CEO, Ben Buckley. Garcia was either wrong or deliberately lying to say this individual was a member of the bid team; he simply never was.

I advised Garcia that he would be better off speaking to another person whose name

I gave him, and spelled, for the purposes of the recording. There is no indication in the Garcia report that he did.

Garcia also failed to acknowledge that it was he who returned to the subject of the spreadsheet at our second face-to-face meeting in April 2014, or that it was his staff who pursued me for the former chief financial officer's contact details even though I said he had no knowledge of the Australian bid.

Garcia said I undermined my 'reliability' by speaking with the media about my communications with him. However, he fails to mention that the communications with the media happened in October 2013, before he informed me in November 2013 that I ought not to speak with the media.

He said the introductory comments to my book excerpts published in 2012 *'disparaged individuals in personal terms, revealing animosity.'* The record shows that Garcia did not mention this to me; he did not ask me who wrote the introductory comments - as it happens, I didn't write them - and he certainly didn't ask me whether I endorsed them, as he summarily assumed in his report.

He also said that some of my statements reflected bias towards some people. This one really made me laugh.

Let's see. I'm bullied and harassed by consultants who he himself in his report condemned in the strongest possible terms. I'm sacked because of the same consultants. I'm disparaged by FFA for years. I'm told I will 'never work again in Australia'. I am threatened by senior staff of FFA, an organisation Garcia accused of *'problematic conduct'* during the bid. Some people in football in Australia no longer talk to me due to fear of retribution from FFA. And I am hacked on websites, email and my phone. Show me someone who wouldn't have some degree of bias in those circumstances, and - to quote an Irish friend - I'll show you Jesus, Mary and Joseph.

For all of these reasons, Garcia concluded that he did not rely on anything from me which he couldn't corroborate elsewhere. Fair enough.

But he should have been honest enough to acknowledge that he was able to corroborate almost everything. Every issue he raised in the report in relation to the Australia bid was identified by me, as the transcript confirms.

What was also noticeable in his report is that Garcia treated bid teams courteously and respectfully. Where something didn't add up, he gave them an opportunity to respond.

He afforded neither Phaedra Almajid nor me such courtesy or natural justice. Instead he condemned both of us, in writing, for evermore.

What I found more unforgivable than what he wrote about me, which I can easily dismiss, is what Garcia wrote about Almajid. He referred to her as 'not credible' and even alleged she had fabricated evidence. A former senior Ethics Committee member told me that Almajid was 'a completely different case' to me.

That may be so, but that is irrelevant.

The fact is there is no justifiable reason in the world why anything needed to be written giving details about Almajid's personal life and concerns, let alone 22 pages of it. As I concluded when Eckert's summary report came out, all Garcia needed to say - if, indeed, it was true - was that he could not corroborate the testimony.

To the extent that the Garcia report was hurtful and damaging was of no consequence in the minds of FIFA.

When I spoke with a senior FIFA manager about this towards the end of 2017, and challenged him on the promises Garcia made to us that were clearly not respected, and what Garcia did, I could see that he had not thought of the report in those terms. It didn't occur to him that the Garcia report - and everything that went on before and after it - had a profound impact on an individual life and the lives of those close to me who had absolutely nothing to do with football.

A former FIFA Ethics Committee member, an experienced prosecutor, told me the report should never have been published in the form that it was because it 'treads on lots of rights'. He told me I had a case against FIFA if I wanted to pursue it as FIFA did not give me a right of reply, Garcia opted not to be neutral and showed bias himself, the report did not honour the promise of confidentiality and, as I have shown here, it was simply incorrect in material ways.

This was confirmed by the Partner of an American law firm who contacted me after publication of the Garcia report. The firm specialises in assisting whistleblowers under US law. He observed that what Garcia had done to Almajid and me was 'Whistleblower Treatment 101'.

'It's textbook stuff that you've been subjected to,' the US lawyer said. 'It doesn't make it any easier for you, but corporations and organisations do this to good people all the time when they want something or someone to just go away.'

While it may be difficult for some to see, considering Garcia has now been appointed a New York state judge, it is he who is the ultimate loser in this episode.

Garcia chose to turn personal and play the woman, when he should have stuck with the issues. He took the equivalent of his 'thirty pieces of silver' from FIFA, conducting an internal inquiry for a disreputable organisation. It started off as an exercise to 'get' Qatar, when that suited FIFA, and finished by concluding that Russia and Qatar had no case to answer.

HOWEVER, FOR ALL that Garcia, Borbely, Eckert and Eckert's then deputy, Alan Sullivan of Australia, were all highly paid 'guns for hire', such nefariousness was not their personal agenda.

It was FIFA's.

If ever there was any doubt, journalist David Conn elicited Blatter's opinion of 'whistleblowers' at a lunch in research for his book *The Rise and the Fall of the House of FIFA* published in 2017. Blatter told Conn that he was 'was not impressed with whistleblowers in general.'

'Because if you are a whistleblower, it's not correct as well,' Blatter told him, using a juvenile analogy likening whistleblowers to a 'snitch' at school.

In Phaedra Almajid's case, she set the original narrative that questioned the winning Qatar bid.

Project Platinum desperately wanted her testimony to count for something. That didn't work out for them, but Louis Freeh found her, dismissed the UK lawyer arranged by *The Sunday Times* and arranged a Washington-based lawyer to represent her. FIFA paid the bills the entire time.

It was because of the audit of the Asian Football Confederation finances, the lifting of documents from AFC servers, as well as Almajid's statements about the Qatar bid, that there was a Garcia inquiry in the first place. Almajid was Garcia's 'Source 1'.

From Blatter's perspective, Almajid was useful when he still intended to take the 2022 tournament away from Qatar as he promised Lowy. When the new Emir figured out what was happening, and reminded Blatter that it would not be in his or FIFA's best interests to take the World Cup away from Qatar, Almajid became a nuisance.

In my case, it was because I placed the conduct of the Australian bid in the big picture context of the FIFA way of doing business. I challenged the status quo, FIFA and FIFA insiders, and upset their world. A truly inconvenient person.

My observations of the 'FIFA way' of doing business struck at the heart of how the 2006 and 2010 World Cups were won. It involved Beckenbauer, Radmann, Abold, elements of the German FA, Bin Hammam, Jack Warner and Hargitay - and all those who knew about it, including Blatter and Valcke.

The decision to award Germany the 2006 World Cup resulted in a 12-11 vote against South Africa. Including those who have died, 15 of the voters have either been banned at one time or another, indicted or are under investigation.

The 2010 World Cup was awarded to South Africa against Morocco, 14-10. Sixteen of the voters have either been banned at some stage, indicted or are under investigation.

For the 2018 and 2022 World Cups, 22 men had a vote after Adamu and Temarii were suspended beforehand. Fourteen have either been banned, indicted or are under investigation.

The pattern of corrupt behaviour didn't just start in 2009 and 2010 in the World Cup bidding process for 2018 and 2022. It has been following the same pattern for some time masterminded by the same people.

IT WAS WITH a heavy heart that I realised almost everything I observed, thought, commented upon and talked about with Garcia in relation to the Australia bid was confirmed by him.

In fact, the Australia bid was the most heavily criticised by Garcia.

He highlighted the deal that was made with the German FA before the bidding phase began but when Australia knew it would bid. It was one of the first issues of concern for FFA lawyers prior to signing the Bidding Agreement in February 2009 because the Bidding Agreement required that there be no relationships entered into with other Member Associations to assist with bidding. Garcia noted that Australia's withdrawal from bidding for the 2011 Women's World Cup gave Germany - the eventual hosts - a free run at it. The former President of the German FA, Theo Zwanziger, who was a party to negotiating the terms of the agreement, told Garcia the only benefit for Germany out of the arrangement was Australia's withdrawal from the 2011 Women's World Cup.

Garcia said the relationship between Franz Beckenbauer, Fedor Radmann and Peter Hargitay raised concerns, especially in light of the conduct of Radmann and Hargitay.

He said that Hargitay and Abold were actively involved in Radmann's engagement and contractual arrangements. The head of the US bid committee, Dr Sunil Gulati, told Garcia that Hargitay pitched his and Radmann's services as a team. Hargitay wrote to Ben in February 2009 outlining the arrangements for Radmann's contract. Radmann insisted that it be via *'AA's Swiss company and not his German company'* - presumably the Beyond Limits Marketing company set-up in St Gallen in 2008.

Garcia said that the coordination of activity between Beckenbauer and Radmann *'cast doubt on the integrity of the bidding process.'*

He said that Andreas Abold, who did not cooperate with the inquiry, *'provided the vehicle for the surreptitious hiring of Fedor Radmann'* and cautioned against hiring him for football business again.

He eviscerated Peter Hargitay in one paragraph, stating that there is a prima facie case that Hargitay violated ethics rules in relation to the payment to Jack Warner. Garcia recommended that any involvement by Hargitay or those associated with him in future bids should be *'carefully reviewed'.*

He noted the inappropriate passing of confidential information from the late Les Murray, then a television journalist and member of the FIFA Ethics Committee, to Hargitay.

The USD$462,200 payment that landed in Jack Warner's personal bank account is the closest he comes to identifying an illicit payment in the entire bidding process. It was as far as Garcia could go. He had no authority to track financial transactions.

He revealed details of the money given to, or attempted to be given to, Oceania, Africa and Trinidad and Tobago in the name of 'international football development'.

He found that Australia paid for the under-20 Trinidad and Tobago team's training camp in Cyprus.

He commented on the relationship between the three international consultants and other Executive Committee members - particularly Sepp Blatter, Mohamed Bin Hammam and Jack Warner. Today, Blatter is suspended from football matters, Bin Hammam is banned for life and Warner has been indicted by the US authorities.

Garcia also followed-up the reference I pointed him to concerning the offer Mali's Amadou Diakite received from Australia. The fact that FFA made a $4 million offer to the African voters via Diakite was not previously reported, yet - what do you know? - it was the same amount allocated for Africa in the internal management budget set out in the spreadsheet. Coincidence?

According to Garcia, Australia's efforts were so clumsy in making this offer that even Issa Hayatou, the former longstanding head of African football implicated in the ISL scandal, objected to it. Hayatou suggested that discussions be held over until after the vote.

Yet Lowy didn't see it that way. In Zurich in December 2010, he thought he had the vote of 'two basic Africans'.

Hayatou was not surprised when he never heard from FFA again. Garcia said that Hayatou *'perceived Mr Lowy's proposal … as an attempt to influence the World Cup vote.'*

Garcia also wrote that there was *'evidence that Hargitay was the guiding hand in making the arrangements as a means of influencing'* a voter.

He said there was *'strong evidence that FFA made improper payments intended to influence the vote of an Executive Committee member.'*

There was *'significant evidence that the AU$500,000 was paid with the intention of influencing Mr Warner's World Cup vote. Australia's bid team perceived the payment as a benefit for Mr Warner, as did Mr Warner himself.'*

While FFA said they had no way of knowing that Jack Warner misappropriated the funding, Garcia concluded that that fact is not relevant to *'an examination of the propriety of the payment'* and that it *'does not change these facts.'*

He added that *'Australia's acquiescence helped create the appearance that benefits were conferred in exchange for a vote, thus undermining the integrity of the bidding process.'*

Garcia indicated in the report that investigation proceedings should be opened against Beckenbauer because of his relationship to the Australian bid.

He wrote of evidence *'concerning possible misconduct by the consultants Peter Hargitay and Fedor Radmann'* as well as Beckenbauer and Warner.

He noted that Andreas Abold did not respond to requests for cooperation with the investigation.

He had specific recommendations in relation to Australia's three international consultants: Hargitay, Radmann and Abold. He concluded that further issues should be pursued, and cautioned against any future involvement with any of the three consultants. Apparently, FIFA has not pursued any of these matters.

Garcia concluded that Australia's conduct revealed *'a disturbing pattern.'*

He noted that: *'There is evidence that individual members of various bid teams violated specific rules governing the bidding process … In Australia, evidence was produced concerning possible misconduct by the consultants Peter Hargitay and Fedor Radmann, as well as by Executive Committee members Jack Warner and Franz Beckenbauer.'*

Garcia decided not to pursue any individual bidding team because they all were so helpful to him, and such help should be weighted in bidders' favour.

Why didn't he extend the same consideration and common decency to Almajid and me?

THE TWO AREAS we discussed that he didn't raise in his report - attempted collusion with Russia and the $5 million mysterious donation to the Asian Football Confederation - were ones about which he presumably could not find any corroborating evidence.

Yet this is curious too.

The assessment of Russia was made by Garcia's deputy Cornel Borbely and the Freeh Group's Tim Flynn. The key person they spoke with was Vitaly Mutko who was Sports Minister at the time of the Russian bid and, until December 2017, was the head of the Organising Committee for Russia 2018. Mutko was banned from all Olympic activity by the International Olympics Committee in December 2017 for his role in state-sponsored doping.

Mutko, along with CEO Alexey Sorokin and deputy CEO Alexander Djordjadze, said there was no alliance with Australia as it would not have been beneficial to them. Mutko also said he declined Lowy's invitation for luncheon on his super yacht.

Lowy also told Garcia that there was no cooperation between Australia and Russia.

Their carefully worded respective responses may well have been accurate. It is why bid teams engage consultants.

But how do they add-up with Frank Lowy, Ben Buckley and Peter and Stevie Hargitay referring time-after-time to a deal with Russia? Why did Hargitay write that the Australian bid through him, was working closely with the Russian bid through Andreas Herren? Why did Hargitay visit Russia on multiple occasions on Australia's behalf? Why did a specialist Olympics journalist say that a vote swap between Russia and Australia was 'the talk of' the IOC? On the day of the vote, why did Lowy sit in a hotel room in Zurich counting on Russia as a vote for Australia? And on the night the vote was announced, why was Lowy outside in the Zurich snow waiting for the Russians to arrive, only to be shunned by them?

Borbely and Flynn actually wrote that: *'On the basis of the relevant documentation made available'* by the Russians, there was no evidence to suggest Russia colluded with anyone.

'No evidence' produced by the Russians?

Could this be like Mutko stating in December 2017 that there was *'No evidence to support state-sponsored doping'*?

And don't forget the computers that went missing.

In respect of Asia, Garcia had access to the same cache of material as Calvert and Blake.

Amongst other things, this included a Memorandum of Understanding between FFA and the Asian Football Confederation for a $5 million grant. Not only do we know there was an MoU, but we know that Bin Hammam wrote two letters in June 2008 suggesting that we give money to Vision Asia for him to determine projects in Asia and Africa; we know that Radmann and Abold visited Bin Hammam in September 2008 to follow-up these letters; and we know that Australia won an award from the Asian Football Confederation for a $5 million contribution. Yet nowhere is this accounted for in total.

Why Garcia chose to ignore this when he had sufficient evidence to ask questions, I guess we'll never know.

OTHER THAN THE two journalists at *The Age* who were on the case since 2010, and literally less than a handful of other journalists, Australia's conduct, as described by Garcia, escaped critical attention within Australia.

The more compliant elements of Australian media characterised what Garcia had to say about the Australian bid as nothing out of the ordinary. One segment in particular involved one journalist giving an interview to another journalist on national radio where the interviewee said twice that I was 'totally discredited'. Neither the interviewer journalist nor the interviewee journalist - supposedly top journalists with the public broadcaster, the Australian Broadcasting Corporation

- bothered to call me for comment beforehand or seek my comment afterwards.

Not one member of the Australian Parliament has raised a question publicly about the Garcia Report.

JUST AS I and others concluded from Calvert and Blake's book that it didn't prove Mohamed Bin Hammam 'bought' the World Cup, Garcia found the same. He wrote:

> *'The record before the Investigatory Chamber does not, however, support the conclusion that the purpose of these payments was to 'help Qatar to win the World Cup bid … Rather, the evidence before the Investigatory Chamber strongly suggests that Mr Bin Hammam paid CAF officials to influence their votes in the June 2011 election for FIFA President.'*

In their book, Calvert and Blake wondered why Garcia didn't want to see their cache of material. Apparently, they never realised he had it from the outset.

THE MAJOR OMISSIONS from the Eckert summary report from three years before, compared with the 'full Garcia', were concerned with recommended action against some individuals and what Garcia had to say about Sepp Blatter.

> *'President Blatter must also take responsibility for the failures that occurred on his watch.*

> *'As the leader of FIFA, responsibility for these failings and for positive steps taken to reform the organization resides with President Blatter.'*

The sentiment was familiar.

It was the same as I said in a 2011 speech to the Governance Institute of Australia, the same speech I sent to Garcia after the first time he contacted me.

'Blatter sets the example to football administrators around the world,' I said.

'He has been at the top of FIFA – either as CEO or President – for 31 years. He must take responsibility for the failures of the organisation and the people who are part of it, as much as he does the successes.'

CHAPTER 38

'You have such an honest face'

Zurich: November 2017

AT THE CENTRE of almost everything at FIFA for 40 years was Sepp Blatter.

Like everyone who has followed the issues of the collapse of FIFA's former marketing partners ISL, World Cup bidding, FIFA governance and more, I was familiar with what he said on the public record.

I also knew that he was a football politician. He was practiced at juggling many balls in the air, treading between the competing views of confederations and member associations, always careful not to upset anyone too much in the pursuit of his number one interest - staying in power - and always secure with his base of support, until it all came tumbling down.

I figured that as someone who was at the centre of everything for so long, it would be worth one more journey for me. What he said publicly might not necessarily be what he believed to be true; and he may be willing to put things on the record where he was once more cautious.

I contacted him in September 2017 to ask if he would meet with me. I told him who I was, that I had worked on the Australian World Cup bid, that I was writing a book, and I thought there were some things he could clear up for me. He responded quickly saying he was happy to meet in Zurich.

Our meeting was a little more than two months later at Blatter's favourite restaurant, the Sonnenberg, next door to the original FIFA headquarters where he started work 42 years beforehand.

Sonnenberg is located in the hills above Zurich, around the corner from where Blatter lives, and not far from the hotel where my former colleague and I encountered him having a quiet drink after work one evening eight years beforehand.

It was a beautiful late autumn day. The sun shone brilliantly, glistening on Lake Zurich, with a clear view of the snow-capped mountains in the distance, and the suburbs below looking neat and pretty amongst the verdant landscape. Winter was on its way, but not quite yet.

We arrived within seconds of one another. Blatter drove the short distance himself in a Mercedes sedan. It surprised me a little because every time I had seen him in a vehicle previously it was a chauffeured limousine. He handed the keys to an attendant to park the car. Blatter was wearing a navy suit with a crisp, white open-neck shirt with matching navy inside trim. I noticed his shoes were shiny.

'Miss Mersiades …. Bonita. Welcome to Zurich.'

We shook hands. I thanked him for making the time to see me.

As we entered the restaurant, he introduced me to the maitre'd and waiter as a visitor from Australia, as they all slipped effortlessly between English and Swiss German. The staff were warm and welcoming: a guest of Herr Blatter's was a friend of theirs. We were shown deferentially to a table by the window, taking in the picture postcard view, a few discreet tables away from the nearest diners.

Blatter looked well. He had slimmed down. He was tanned. Gone were the plasters from his face covering melanoma extractions, and the haunted look he had when it all began to fall apart for him. He looked older and he was quieter, less forthright. He seemed to me to be relaxed into his 81 - getting on for 82 - years.

I gave him a gift I brought from home. Remembering the wine he served to Prime Minister Kevin Rudd, Frank Lowy and others years before, I found a bottle of a straw-coloured chardonnay from Margaret River. It wouldn't have rated as a gift in FIFA terms - Peter Hargitay would absolutely scoff - but it wasn't something that you'd drink every night either. He graciously accepted it.

WE STARTED WITH small talk, mostly about the recent qualification of both Switzerland and Australia for the 2018 World Cup.

He said he thought Switzerland were lucky - 'It was never a penalty!' he said, referring to the sole and controversial goal that separated Switzerland and Northern Ireland from getting to Russia. He commented that Australia had done well to get to its fourth successive World Cup, but said that we should have made it in the group stage of the Asian qualifiers.

The conversation moved easily to the matters that had occupied both of us - many people - over the past seven years. I was prepared with a list of questions, but it wasn't necessary to open my notebook to be reminded of them. I asked him would he mind if I took notes. 'Not at all,' he said.

The first matter he talked about was his former nemesis, Mohamed Bin Hammam. He said that he thought Bin Hammam wanted the FIFA Presidency more than he did Qatar winning the 2022 World Cup.

'For years he was doing things for people to help him win the Presidency.'

'We gave him $5 million,' I told him.

'What for?' he asked.

'Not exactly him, but Vision Asia. We had a memorandum of understanding that granted Vision Asia $5 million. We even won an award for it.'

Blatter laughed. He genuinely thought it was funny. 'Vision Asia, Bin Hammam, same thing. Why would you give money to someone who is already rich?'

'It was supposed to help us get votes from Asia and Africa,' I said.

'Do you know what happened to it?' he asked.

I shrugged my shoulders. 'Not as far as I'm aware. Some may have gone to Chonburi,'

Blatter laughed again. Chonburi was the club owned by former Executive Committee member, Worawi Makudi of Thailand, an ally of Bin Hammam. Makudi was banned from all football activity for five years in October 2016.

'He wasn't supposed to run in 2011,' Blatter told me, referring again to Bin Hammam. 'He went against his Emir.'

Blatter continued. 'In December 2010, soon after the vote, I went to a meeting in Doha at the Palace with the Emir, the young one who is now the Emir, Sheikh Jassim and Bin Hammam.'

Sheikh Jassim is the new Emir's older brother who renounced his rights as heir apparent in favour of his younger brother in 2003. He is the patron of the Aspire Academy.

Blatter continued. 'The Emir knew that I wasn't happy that they won. He knew I wanted America to win, but he also knew that FIFA couldn't have a World Cup in Qatar in 2022 and a Qatari as President of FIFA. He wanted to keep the World Cup. He told me in front of Bin Hammam that Bin Hammam would not run. I thought that was that. I returned to Zurich.

'Next thing' he continued, breaking some bread, 'he is running. He gave an interview. I read it in the paper one morning.'

'What did you do?' I asked.

'Well straight away, I wrote an email and asked them *What is going on? Why is he running?'* We had an agreement.'

'Did they respond?'

'Sheikh Jassim did. He told me *Don't worry. We will fix it.'*

He watched me as I completed my notes.

'You remember when Bin Hammam pulled out of the Presidential race?' he asked.

'Yes, a night or two before the election.'

'Everyone thinks he pulled out because of the ethics charges. It was nothing to do with the ethics charges,' Blatter said.

'It was because he was told to. By Qatar. Because they promised me he would not stand. Sheikh Jassim was here in Zurich. We were at a meeting, the three of us. Sheikh Jassim told him to withdraw.'

Blatter picked up a piece of proscuitto - he told me it was a traditional Swiss way of procuring it - and tore another corner of his bread roll.

'And that was that,' he said.

'WHEN DID YOU know that Qatar was going to win?' I asked.

'As soon as Michel told me his votes had shifted,' he replied referring to Michel Platini. 'We had talked about the bidding contest in the Executive Committee, that it would go to Russia and America.'

He explained why.

'Russia because 2018 had to go to Europe, and they had not hosted it. This big country in Europe, as well as Asia you know. We knew they were capable.'

'Because of the 1980 Olympic Games,' I said.

'Yes, they are a very competent country, a football country,' he continued. 'America because it was really CONCACAF's turn. Not Asia's. CONCACAF. And America is very good for us. The sponsors, the broadcasters, the fans. It would help football there after 1994, almost 30 years, and that is good for football.'

'When did Platini tell you his votes shifted?'

'He told me that his votes were shifting. Him, Lefkaritis, Erzik, D'Hooghe. They all went to Qatar. After the meeting with Sarkozy.'

Platini was reported to have met with the then French President, Nicolas Sarkozy, on 23 November 2010, nine days before the FIFA Executive Committee meeting. Also at the meeting was Sheikh Tamim of Qatar, the man who would later become the Emir, succeeding his father in 2013.

The following year, in 2011, Qatar Airways purchased 90 aircraft at the annual Dubai Air Show: 88 of them were French-manufactured Airbus aircraft, two were US-manufactured Boeing aircraft. Al Jazeera subsequently purchased the TV rights to the French Ligue 1 and Qatar Sports Investments purchased Paris St Germain.

'I didn't believe D'Hooghe until I saw the job his son got,' Blatter added.

Michel D'Hooghe's son, Pieter, also a medical specialist was offered a role as a surgeon at a private hospital in Qatar in 2012.

'What did you do when you found out?'

'I called President Obama. With Sunil.' He was referring to the then longstanding President of US Soccer and head of the US bid, Dr Sunil Gulati. 'We phoned President Obama together the night or two before and I told him *'It is going to be very difficult for you to win'*.

'What did President Obama say?' I asked.

'He understood what had gone on. He thanked me for telling him.'

'What did you think when the Emir of Qatar came to you asking how much it would cost to buy the World Cup?' I asked.

'That didn't happen.'

'It didn't happen?'

'No.'

'So why did Peter Hargitay tell us that? My boss told me that you or Valcke told Hargitay that's what happened.'

'No.'

'What about the bonus from Al Jazeera?'

'I don't remember those details,' he said. 'But sponsors and broadcasters pay bonuses all the time. That is not unusual.'

'A $100 million dollar bonus is normal?'

He shrugged.

'And did any American companies pay bonuses?' I asked.

'I don't remember.'

I couldn't help but notice the difference in his demeanour. When he was talking about Bin Hammam, his arrangement with Qatar and calling President Obama, he was clear, confident, certain of his facts and eager to share.

When the conversation turned to money, and whether the Emir of Qatar offered to 'buy' the World Cup and the quantum of Al Jazeera's bonus, he was almost monosyllabic.

'AUSTRALIA HAD NO chance,' he told me. 'Not a chance. Never.'

'If that's the case, why did the Germans tell us that we did?'

'I don't know why the Germans did what they did.' He thought for a moment. 'I don't know why they told you you could win when you had no chance. That was very bad of them. No doubt Radmann had some scheme going. I know that he got a lot of money and so did Franz.'

'You know that Beckenbauer was paid by us?'

'Of course. Franz wouldn't do what he did for Australia for nothing.'

'But he didn't vote for us? You did.'

'Yes, I did.' He beamed at me. 'For two reasons. Let me tell you. One. My daughter wanted me to vote for Australia so I could not go home and tell her I did if I didn't. Two. I knew if I didn't vote for Australia, no-one else would and I wanted you to get at least one vote.'

'Why did you tell Frank to ask the Germans to help him?' I asked.

'We were in Germany at the time I think. It was 2006, or soon after. Obviously they knew how to win. I told him to find out from them. And I told him to talk to Bin Hammam because he was the head of the Asian confederation. Bin Hammam only wanted one Asian bidder,' he said.

There was a brief silence.

'Now listen to me,' he said learning forward on the table. 'You never had a chance because you were never going to be competitive for the broadcasters. Not the time zone, not the money. It is obvious. We have to make enough money at the World Cup for the next four years and Australia wouldn't be able to do it.'

We ate in silence for a few moments.

My mind took me back to the brief conversation with Jerome Valcke in the foyer of FIFA headquarters where he told us precisely that in July 2009. I thought about the meeting with Hany Abo Rida in Cairo in October of that year where he highlighted the same issue. I thought about the McKinsey report published a few days before the vote that said the same thing.

I thought about all the wasted time, money, effort and emotional energy for so many people; the impact this bid that we were 'never' going to win had on so many people.

And I thought about the fact that I said from the outset that the consultants were taking us for a ride. No wonder they were keen to get rid of me!

'Did you know Jerome Valcke told us this in 2009 when our Prime Minister visited you?'

He shook his head.

'So why didn't you tell Frank this?' I asked Blatter.

He leaned back in his seat, hunched his shoulders a little and held out his hands, palms facing upwards.

'How could I?' he asked. 'I was the FIFA President. If a member association wants to bid, I have to welcome it. I cannot tell them not to do so. They have a right.'

He was silent for a few moments before continuing.

'What would people say if I went around saying they shouldn't bid? Then they would say I was interfering, that I was - what's the word in English? .... '

'Pre-empting?' I suggested.

'Yes, then they would say I was pre-empting the decision of the Executive Committee. From my point of view, it is good to have the interest. It is good to have the competition.'

'But it was taxpayers' money,' I said.

'Well that is not my fault!' he replied. 'I didn't ask your government to pay, did I?'

'HOW IS FRANK?' Blatter asked.

'He's well enough. He was walking around the pitch after the World Cup qualifier. He seemed fine.'

'Frank is an exceptional businessman. I've lost contact with him. But he and I got on well. I liked him.' He had a sip of wine. 'You know I responded to pleas from Frank.'

'Yes, I do.'

'I didn't ever hear from the federation, but I did from Frank. Personally. A number of times. He came to see me. Not like England. They were the worst losers. Always complaining. Frank pleaded with me to investigate what went on. And we did.'

'I understand he presented to you the evidence his investigators had gathered, and you told him that you would get rid of the Qatar World Cup, when he visited you in January 2012.'

'I told Frank I would investigate. And we did,' he said again.

'Did Murdoch offer to help you?'

'What do you mean?'

'Did Rupert Murdoch offer to support you in the media? He visited you at the same time.'

He still wore a blank expression, so I continued. 'In his newspapers and television stations. Before this visit took place. Did he write or talk to you about this?'

Blatter shrunk back into his seat and paused. 'I don't remember.'

'WHAT DO YOU think of the Garcia Report?' I asked.

He guffawed, and rolled his eyes.

'The Americans had the Garcia Report immediately,' he said. 'Before FIFA. Garcia and his wife - she is CIA ....'

'FBI,' I corrected him.

'FBI. He was in with them the entire time. And then there is Christopher Steele as well. He encouraged the Americans to take a look at FIFA too.'

He put down his knife and fork.

'Here is the thing. Garcia gives us the report in September. In December after all that performance in the media, he resigns. And at the same time, Quinn Emanuel writes to FIFA offering their services for the issues with the Justice Department. But I didn't know any of this about Quinn Emanuel until I read it in the paper earlier this year.'

He was most indignant.

'But Valcke and Kattner and Villiger, they knew, because they signed it in January 2015. I have never seen the document, other than in the newspaper. They didn't tell me. Then I find out that in March 2015, the US asked the Swiss to help to arrest some people. Villiger, he kept telling me '*I'm your lawyer too. I am FIFA lawyer and I am your lawyer.*' Then all this happened. Everyone is gone, they are sacked, they are all gone except one man.'

'Marco Villiger,' I say.

He nodded. 'So I ask him: '*Where is my lawyer now?*' And I wonder: what else did they not tell me?'

'So are you saying that there were things going on in FIFA that you didn't know about?'

He gave a half-shrug of his shoulders, looked at me, raising his hands a little. Clearly that's what he was implying.

I returned to my original question. 'What do you think of the Garcia report?'

He took a mouthful of food and did not respond. Deliberately so, I judged.

'Well what did you think of how the Garcia report dealt with Phaedra Almajid and me?'

'Who?'

'The Qatar whistleblower and me.'

He sat back in his chair. He let out a long sigh, and turned his head to the right to gaze out of the window at the picture postcard view. He looked back at me and spoke very quietly.

'You're the whistleblower?'

I knew he already knew this as a former FIFA executive had told me he did ahead of the meeting. 'Yes,' I replied.

'You have such an honest face,' he said. He seemed taken aback by the concept of a whistleblower being honest.

He peered at me. 'I believe you. I believe you.' He said it the second time almost as if he surprised himself.

When we finished our lunch, we had our photo taken on the terrace. He insisted on waiting with me until my taxi arrived, seated at an outdoor table.

He pointed in the direction of the original FIFA headquarters adjacent to the restaurant. 'When I arrived at FIFA in 1975, my employee number was 12. A substitute. I worked hard because I wanted to be in the first eleven.'

A FEW DAYS later we caught up briefly again at a coffee bar in a hotel on Zurich's Bahnhofstrasse. This time Blatter brought a gift - two, in fact.

One was a small teddy bear, about 14 centimetres from top to toe, with a scarf on it printed with *Lighthouse.*

'You know I have a small zoo in my apartment?' he asked. 'I have hundreds of stuffed toys. These teddy bears, which are for a HIV charity I have supported for many years. Plus others from everywhere I've visited. Africa, Australia of course. All kinds of animals.'

The other gift was something I instinctively refused. It was a silver coin-size medallion of the 2014 FIFA World Cup.

'I am sorry, but I can't accept that,' I told him.

'But you must, you must. It is mine to give. It is not FIFA's.'

'It's too valuable. It wouldn't feel right,' I said.

'Please, please. You must accept it. I would be most embarrassed if you didn't, especially here in this hotel. This is like my home. You are my guest. This is something that is mine to give and I want you to have it.'

His eyes looked far away and sad as he said this. I thought that it would be ungracious not to accept it so I thanked him, and resolved to donate it for a football charity fundraiser. The teddy bear sits on my desk.

It was a quick meeting. Blatter had an appointment; I was meeting friends. He thanked me for visiting him in Zurich.

He told me to let him know when my book is finished so he can get a copy.

'You probably won't like it,' I said.

'There are many things written I don't like. But you invited me to speak. You came here. You had the courage to see me. That is kind, that is good, that is strong-hearted. I wish you all the best,' he said as he put on his overcoat and scarf.

I thought it might be as close I would ever get to an acknowledgement that he and FIFA had conducted themselves shamefully.

He added: 'I had a wonderful life at FIFA for 40 years. Nothing can change that.'

CHAPTER 39
The right side of history

Sydney: January 2018

HOW DID IT get to this?

Football got to this point because Sepp Blatter, and Joao Havelange before him, took FIFA and football from being what journalist and writer David Conn characterises as an amateur, cottage industry with genteel values to an international commercial behemoth.

Together with enablers who helped form the 'Enterprise', as characterised by the FBI and IRS, they built the World Cup into the most prestigious sporting event on the planet. But it has been at the expense of the reputation of world football and without any regard for the forgotten stakeholders of the game - players and fans.

Those who have worked closely with Blatter say that it is FIFA's system of governance built around the confederations, and Blatter's unwillingness to take the hard decisions towards the end, that brought it to the precipice in May 2015. Unless there is significant governance change FIFA may, ultimately, either stay on the precipice for some time before it eventually tips over.

They reason that the FIFA president is a politician elected at the pleasure of the 200 plus member associations, who has to work with an Executive Committee, now Council, drawn from across the globe. The individuals who are elected to serve on the Executive Committee are not necessarily aligned with the elected President, and are themselves football politicians within their own confederations and national jurisdictions, who bring their own diverse standards of probity with them.

FIFA insiders say repeatedly that Sepp Blatter's overwhelming objective was to be at the top of world football, and he did whatever it takes to do just that.

In staying at the top for so long, at best, he turned a blind eye to all that was going on around him and, at worst, he was a party to it. All those who are closest to Blatter, and Blatter himself, say he was not corrupt but he did enjoy the trappings of office.

Blatter was at the helm of FIFA, either as its chief executive or president, for 34 years. Yet, to this day, he accepts no responsibility for the 'devils' in football.

THE QATAR 2022 decision gave rise to widespread concerns about the bidding process because it seemed such an outrageous choice. While Mohamed Bin Hammam did not actively get behind his own country's bid for some time, he knew what it takes to get business done in FIFA. He knew the FIFA way inside-out.

Blatter might have gone some way to rehabilitating his image if, after the farcical 2011 election when he could have argued he had a mandate to do so, he had moved to fundamentally reform the structure and governance of the organisation. He engaged the calibre of experts in place to make that happen - such as Professor Mark Pieth and some of the other members of the 2012 Governance Committee - but then he did nothing more than introduce marginal change. Almost everyone associated with that committee resigned in protest about the lack of interest and conviction in real reform.

The modest Carrard reforms of 2016 also do not go far enough.

While FIFA has improved its public image at one level, and introduced some bureaucratic discipline and process to some of its systems, many observers - both inside and outside FIFA - believe the current president, Gianni Infantino, is no different from his predecessors. When it boils down to it, he's a politician who wants to stay in power, beholden to the same confederations and national associations.

FIFA is a case study of what happens when organisations and people are able to continue unchallenged, without renewal and without accountability. Any organisation that is not routinely subject to external scrutiny based on full transparency will inevitably become self-serving, arrogant and beholden to no-one except the long serving privileged and sinecured individuals who control the organisation.

Without transparency and external scrutiny, flawed governance practices - and in the case of football, corruption - inevitably emerge and pervade the culture of an organisation.

Regrettably, for those of us who play and love sport, FIFA and its confederations are not the only culprits in world sport.

AUSTRALIA PAID a high price for its World Cup bid.

It wasn't just the $50 million of taxpayers' money.

It wasn't just the $9.5 million given in the name of 'football development' in the hopeful exchange for a vote: $4 million for Oceania, $5 million for Asia, and USD$462,200 which ended up with Jack Warner.

It wasn't just that someone had discussions with Issa Hayatou and Amadou Diakite on our behalf about how we might fund $4 million worth of projects in Africa, or that we signed an agreement with Jamaica that might have seen them receive $2.5 million.

It wasn't just that Garcia wrote that there was 'significant evidence' that Australia made payments with the intention of influencing votes.

It wasn't just that Garcia found that the Australian bid concealed its relationship with the German FA, Franz Beckenbauer and Fedor Radmann - as well as Peter Hargitay until journalist Matthew Hall wrote about him.

It wasn't just that we were humiliated with one vote, or embarrassed by the dreadful final presentation in Zurich put together by Andreas Abold.

It wasn't just that the Australian bid was talked about amongst the other bidders as the 'dirty bid', or that it was seen as 'deeply unpleasant to deal with' according to one senior journalist, or that 'they've put people off everywhere' according to US bid CEO, David Downs.

It wasn't just that we engaged three consultants at a cost of approximately $14.5 million whom Garcia cautioned about ever being employed by world football again; the same three men I expressed concern about in the first place as being a 'reputational risk' for Australia.

It was because we played the game the FIFA way.

We were diminished. My country, and the game I love.

WHEN I WAS talking with a publisher about the final draft of this book, she said to me '*I want to know about you, how you feel, how outraged you must be that this happened to you, what it feels like to be a victim of these outrageous men.*'

I don't feel outraged. I accept that what I have experienced comes with the territory of speaking out. I also don't feel a victim.

But there is a victim. It is the Australian public.

And it is football.

It's the seven-year-old child who pulls on their boots terribly excited to be running around a pitch with their friends, chasing a ball like bees to a honeypot.

It's the next door neighbour who heads to the park at 6am on Saturdays and Sundays to put up the nets and set-up the canteen for a weekend's worth of games for his or her children.

It's the work colleague who saves up their money to buy a season ticket to the club he or she supports through thick or thin, rain or shine, to sing their heart out from the terraces every home game.

It's the referee who spends hours improving their fitness, improving their decision-making, and understanding the laws of the game inside-out - even if they don't always get it right on the day!

It's the coach who can break down play, analyse the game, know the opposition and understand the strengths and weaknesses of a squad to bring out the best in them.

It's the player who has spent the best part of their life so far training harder, getting fitter, improving their skills, and sacrificing other parts of their life in order to be the best possible player they can be – whether amateur or professional.

I know all those people. I am most of those people.

Those at the very top of football - whether it be FIFA, the confederations, member associations and particularly my own in Australia - long ago lost what it was to be a 'real football' person.

But it was about such real football people that former US Attorney-General Loretta Lynch said in 2015 that *'The betrayal of trust is outrageous. The scale of corruption is unconscionable.'*

Because a sport like football exemplifies values such as integrity, fair play and team work which form the guiding principles that underpin our society, fighting corruption in football isn't simply about fighting corruption in football. Again, to quote Lynch, it also *'reaffirms the ideals that have always guided our society - and most importantly, our young people, toward the fair and just future they deserve.'*

AUSTRALIA'S FIRST EVER World Cup Finals Coach from the 1974 tournament, Rale Rasic, said to me over coffee not long after I left FFA in 2010 that *'You can leave football, but it will never leave you.'*

He's right.

Over the years, and particularly in the years since the Garcia inquiry, a small community has developed amongst those of us who have worked inside football and who are now outside. As one of them said to me as I was writing the final words of this book, we have been 'airbrushed' out of the game officially. And yet, we still continue the fight for football.

Some of us left football at a professional level by choice. Others, like me, were given no choice.

All of us feel a sense of having been a small part of something much bigger. All of us feel that so much that happened was beyond our control. All of us believe that there are still many things yet to be uncovered. All of us have assisted one or more of the various authorities who are investigating world football. All of us are hopeful that the authorities continue their investigations, that the 'bad guys' are brought to justice, and genuine, independent reform and change can happen.

We feel that we've done our fair share of heavy-lifting.

Many of us have paid a high price. We've lost jobs; we've lost livelihoods; we've had illnesses; we've been abused by people who don't even know us; we've been disowned by people who once called themselves friends; we've been attacked personally, professionally and in cyberspace; we've been threatened; the same organisations that we once worked so diligently and loyally for have disparaged and demeaned us, campaigned against us and tried to rob us of dignity and respect; our self-esteem, confidence, resolve and resilience have been tested.

As I complete this book, and with many people knowing its publication is imminent, I have once again had a cyber attack against me. Once the book is published, I anticipate a barrage of criticism and more dirty tricks against me.

But you get up. You walk on.

I hope this book encourages others to do so too.

All of us have had nothing to gain, and everything to lose - except for one thing. We are on the right side of history.

Who's Who

FIFA Executive Committee

UNTIL FEBRUARY 2015, the FIFA Executive Committee comprised the President of FIFA and the top elected officials from each continental Confederation, drawn from Africa (4 members), Asia (4), Europe (8), North and Central America and the Caribbean (3), Oceania (1), and South America (3). The following are the 24 men who formed the Executive Committee throughout the period of the bidding process in 2009 and 2010.

Amos Adamu, Nigeria

Former sports bureaucrat, he was on the Executive Committee from 2006 to November 2010, when he was caught by a *Sunday Times* sting. Because of his suspension, he did not vote.

Jacques Anouma, Cote d'Ivoire

Financial manager who worked for the Ivoirian government as well as the private sector. He was a member of the Executive Committee from 2007 to April 2015 when he lost his bid for re-election.

Franz Beckenbauer, Germany

Playing legend and coaching great. Executive Committee member from 2007 until he retired, ostensibly to spend more time with his family, in 2011. He is currently under investigation by the Swiss authorities. While he publicly supported the Australian bid, he has not confirmed who he voted for.

Sepp Blatter, Switzerland

President of FIFA from 1998 to 2015 when he was suspended from football. He is currently serving a ban until 2021 because of the 'dishonest payment' to Michel Platini, and is under investigation by the FIFA Ethics Committee for further matters concerned with executive bonuses. He has publicly stated on a number of occasions, including to me, that he was Australia's sole vote in the first round.

Chuck Blazer, USA

General Secretary of CONCACAF from 1990 to 2011 and on the FIFA Executive Committee from 1996 to 2013 when he resigned ahead of his guilty plea to the US authorities. He died in July 2017.

Mong-Joon Chung, South Korea

Former President of the Korean FA, he was a member of the FIFA Executive Committee from 1994 to 2011. He is also Chairman of Hyundai Heavy Industries, twice a Presidential candidate in South Korea, and with a PhD in International Relations from Johns Hopkins University. Chung received a six-year ban by the FIFA Ethics Committee in 2016 for his role in the South Korea 2022 World Cup bid. The Garcia report showed that the activity for which he was banned was not as egregious as others who have not been investigated.

Senes Erzik, Turkey

Former longstanding UEFA and FIFA Executive Committee member and former pharmaceutical executive. He was one of the last remaining members of the FIFA Executive Committee who voted in 2010, retiring in 2017.

Julio Grondona, Argentina

A FIFA Executive Committee member from 1988 until his death in 2014, he was the senior vice-president and chairman of FIFA's finance committee. Since his death, FIFA has said he is responsible for authorising the USD$10 million payment to CONCACAF for the South African World Cup. In 2017, a Swiss banker admitted to facilitating bribes to Grondona as part of the US investigations.

Mohamed Bin Hammam, Qatar

President of the AFC from 2002 to July 2012, and on the FIFA Executive Committee from 1996 to 2011. He was banned from football for life in July 2012 for payments made to delegates of the Caribbean Football Union in 2011 during his election bid for the FIFA Presidency.

Issa Hayatou, Cameroon

President of CAF since 1988 and a member of the FIFA Executive Committee from 1990 until he lost his positions in the 2017 CAF elections. Hayatou became senior vice-president and chairman of the finance committee after Grondona's death.

Michel D'Hooghe, Belgium

Medical specialist and member of the FIFA Executive Committee from 1988 to 2017.

Marios Lefkaritis, Cyprus

Owner of a petrochemical company, Lefkaritis was Treasurer of UEFA and on the FIFA Executive Committee from 2007 to 2017.

Nicolas Leoz, Paraguay

A lawyer, Leoz was President of CONMEBOL from 1986 and on the FIFA Executive Committee from 1998 until he retired in 2013 shortly before being named officially as a recipient of bribes in the ISL scandal. He was indicted by the US authorities in May 2015.

Worawi Makudi, Thailand

A longstanding Thai football official, Makudi was on the FIFA Executive Committee from 1997 until he lost his seat at the 2015 election. He was banned by the FIFA Ethics Committee for five years in 2016 due to domestic issues in Thailand.

Vitaly Mutko, Russia

Then Deputy Chair of the Russia 2018 Bid and Sports Minister of Russia, now deputy Prime Minister, President of Russian FA and Chairman of Organising Committee for Russia 2018. He was a member of the FIFA Executive Committee from 2009 to 2017, when he was declared ineligible to stand again by the FIFA Governance Committee because of his government role. In December 2017, he received a lifetime ban from the International Olympic Committee because of his part in state-sponsored doping related to the Sochi Winter Olympics in 2014.

Junji Ogura, Japan

A former football administrative employee, Ogura was a member of FIFA Executive Committee from 2002 until he retired in 2011. Other than early round voting for Japan, he has not disclosed who he voted for.

Michel Platini, France

Playing great. President of the UEFA from 2007 and on the FIFA Executive Committee from 2002. He was banned for four years in 2015 over the 'dishonest payment' between Blatter and him. The ban prevented Platini from running for the FIFA Presidency in 2016. He is one of three people who has disclosed his entire vote: he says he voted for Russia 2018 and Qatar 2022.

Hany Abo Rida, Egypt

Owner of an engineering company, Abo Rida joined the FIFA Executive Committee in 2009. He is the only voter from 2010 who is still a member of the larger FIFA Council at the end of 2017.

Rafael Salguero, Guatemala

A lawyer, Salguero was on the FIFA Executive Committee from 2007 to 2015. He is one of three people who has disclosed his entire vote: he says he voted for Russia 2018 and USA 2022.

Ricardo Teixeira, Brazil

A former son-in-law to Joao Havelange, Teixeira was President of the Brazil Football Federation from 1989 and was on the FIFA Executive Committee from 1994 until 2012 when he retired, shortly before being named in the Swiss prosecutors' report into the ISL scandal. He was indicted by US authorities in May 2015 and by Spanish authorities in 2017.

Reynald Temarii, Tahiti

Former national team player. He was president of Oceania confederation and a FIFA Executive Committee member from 2004 until November 2010, when he was caught by a *Sunday Times* sting. He did not vote.

Geoff Thompson, England

A magistrate, he was Chairman of the English FA for eight years until 2008 and on the FIFA Executive Committee from 2007 to 2011 when he retired. He remains a member of FIFA's Player Status Committee. He is one of three people who has disclosed his entire vote: he says he voted for England 2018 followed by Belgium/Netherlands 2018, and South Korea 2022 followed by USA 2022.

Angel Maria Villar Llona, Spain

Former national team player. A FIFA Executive Committee member from 1998 until 2017. He was a vice-president of UEFA and President of the Spanish FA at the time of his arrest by Spanish authorities in July 2017.

Jack Warner, Trinidad and Tobago

A property developer and former government Minister and deputy leader of the Opposition, Warner ran CONCACAF from 1990 and was on the FIFA Executive Committee from 1983. He resigned from all positions in the wake of the Bin Hammam payments in the Caribbean in 2011. He was indicted by the US authorities in May 2015 and, at December 2017, is continuing to fight extradition to the United States.

Others

The 'A' Team

The nickname given internally to the Australian World Cup bid's strategy committee comprising Frank Lowy, his two closest Board members, Brian Schwartz and Philip Wolanski; CEO Ben Buckley; and international consultants Andreas Abold, Peter Hargitay and Fedor Radmann.

AFC

Asian Football Confederation.

AFL

Australian Football League. Australian Rules football is the major football code in Australia.

Alexey Sorokin

Then: CEO of the Russia 2018 bid, former CEO of the Russian FA. Now: CEO of the Russia 2018 World Cup and member of the FIFA Executive Committee.

Andreas Herren

Former senior media manager with FIFA who worked closely with Markus Siegler. He was a consultant to the Russia 2018 bid, along with Siegler.

Ben Buckley

Chief Executive Officer (CEO) of Football Federation Australia, and of Australia's World Cup bid. My immediate boss. Buckley left the role in November 2012 to be replaced by the former CEO of the National Rugby League. After a few years working with Foxtel, Buckley is now working again with his best mate and former boss, Andrew Demetriou who ran the AFL during the World Cup bid, as co-founder and chief executive of a sports marketing company.

Brian Schwartz

Deputy Chairman of the FFA Board, and one of Frank Lowy's closest confidants. Also Deputy Chairman of Westfield. A member of the 'A' Team.

CAF

Confederation of African Football.

CONCACAF

Confederation of North, Central American and Caribbean Association Football.

CONMEBOL

Confederation of South American Football.

David Chung

Not to be confused with Dr Moon-Jung Chung of South Korea, David Chung was the senior vice-president of Oceania at the time Reynald Temarii was suspended. He is now the President of Oceania and on the FIFA Executive Committee.

ExCo

The shorthand version for the FIFA Executive Committee (see above for explanation and separate list of members).

FIFA

No-one reading this book will not be aware of this but, for good measure, world football's governing body. FIFA comprises six geographic confederations and more than 200 national Member Associations. Each Member Association is also a member of one of the confederations.

FIFA Congress

World football's overarching body - often referred to as its 'parliament' - formed by the Member (national) Associations of world football with one vote for each football association.

FFA

Football Federation Australia, the national governing body of football in Australia.

Frank Lowy

The Chairman (or President) of FFA from July 2003 to November 2015. He was also the owner of the global retail property group co-founded by him in 1957, Westfield, until he announced its sale at the end of 2017. Lowy was knighted by the Queen of England in her 2017 birthday honours for his contribution to the British economy. He was succeeded as FFA President by his youngest son, Steven, who was also co-managing director of Westfield with his brother, until the Westfield sale.

Kate Ellis

Australia's Sports Minister from December 2007 to June 2010.

Kevin Rudd

Australia's Prime Minister from November 2007 to June 2010 and again from June 2012 to September 2013.

Markus Siegler

Former head of communications with FIFA, former business partner of Peter Hargitay. He was a consultant to the Russia 2018 bid, along with Andreas Herren.

Moya Dodd

Member of FFA Board since 2007. Member of AFC Executive Committee since 2009. Co-opted member of FIFA Executive Committee from 2013 to 2017.

Oceania

Oceania Football Confederation.

Peter Kenyon

Long time football senior executive with Manchester United. He was CEO of Chelsea Football Club at the time of the bids.

Philip Wolanski

Member of FFA Board, and one of Frank Lowy's closest confidants. Childhood friend of Lowy's sons. He was a member of the 'A' Team.

PwC (PricewaterhouseCoopers)

A global consulting firm of which FFA was a client of the Sydney Office.

Richard Scudamore

Long time CEO of the English Premier League.

Stuart Taggart

Head of Operations for Australia's World Cup bid, responsible for technical issues for the bid such as stadiums, accommodation and other infrastructure, relationships with state governments, hotel providers, venue managers and host cities; and for coordinating the Bid Book.

Tai Nicholas

CEO of Oceania Football Confederation.

UEFA

Union of European Football Associations, the powerful confederation of European football.

Acknowledgements

FIRST, THANK YOU to the crew at Powderhouse Press for taking on this book, and for all their help; and to Leslie Priestley, a Liverpool fan, who made the book actually look like a book in record time.

Thank you to the people who I have spoken with and met with over the years who have assisted with my research and investigations. That includes the former FIFA President, Sepp Blatter, as well as many others I can't name, especially some former and current officials and employees within football. We know who you are, and I appreciate your time, your stories and your willingness to share information.

Thank you to the following people for friendship and support.

Adam Howard, Amanda Hackett, Ange Postecoglou, Anthony Siokos, Archie Fraser, Benjamin Fitzmaurice, Beverly Goldsmith, Boutros Boutros, Chris Tanner, Christine Whyte, Clare Sambrook, Daryl Adair, Dina Durrant, Elia Santoro, Emma McLarkin MEP, Eva Havas, Ezequiel Trumper, Frank Farina, Francis Awaritefe, Georgina Halford-Hall, Graeme Joffe, Guido Tognoni, Harold Mayne-Nicholls, Ian Ferguson, James Corbett, Jen Dobbie, Jens Sejer Andersen, Jerome Champagne, John Carrick, John Havas, John Sigur, Julie Farina, Kate McQuestin, Kimon Taliadoros, Liz Roadley, Lord David Triesman, Lucas Neill, Maria Suurballe, the late Michael Cockerill, Neil Favager, Nick Bogiatzis, Nick Harris, Paul Bateson, Paul Templeman, Paul Williams, Rabieh Krayem, Ray Gatt, Richard Vaughan, Roger Sleeman, Russell Atwood, Sam Macri, Sam Williams, Simon Hill, Simon Pearce, Stephan Havas, Steve Macri, Ted Mulder, Terry Moran, Terry Steans, Thomas Broich, Tim Cahill, Tim McCormack, the late Tom Havas, Tony Pignata, Tony Tannous, Vasiliki Nihas, Vicky Krayem.

Phaedra Almajid, In'shallah. Peace be with you. You deserve it.

Thank you to the journalists from around the world who have asked questions, who were always courteous and professional, and who understood that my motivation was about advancing football.

Of course, there is the 'Oracle' of FIFA corruption, Andrew Jennings. I don't think there is one thing he has said about this entire FIFA business that has been wrong. Andrew is not just thoroughly professional, but he has taught me so much. Best of all, he gets to enjoy the last laugh at all the people he has pursued for so long.

Damian Collins MP and Jaimie Fuller: your support, professionalism, friendship, kindness and 'can-do' attitude will always be appreciated. Working with you to fight the good fight is a privilege.

And finally my personal 'A' team.

My late big brother read an earlier draft of this book on summer holidays in Tasmania quite a few years ago. He didn't live to read the final version, but putting the final bits of the puzzle together was only possible due to his love and generosity.

Michael and Antony, seeing your values, intelligence, loyalty, humour, and innate sense of fairness develop and mature is one of the great pleasures of life.

And, of course, Nick. Thank you for everything. You are the most decent, honourable person I know. If the rest of the world was half the person you are, the rest of us would have absolutely nothing to worry about. 'Σ'αγαπώ πάντα'.

About the Author

BONITA MERSIADES' life has always had football in it. She was given her love of it courtesy of her refugee father from eastern Europe, and grew-up surrounded by the game amongst the many and diverse ethnic communities in Australia who helped nurture and build it.

As a grassroots football club volunteer in four cities – Canberra, Brisbane, Sydney and Townsville – she has done what all volunteers do: put up nets, helped dress grounds, managed teams, been a 'soccer mum', worked in the canteen and merchandise shop, done social media and websites, created an under-5 competition, and run competitions and carnivals. She was previously on the executive committee of the Football Media Association in Australia. She remains an active volunteer in football, and is a member of an A-League club.

Her early career was principally in government where she worked at senior executive level on measures including Australia's first National HIV/AIDS Strategy, coordination of employment initiatives, the introduction of the Higher Education Contribution Scheme, a national access and equity strategy for vocational education, and advancing Australian food exports.

Mersiades happened to find herself working professionally in the game for a national league club, a state federation, as team operations manager for the men's national team the Socceroos, and as head of corporate and public affairs for Football Federation Australia. In the latter role, she was involved in Australia's bid to host the 2022 World Cup until January 2010.

She is the ghost-writer of the playing biography of Frank Farina, *My World is Round* (1998).

Along with British MP Damian Collins, and Swiss-based Australian businessman Jaimie Fuller, Mersiades is a co-founder of #NewFIFANow, the campaign group established in the wake of the Garcia inquiry that advocates for independent governance reform of world football administration.

In addition to her volunteer duties, Mersiades is editor and founder of a football news and opinion website, footballtoday.news. She has also established a niche publishing company, Fair Play Publishing, which is focused on the publication of 'really good football books'.

Bonita Mersiades was one of the first people in the world to speak out about, and highlight, the environment and culture within which world football and FIFA operated.

About Powderhouse Press

POWDERHOUSE PRESS IS a small publishing company that aims to do one thing: publish outstanding work especially in the genre of anti-corruption and whistleblowing. Because we are small, we publish work that interests us and which we think tells an important story that deserves telling.

For further information, see www.powderhousepress.com

CPSIA information can be obtained
at www.ICGtesting.com
Printed in the USA
LVOW10s2154270118
564266LV00026B/333/P